Microsoft

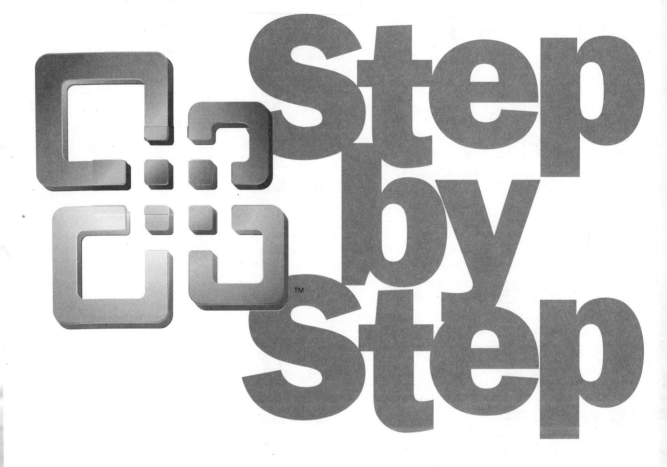

Step by Step

Microsoft® Office
PowerPoint® 2003

Online Training Solutions, Inc.

PUBLISHED BY
Microsoft Press
A Division of Microsoft Corporation
One Microsoft Way
Redmond, Washington 98052-6399

Library of Congress Cataloging-in-Publication Data
Microsoft Office PowerPoint 2003 Step by Step / Online Training Solutions, Inc.
     p. cm.
   Includes index.
   ISBN 0-7356-1522-5
   1. Computer graphics.   2. Microsoft PowerPoint (Computer file).   3. Business presentations--Graphic methods--Computer programs.   I. Online Training Solutions (Firm)

T385.M515   2003
006.6'869--dc21   2003052653

Printed and bound in the United States of America.

1 2 3 4 5 6 7 8 9   QWE   8 7 6 5 4 3

Distributed in Canada by H.B. Fenn and Company Ltd.

A CIP catalogue record for this book is available from the British Library.

Microsoft Press books are available through booksellers and distributors worldwide. For further information about international editions, contact your local Microsoft Corporation office or contact Microsoft Press International directly at fax (425) 936-7329. Visit our Web site at www.microsoft.com/mspress. Send comments to mspinput@microsoft.com.

Acquisitions Editor: Alex Blanton
Project Editor: Aileen Wrothwell

Body Part No. X09-71464

Contents

Contents

What's New in Microsoft Office PowerPoint 2003

You'll notice some changes as soon as you start Microsoft Office PowerPoint 2003. The program has a new look, and many tasks are now performed from easy-to-use task panes, such as Getting Started, Help, Search, and Research, which open when you need them.

New In Office 2003

Many of the features that are new or improved in this version of PowerPoint won't be apparent to you until you start using the program. To help you quickly identify features that are new or improved with this version, this book uses the icon in the margin whenever those features are discussed or shown.

The following table lists the new features that you might be interested in, as well as the chapters in which those features are discussed.

To learn how to	Using this feature	See
Choose words that suit your presentation and your audience and research information on the Web	Thesaurus and Research task pane	Chapter 4
Track types of data that can be used in multiple ways, such as dates, names, and addresses	Smart Tags	Chapter 5
Get superior performance when playing video or sound	Improved media playback	Chapter 10
Edit a presentation in your own handwriting	Tablet PC support	Chapter 11
Work on presentations as part of a team	Document Workspaces	Chapter 11
Restrict who can work on a presentation	Information Rights Management Improved password protection Digital Signatures	Chapter 11
Deliver a presentation on a computer on which PowerPoint is not installed	Updated PowerPoint Viewer program	Chapter 13
Make sure you include all the files you need when you transfer a presentation to a CD	Package for CD	Chapter 13

To learn how to	Using this feature	See
Move smoothly from slide to slide when delivering an electronic slide show	New slide show navigation tools	Chapter 13
Mark up slides during a presentation	Improved ink annotations	Chapter 13

Getting Help

Every effort has been made to ensure the accuracy of this book and the contents of its CD-ROM. If you do run into problems, please contact the appropriate source for help and assistance.

Getting Help with This Book and Its CD-ROM

If your question or issue concerns the content of this book or its companion CD-ROM, please first search the online Microsoft Press Knowledge Base, which provides support information for known errors in or corrections to this book, at the following Web site:

www.microsoft.com/mspress/support/search.asp

If you do not find your answer at the online Knowledge Base, send your comments or questions to Microsoft Press Technical Support at:

mspinput@microsoft.com

Getting Help with Microsoft Office PowerPoint 2003

If your question is about Microsoft Office PowerPoint 2003, and not about the content of this Microsoft Press book, your first recourse is PowerPoint's Help system. This system is a combination of help tools and files stored on your computer when you installed The Microsoft Office System 2003 and, if your computer is connected to the Internet, help files available from Microsoft Office Online.

To find out about different items on the screen, you can display a *ScreenTip*. To display a ScreenTip for a toolbar button, for example, point to the button without clicking it. Its ScreenTip appears, telling you its name. In some dialog boxes, you can click a question mark icon to the left of the Close button in the title bar to display the Microsoft Office PowerPoint Help window with information related to the dialog box.

When you have a question about using PowerPoint, you can type it in the "Type a question for help" box at the right end of the program window's menu bar. Then press Enter to display a list of Help topics from which you can select the one that most closely relates to your question.

Another way to get help is to display the Office Assistant, which provides help as you work in the form of helpful information or a tip. If the Office Assistant is hidden when a tip is available, a light bulb appears. Clicking the light bulb displays the tip, and provides other options.

If you want to practice getting help, you can work through this exercise, which demonstrates two ways to get help.

BE SURE TO start PowerPoint before beginning this exercise.

1   At the right end of the menu bar, click the **Type a question for help** box.

2   Type How do I get help?, and press Enter .

A list of topics that relate to your question appears in the Search Results task pane.

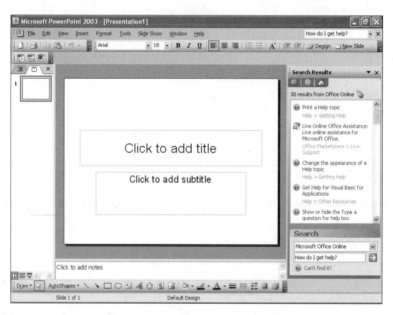

You can click any of the help topics to get more information or instructions.

3   In the **Search Results** task pane, scroll down the results list, and click **About getting help while you work**.

The Microsoft Office PowerPoint Help window opens, displaying information about that topic.

Maximize

4   At the right end of the Microsoft Office PowerPoint Help window's title bar, click the **Maximize** button, and then click **Show All**.

The topic content expands to provide in-depth information about getting help while you work.

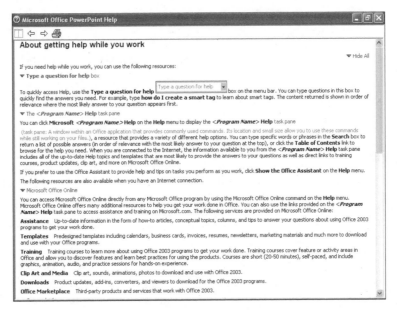

Close

5 At the right end of the Microsoft Office PowerPoint Help window's title bar, click the **Close** button, to close the window.

6 On the **Help** menu, click **Microsoft Office PowerPoint Help**.

The PowerPoint Help task pane opens.

7 In the task pane, click **Table of Contents**.

8   The task pane now displays a list of help topics organized by category, like the table of contents in a book.

Back

9   On the toolbar at the top of the task pane, click the **Back** button.

Notice the categories of information that are available from the Microsoft Office Online Web site. You can also reach this Web site by clicking Microsoft Office Online on the Help menu.

More Information

If your question is about a Microsoft software product, including PowerPoint 2003, and not about the content of this Microsoft Press book, please search the appropriate product support center or the Microsoft Knowledge Base at:

support.microsoft.com

In the United States, Microsoft software product support issues not covered by the Microsoft Knowledge Base are addressed by Microsoft Product Support Services. The Microsoft software support options available from Microsoft Product Support Services are listed at:

support.microsoft.com

Outside the United States, for support information specific to your location, please refer to the Worldwide Support menu on the Microsoft Product Support Services Web site for the site specific to your country:

support.microsoft.com

Using the Book's CD-ROM

The CD-ROM included with this book contains all the practice files you'll use as you work through the exercises in this book. By using practice files, you won't waste time creating sample content with which to experiment—instead, you can jump right in and concentrate on learning how to use Microsoft Office PowerPoint 2003.

What's on the CD-ROM?

In addition to the practice files, the CD-ROM contains some exciting resources that will really enhance your ability to get the most out of using this book and PowerPoint 2003, including the following:

- *Microsoft Office PowerPoint 2003 Step by Step* in e-book format.
- *Insider's Guide to Microsoft Office OneNote 2003* in e-book format.
- *Microsoft Office System Quick Reference* in e-book format.
- *Introducing the Tablet PC* in e-book format.
- *Microsoft Computer Dictionary, Fifth Edition* in e-book format.
- 25 business-oriented templates for use with programs in The Microsoft Office System.
- 100 pieces of clip art.

Important The CD-ROM for this book does not contain the PowerPoint 2003 software. You should purchase and install that program before using this book.

Minimum System Requirements

To use this book, you will need:

- **Computer/Processor**

  Computer with a Pentium 133-megahertz (MHz) or higher processor
- **Memory**

  64 MB of RAM (128 MB recommended) plus an additional 8 MB of RAM for each program in The Microsoft Office System (such as PowerPoint) running simultaneously
- **Hard Disk**
  - 245 MB of available hard disk space with 115 MB on the hard disk where the operating system is installed

■   An additional 20 MB of hard disk space is required for installing the
     practice files.

Hard disk requirements will vary depending on configuration; custom installation choices may require more or less hard disk space

■ **Operating System**

   Microsoft Windows 2000 with Service Pack 3 (SP3) or Microsoft Windows XP
   or later

■ **Drive**

   CD-ROM drive

■ **Display**

   Super VGA (800 × 600) or higher-resolution monitor with 256 colors

■ **Peripherals**

   Microsoft Mouse, Microsoft IntelliMouse, or compatible pointing device

■ **Software**

   Microsoft Office PowerPoint 2003, Microsoft Office Word 2003, Microsoft
   Office Outlook 2003, Microsoft Producer, and Microsoft Internet Explorer 5
   or later

Installing the Practice Files

You need to install the practice files on your hard disk before you use them in the
chapters' exercises. Follow these steps to prepare the CD's files for your use:

1   Insert the CD-ROM into the CD-ROM drive of your computer.

   The Step by Step Companion CD End User License Agreement appears. Follow the
   on-screen directions. It is necessary to accept the terms of the license agreement
   in order to use the practice files. After you accept the license agreement, a menu
   screen appears.

   Important   If the menu screen does not appear, start Windows Explorer. In the
   left pane, locate the icon for your CD-ROM drive and click this icon. In the right
   pane, double-click the **StartCD** executable file.

2   Click **Install Practice Files**.

3   Click **Next** on the first screen, and then click **Yes** to accept the license agreement
   on the next screen.

4   If you want to install the practice files to a location other than the default folder
   (*My Documents\Microsoft Press\PowerPoint 2003 SBS*), click the **Browse** button,
   select the new drive and path, and then click **OK**.

5   Click **Next** on the **Choose Destination Location** screen, click **Next** on the **Select Features** screen, and then click **Next** on the **Start Copying Files** screen to install the selected practice files.

6   After the practice files have been installed, click **Finish**.

Within the installation folder are subfolders for each chapter in the book.

7   Close the Step by Step Companion CD window, remove the CD-ROM from the CD-ROM drive, and return it to the envelope at the back of the book.

Using the Practice Files

Each exercise is preceded by a paragraph or paragraphs that list the files needed for that exercise and explains any file preparation you need to take care of before you start working through the exercise, as shown here:

BE SURE TO start PowerPoint before beginning this exercise.
USE the *TrackChange* document in the practice file folder for this topic. This practice file is located in the *My Documents\Microsoft Press\PowerPoint 2003 SBS\WorkingText\Adding* folder and can also be accessed by clicking *Start/All Programs/Microsoft Press/PowerPoint 2003 Step by Step*.
OPEN the TrackChange document.

Usually you will be instructed to open the practice files form within the application in which you are working. However, you can also access the files directly from Winows by clicking the Start menu items indicated. Locate the file in the chapter subfolder and then double-click the file to open it.

The following table lists each chapter's practice files.

Chapter	Folder	Subfolder	Files
Chapter 1: Creating Presentations	CreatingPresent	Opening Viewing	OpenSave ViewPres
Chapter 2: Working with Slides	WorkingSlide	EnteringText Changing Inserting Rearranging EnteringNotes	EnterText ChangeLayout InsertSlide SlideInsert OrderSlides EnterNotes

Chapter	Folder	Subfolder	Files
Chapter 3: Working with Outlines	WorkingOutline	Entering Editing Arranging Formatting Importing Exporting	TextOutline EditText ArrangeText FormatText InsertOutline Outline SendOutline
Chapter 4: Working with Slide Text	WorkingText	Adding Aligning Finding Correcting Spelling Choosing	AddText AlignText ReplaceText CorrectText SpellCheck Thesaurus
Chapter 5: Applying and Modifying Design Templates	ApplyingDesign	MakingLook ViewingMaster FormattingText SavingPresent	AddTemplate ApplyTemplate ChangeMaster Bamboo FormatMaster SaveTemplate
Chapter 6: Changing Presentation Colors	ChangingColor	SwitchingScheme CreatingScheme AddingColor ColoringSlide	ColorScheme CreateScheme AddColor AddBackground
Chapter 7: Creating Shapes	CreatingShape	DrawingShape ChangingShape AligningShape StackingShape	DrawShape ChangeShape AlignShape StackShape

Chapter	Folder	Subfolder	Files
Chapter 8: Adding Graphics	AddingPicture	InsertingClip ModifyingClip InsertingPic	InsertArt ChangeClip InsertPic Picture01 Picture02 Picture03 Picture04 Picture05 Picture06 Picture07 Picture08 Picture09 Picture10 Picture11 Picture12
		ModifyingPic InsertingArt	ModifyPic InsertWordArt
Chapter 9: Adding Tables, Charts, and Diagrams	AddingTable	InsertingTable InsertingWork InsertingChart InsertingOrg	InsertTable InsertWorksheet Budget InsertChart Sales InsertOrg
Chapter 10: Creating a Multimedia Presentation	CreatingMultimedia	Animating AddingTransition InsertingSound ModifyingSound	AnimateSlide AddTrans InsertMedia InsertMovie ModMedia InsertMovie

Chapter	Folder	Subfolder	Files
Chapter 11: Reviewing and Sharing a Presentation	ReviewingShare	AddingComment ProtectingPresent SendingPresent MergingVersion	AddComments AddPassword EmailPres CompareMerge CompareMerge _KA CompareMerge _KB
Chapter 12: Printing Presentations	PrintingPresent	AddingHeader PreviewingPresent SendingPrint	HeaderFooter PrintPreview PrintFile
Chapter 13: Setting Up and Delivering Slide Shows	SettingShow	TakingPresent DeliveringShow CreatingCustom AddingTiming BroadcastingPresent	RoadPres DeliverShow CustomShow AddTimings Broadcast
Chapter 14: Creating Web Presentations	CreatingWeb	CreatingSummary CreatingHyperlink PreviewingPage	CreateAgenda CreateLink CreateWeb
Chapter 15: Customizing PowerPoint	No practice files		

Uninstalling the Practice Files

After you finish working through this book, you should uninstall the practice files to free up hard disk space.

1   On the Windows taskbar, click the **Start** button, and then click **Control Panel**.

2   In Control Panel, click **Add or Remove Programs**.

3   In the list of installed programs, click **Microsoft Office PowerPoint 2003 Step By Step**, and then click the **Remove** or **Change/Remove** button.

4   In the **Uninstall** dialog box, click **OK**.

5   After the files are uninstalled, click **Finish**, and then close the Add or Remove Programs window and Control Panel.

Important   If you need additional help installing or uninstalling the practice files, please see "Getting Help" earlier in this book. Microsoft Product Support Services does not provide support for this book or its CD-ROM.

Conventions and Features

You can save time when you use this book by understanding how the *Step by Step* series shows special instructions, keys to press, buttons to click, and so on.

Convention	Meaning
Microsoft Office Specialist	This icon indicates a topic that covers a Microsoft Office Specialist exam objective.
New In Office 2003	This icon indicates a new or greatly improved feature in Microsoft Office PowerPoint 2003.
	This icon indicates a reference to the book's companion CD.
BE SURE TO	These words are found at the beginning of paragraphs preceding or following step-by-step exercises. They point out items you should check or actions you should carry out either before beginning an exercise or after completing an exercise.
USE OPEN	These words are found at the beginning of paragraphs preceding step-by-step exercises. They draw your attention to practice files that you'll need to use in the exercise.
CLOSE	This word is found at the beginning of paragraphs following step-by-step exercises. They give instructions for closing open files or programs before moving on to another topic.
1 2	Numbered steps guide you through hands-on exercises in each topic.
●	A round bullet indicates an exercise that has only one step.
Troubleshooting	These paragraphs show you how to fix a common problem that might prevent you from continuing with the exercise.
Tip	These paragraphs provide a helpful hint or shortcut that makes working through a task easier.
Important	These paragraphs point out information that you need to know to complete a procedure.

Convention	Meaning
⊡ Save	The first time you are told to click a button in an exercise, a picture of the button appears in the left margin. If the name of the button does not appear on the button itself, the name appears under the picture.
Ctrl + Home	A plus sign (+) between two key names means that you must hold down the first key while you press the second key. For example, "press Ctrl+Home" means "hold down the Ctrl key while you press the Home key."
Black bold characters	In steps, the names of program elements, such as buttons, commands, and dialog boxes, are shown in black bold characters.
Blue bold characters	Anything you are supposed to type appears in blue bold characters.
Blue italic characters	Terms that are explained in the glossary at the end of the book are shown in blue italic characters.

Taking a Microsoft Office Specialist Certification Exam

As desktop computing technology advances, more employers rely on the objectivity and consistency of technology certification when screening, hiring, and training employees to ensure the competence of these professionals. As a job seeker or employee, you can use technology certification to prove that you have the skills businesses need, and can save them the trouble and expense of training. Microsoft Office Specialist is the only Microsoft certification program designed to assist employees in validating their Microsoft Office System skills.

About the Microsoft Office Specialist Program

A Microsoft Office Specialist is an individual who has demonstrated worldwide standards of Microsoft Office skill through a certification exam in one or more of The Microsoft Office System desktop programs including Microsoft Word, Excel, PowerPoint®, Outlook®, Access and Project. Office Specialist certifications are available at the "Specialist" and "Expert" skill levels. Visit *www.microsoft.com /officespecialist/* to locate skill standards for each certification and an Authorized Testing Center in your area.

What Does This Logo Mean?

This Microsoft Office Specialist logo means this courseware has been approved by the Microsoft Office Specialist Program to be among the finest available for learning PowerPoint 2003. It also means that upon completion of this courseware, you might be prepared to become a Microsoft Office Specialist.

Selecting a Microsoft Office Specialist Certification Level

When selecting the Microsoft Office Specialist certification(s) level that you would like to pursue, you should assess the following:

■ The Office program ("program") and version(s) of that program with which you are familiar

■ The length of time you have used the program

■ Whether you have had formal or informal training in the use of that program

Candidates for Specialist-level certification are expected to successfully complete a wide range of standard business tasks, such as formatting a document or spreadsheet. Successful candidates generally have six or more months of experience with the program, including either formal, instructor-led training or self-study using Microsoft Office Specialist-approved books, guides, or interactive computer-based materials.

Candidates for Expert-level certification are expected to complete more complex, business-oriented tasks utilizing the program's advanced functionality, such as importing data and recording macros. Successful candidates generally have one or more years of experience with the program, including formal, instructor-led training or self-study using Microsoft Office Specialist-approved materials.

Microsoft Office Specialist Skill Standards

Every Microsoft Office Specialist certification exam is developed from a set of exam skill standards that are derived from studies of how the Office program is used in the workplace. Because these skill standards dictate the scope of each exam, they provide you with critical information on how to prepare for certification.

Microsoft Office Specialist Approved Courseware, including the Microsoft Press Step by Step series, are reviewed and approved on the basis of their coverage of the Microsoft Office Specialist skill standards.

The Exam Experience

Microsoft Office Specialist certification exams for Office 2003 programs are performance-based exams that require you to complete 15 to 20 standard business tasks using an interactive simulation (a digital model) of a Microsoft Office System program. Exam questions can have one, two, or three task components that, for example, require you to create or modify a document or spreadsheet:

Modify the existing brochure by completing the following three tasks:

1   Left-align the heading, *Premium Real Estate*.

2   Insert a footer with right-aligned page numbering. (Note: accept all other default settings.)

3   Save the document with the file name Broker Brochure in the My Documents folder.

Candidates should also be aware that each exam must be completed within an allotted time of 45 minutes and that in the interest of test security and fairness, the Office Help system (including the Office Assistant) cannot be accessed during the exam.

Passing standards (the minimum required score) for Microsoft Office Specialist certification exams range from 60 to 85 percent correct, depending on the exam.

The Exam Interface and Controls

The exam interface and controls, including the test question, appear across the bottom of the screen.

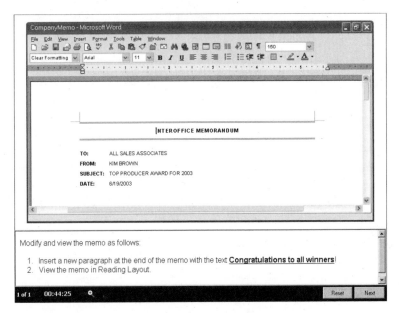

- The **Counter** is located in the left corner of the exam interface and tracks the number of questions completed and how many questions remain.

- The **Timer** is located to the right of the Counter and starts when the first question appears on the screen. The Timer displays the remaining exam time. If the Timer is distracting, click the Timer to remove the display.

   Important   Transition time between questions is not counted against total allotted exam time.

- The **Reset** button is located to the left of the **Next** button and will restart a question if you believe you have made an error. The **Reset** button will not restart the entire exam nor extend the total allotted exam time.

- The **Next** button is located in the right corner. When you complete a question, click the **Next** button to move to the next question. It is not possible to move back to a previous question on the exam.

Test-Taking Tips

- Follow all instructions provided in each question completely and accurately.

- Enter requested information as it appears in the instructions, but without duplicating the format. For example, all text and values that you will be asked to enter will appear in the instructions with bold and underlined text formats (for example, text), however, you should enter the information without applying these formats unless you are specifically instructed to do otherwise.

■ Close all dialog boxes before proceeding to the next exam question unless you are specifically instructed otherwise.

■ There is no need to close task panes before proceeding to the next exam question unless you are specifically instructed otherwise.

■ There is no need to save your work before moving on to the next question unless you are specifically instructed to do otherwise.

■ For questions that ask you to print a document, spreadsheet, chart, report, slide, and so on, please be aware that nothing will actually be printed.

■ Responses are scored based on the result of your work, not the method you use to achieve that result (unless a specific method is indicated in the instructions), and not the time you take to complete the question. Extra keystrokes or mouse clicks do not count against your score.

■ If your computer becomes unstable during the exam (for example, if the exam does not respond or the mouse no longer functions) or if a power outage occurs, contact a testing center administrator immediately. The administrator will restart the computer and return the exam to the point where the interruption occurred with your score intact.

Certification

At the conclusion of the exam, you will receive a score report, which you can print with the assistance of the testing center administrator. If your score meets or exceeds the passing standard (the minimum required score), you will be mailed a printed certificate within approximately 14 days.

College Credit Recommendation

The American Council on Education (ACE) has issued a one-semester hour college credit recommendation for each Microsoft Office Specialist certification. To learn more, visit *www.microsoft.com/traincert/mcp/officespecialist/credit.asp*.

For More Information

To learn more about Microsoft Office Specialist certification, visit *www.microsoft.com /officespecialist/*.

To learn about other Microsoft Office Specialist approved courseware from Microsoft Press, visit *www.microsoft.com/mspress/certification/officespecialist/*.

Microsoft Office Specialist Skill Standards

Each Microsoft Office Specialist certification has a set of corresponding skill standards that describe areas of individual, Microsoft Office program use. You should master each skill standard to prepare for the corresponding Microsoft Office Specialist certification exam.

Microsoft Office Specialist

This book will fully prepare you for the Microsoft Office Specialist certification at the Specialist level. Throughout this book, content that pertains to a Microsoft Office Specialist skill standard is identified with the logo shown in the margin.

Standard	Skill	Page
PP03S-1	**Creating Content**	
PP03S-1-1	Create new presentations from templates	14, 17
PP03S-1-2	Insert and edit text-based content	23, 39, 44, 52, 60, 74
PP03S-1-3	Insert tables, charts, and diagrams	165
PP03S-1-4	Insert pictures, shapes, and graphics	117, 128, 139, 145, 155, 169, 175
PP03S-1-5	Import objects	165, 174, 189, 195
PP03S-2	**Formatting Content**	
PP03S-2-1	Format text-based content	50, 64, 68
PP03S-2-2	Format pictures, shapes, and graphics	123, 133, 145, 152
PP03S-2-3	Format slides	28, 83, 105, 108, 110
PP03S-2-4	Apply animation schemes	181
PP03S-2-5	Apply slide transitions	187
PP03S-2-6	Customize slide templates	86
PP03S-2-7	Work with masters	92, 222
PP03S-3	**Collaborating**	
PP03S-3-1	Track, accept, and reject changes in a presentation	212
PP03S-3-2	Add, edit, and delete comments in a presentation	201, 212
PP03S-3-3	Compare and merge presentations	212

Microsoft Office Specialist Skill Standards

Standard	Skill	Page
PP03S-4	**Managing and Delivering Presentations**	
PP03S-4-1	Organize a presentation	9, 23, 32, 44, 48, 270
PP03S-4-2	Set up slide shows for delivery	246, 270
PP03S-4-3	Rehearse timing	250
PP03S-4-4	Deliver presentations	241
PP03S-4-5	Preparing presentations for remote delivery	238, 256
PP03S-4-6	Save and publish presentations	5, 98, 270
PP03S-4-7	Print slides, outlines, handouts, and speaker notes	224, 228
PP03S-4-8	Export a presentation to another Microsoft Office program	54

About the Authors

Online Training Solutions, Inc. (OTSI)

OTSI is a traditional and electronic publishing company specializing in the creation, production, and delivery of computer software training. OTSI publishes the Quick Course® series of computer and business training products. The principals of OTSI are:

Joyce Cox has over 20 years' experience in writing about and editing technical subjects for non-technical audiences. For 12 of those years she was the principal author for Online Press. She was also the first managing editor of Microsoft Press, an editor for Sybex, and an editor for the University of California.

Steve Lambert started playing with computers in the mid-seventies. As computers evolved from wire-wrap and solder to consumer products, he evolved from hardware geek to programmer and writer. He has written over 14 books and a wide variety of technical documentation and has produced training tools and help systems.

Gale Nelson honed her communication skills as a technical writer for a SQL Server training company. Her attention to detail soon led her into software testing and quality assurance management. She now divides her work time between writing and data conversion projects.

Joan Preppernau has been contributing to the creation of excellent technical training materials for computer professionals for as long as she cares to remember. Joan's wide-ranging experiences in various facets of the industry have contributed to her passion for producing interesting, useful, and understandable training materials.

The OTSI publishing team includes the following outstanding professionals:

Susie Bayers
Jan Bednarczuk
Keith Bednarczuk
RJ Cadranell
Liz Clark
Nancy Depper
Leslie Eliel
Joseph Ford
Jon Kenoyer
Marlene Lambert
Aaron L'Heureux
Lisa Van Every
Michelle Ziegwied

For more information about Online Training Solutions, Inc., visit *www.otsi.com*.

Perspection, Inc.

Microsoft PowerPoint Version 2002 Step by Step, on which this book was based, was created by the professional trainers and writers at Perspection, Inc. Perspection writes and produces software training books, and develops multimedia and Web-based training.

Quick Reference

4   Select the **On-screen presentation** option, if necessary, to select that presentation type, and then click **Next**.

5   Type a name in the **Presentation title** and **Footer** boxes.

6   Click **Next**, and then click **Finish**.

17   **To start a new presentation with a design template**

1   In the **New Presentation** task pane, click **From Design Template**.

2   In the **Slide Design** task pane, click the slide design you want.

3   In the **Slide Design** task pane, click the **Other Task Panes** down arrow to display a list of the task panes, and then click **Slide Layout**.

4   In the **Slide Layout** task pane, click a slide layout.

20   **To create a blank presentation**

1   In the **New Presentation** task pane, click **Blank Presentation**.

2   On the Standard toolbar, click the **New** button.

Chapter 2   **Working with Slides**

Page 23   **To enter text in a slide**

●   In the **Slides** pane, click the text placeholder and begin typing.

23   **To create a new slide**

●   On the Formatting toolbar, click the **New Slide** button.

23   **To insert a bulleted list in a slide**

1   On the **Outline** tab of the **Outline/Slides** pane, point to the right of the line after which the list should appear.

2   Press Enter, and then press Tab.

28   **To apply a new format to a slide**

1   Select the slide you want to reformat.

2   In the **Slide Layout** task pane, scroll down until you see the layout you want to apply, and then click it.

28   **To reapply a slide's original formatting**

1   Select the slide you want to format.

2   On the **Format** menu, click **Slide Layout**.

3   Click the down arrow to the right of the selected slide layout.

4   On the menu, click **Reapply Layout**.

60 **To create a word processing box**

    1   On the Drawing toolbar, click the **Text Box** button.

    2   Position the upside-down T-pointer where you want the word processing box to appear, and then drag the pointer to create a box that is roughly the size you want.

    3   Release the mouse button.

60 **To copy a text object**

    ●   Hold down the Ctrl key, and then drag the selection box of the text object to a new location on the slide.

60 **To adjust a text object to fit the size of the text**

    1   On the **Format** menu, click **Placeholder**.

    2   Click the **Text Box** tab to display text spacing and alignment options.

    3   Select the **Resize AutoShape to fit text** check box, and then click **OK**.

64 **To change paragraph spacing**

    ●   On the Formatting toolbar, click the **Increase Paragraph Spacing** button or the **Decrease Paragraph Spacing** button.

74 **To mark a word as a foreign language word**

    1   Select the word.

    2   On the **Tools** menu, click **Language**.

    3   Scroll down the list, click the language you want to mark the phrase as, and click **OK**.

74 **To spell check a whole document**

    ●   On the Standard toolbar, click the **Spelling** button.

74 **To check the style of a document**

    1   On the **Tools** menu, click **Options**.

    2   Click the **Spelling and Style** tab to display a list of options.

    3   Select the **Check style** check box, and then click **Style Options**.

    4   Select the options that you want and click **OK**.

79 **To change the text case**

    1   Select the text that you want to change.

    2   On the **Format** menu, click **Change Case**.

    3   Click the change case option that you want to apply to the selected text.

    4   Click **OK** to apply the change option to the presentation.

105 To change a color in a color scheme

  1   In the **Slide** pane, click a slide.

  2   On the Formatting toolbar, click the **Slide Design** button, and in the **Slide Design** task pane, click **Color Schemes**.

  3   Click **Edit Color Schemes** at the bottom of the **Slide Design** task pane.

  4   In the **Scheme colors** area, click the color box you want to change.

  5   Click **Change Color**.

  6   In the color palette, click the color you want, click **OK**, and click **Apply**.

108 To add a color to the color palette

  1   In the **Slide** pane, click a slide.

  2   Select a text object to display the dotted selection box.

  3   On the Drawing toolbar, click the down arrow to the right of the **Font Color** button.

  4   On the drop-down color palette, click **More Colors**.

  5   Click the color you want to add.

  6   Click **OK**.

110 To add a shade to a slide background

  1   In the **Slide** pane, click a slide.

  2   On the **Format** menu, click **Background**.

  3   Click the down arrow to the right of the **Background fill** box.

  4   On the **Background Fill** menu, click **Fill Effects**.

  5   In the **Colors** area, select the **One color** option.

  6   Click the down arrow to the right of the **Color 1** box, and then click the color box that you want to change.

  7   Select the options you want to apply, click **OK**, and click **Apply**.

110 To apply a texture to a slide background

  1   In the **Slide** pane, click a slide.

  2   On the **Format** menu, click **Background**.

  3   Click the down arrow to the right of the **Background fill** box, and then click **Fill Effects**.

  4   Click the **Texture** tab, and then select the textured fill option you want to apply.

  5   Click **OK** to display the **Background** dialog box, and then click **Apply**.

1   In the **Slide** pane, click the slide on which you want to draw a shape.

2   On the Drawing toolbar, click **AutoShapes**.

3   Click the shape you want to draw.

4   Position the crosshair pointer where you want the shape to be placed, and then drag to draw the shape.

1   Select the shape.

2   Drag a sizing handle until the shape is the size you want (holding down the ⌷Shift⌷ key if you want to preserve the shape's proportions).

1   Click the shape to select it.

2   On the Standard toolbar, click the **Copy** button. To move the shape, click the **Cut** button.

3   Position the insertion point where you want to paste the shape, and on the Standard toolbar, click the **Paste** button.

1   Select the shape.

2   On the Drawing toolbar, click the down arrow to the right of the **Fill Color** button, and click **Fill Effects**.

3   Click the tab for the type of fill effect you want to apply.

4   Click the textured fill you want to apply, and click **OK**.

1   Select the shape.

2   On the Drawing toolbar, click the down arrow to the right of the **Line Color** button, and click the color box you want.

1   Select the shape.

2   On the Drawing toolbar, click the **Shadow Style** button.

3   On the **Shadow Style** menu, click the button for the shadow style you want to apply.

123 **To change the font attributes of a shape**

   1   Select the shape.

   2   On the Drawing toolbar, click the down arrow to the right of the **Font Color** button, and then click the color you want to apply.

   3   On the Formatting toolbar, click the down arrow to the right of the **Font** button, and then click the font you want to apply.

128 **To align a shape with another shape**

   1   Select the shapes.

   2   On the Drawing toolbar, click the **Draw** button, point to **Align or Distribute**, and then click **Align Center**.

128 **To align a shape to guides**

   1   On the **View** menu, click **Grid and Guides**.

   2   Select the **Display grid on screen** and **Display drawing guides on screen** check boxes, then click **OK** to close the **Grid and Guides** dialog box.

   3   Select the shapes, hold down the [Shift] key, and then drag the selected shapes to the left until their edges touch or snap to the grid.

128 **To add a connecting line to shapes**

   1   On the Drawing toolbar, click **AutoShapes**, point to **Connectors**, and then click the style of connecting line you want.

   2   Position the center of the pointer at the point in the first shape where you want to attach the connecting line, and then click the shape to select a connection point.

   3   Position the pointer at the point in the second shape where you want to attach the connecting line, and then click the shape to select another connection point.

128 **To change the format of the connecting lines**

   1   Select the connector lines.

   2   On the Drawing toolbar, click the **Dash Style** button, and then click a line style.

   3   On the Drawing toolbar, click the **Line Style** button, and then click a line style.

133 **To change the stacking order of shapes**

   1   Select the shape whose order you want to change.

   2   On the Drawing toolbar, click the **Draw** button, point to **Order**, and then click **Send to Back**, **Bring to Front**, or **Send Backward**.

145   To change the color of a clip art image

1   Select the clip art image.

2   On the **View** menu, point to **Toolbars,** and then click **Picture** to display the Picture toolbar, if necessary.

3   On the **Picture** toolbar, click the **Recolor Picture** button.

4   Select the **Fills** option to display the fill colors in the image.

5   In the **New** area, click the down arrow to the right of the color you want to change, and then click a new color.

6   Click **OK** to close the **Recolor Picture** dialog box.

147 To insert a picture from a file

1   Position the insertion point where you want to insert the picture.

2   On the **Insert** menu, point to **Picture,** and then click **From File.**

3   Navigate to the folder where the picture is stored.

4   Click the file you want to insert, and then click **Insert.**

147 To create a new photo album

1   On the **Insert** menu, point to **Picture,** and then click **New Photo Album.**

2   Click **File/Disk.**

3   Navigate to the folder where the pictures are stored.

4   Click the pictures you want to add to the photo album, and click **Insert.**

5   In the **Album Layout** area, click the down arrow to the right of the **Picture layout** box, and then click the layout you want.

6   Click the down arrow to the right of the **Frame shape** box, click the frame shape you want, and click **Create.**

152 To crop a picture

1   Select the picture on the slide.

2   On the **Picture** toolbar, click the **Crop** button.

3   Position the center of the cropping tool over the handle, and then drag until the picture is cropped how you want it.

152 To compress a picture

1   Select the picture on the slide.

2   On the **Picture** toolbar, click the **Compress Pictures** button.

3   Click **OK,** and then click **Apply.**

1 On the Drawing toolbar, click the **Insert WordArt** button.

2 Click the style you want, and then click **OK**.

3 In the **Text** box, type the WordArt text, and click **OK**.

4 Click the WordArt object and, on the **WordArt** toolbar, click the buttons for the adjustments you want to make.

1 Position the insertion point where you want to place the table.

2 On the **Insert** menu, click **Table**.

3 Click the up arrow to the right of the **Number of rows** box until it displays the number of rows you want.

4 Click the up arrow to the right of the **Number of columns** box until it displays the number of columns you want.

5 Click **OK**.

1 In PowerPoint, on the **Insert** menu, click **Object**.

2 In the **Insert Object** dialog box, click **Create new**.

3 In the **Object type** box, click **Microsoft Word Document**, and then click **OK**.

4 Use the commands on the **Table** menu to create the table that you want.

5 Click outside of the table to return to Microsoft PowerPoint.

1 Position the insertion point where you want to place the worksheet.

2 On the **Insert** menu, click **Object**.

3 Select the **Create from file** option, and then click **Browse**.

4 Navigate to the folder that contains the worksheet you want to insert.

5 In the list of file and folder names, click the file, and then click **OK** to close the **Browse** dialog box.

169   **To create a graph**

1   Position the insertion point where you want to place the graph.

2   On the **Insert** menu, click **Chart**.

3   In the datasheet of placeholder data, click the blank cell above the **East** data label.

4   On the Graph Standard toolbar, click the **Import File** button.

5   Navigate to the file that contains the graph data you want to insert, and then double-click the file.

6   Click **OK** to overwrite the current data in the datasheet.

169   **To change the graph type**

●   On the Graph Standard toolbar, click the down arrow to the right of the **Chart Type** button, and then click the chart type you want.

174   **To insert an Excel chart**

1   Position the insertion point where you want to place the chart.

2   On the **Insert** menu, click **Object**.

3   Select the **Create from file** option, and then click **Browse**.

4   Navigate to the folder that contains the chart you want to insert.

5   In the list of file and folder names, click the file, and then click **OK** to close the **Browse** dialog box.

175   **To create an organization chart**

1   Position the insertion point where you want to place the org chart.

2   On the **Insert** menu, click **Diagram**.

3   Click **OK**.

175   **To add a chart box to an org chart**

1   Click the chart box to which you want to add a related chart box.

2   On the **Organization Chart** toolbar, click the down arrow to the right of the **Insert Shape** button, and then click the type of chart box shape you want to add.

179   **To create a diagram**

1   Position the insertion point where you want to place the diagram.

2   On the Drawing toolbar, click the **Insert Diagram or Organization Chart** button.

3   Select the diagram that you want to add, and then click **OK**.

1   Click the **Slide Sorter View** button, and then click the slide to which you want to add the animation scheme.

2   On the **Slide Show** menu, click **Animation Schemes**.

3   In the **Apply to selected slides** area of the **Slide Design** task pane, click the scheme you want to apply.

1   Display the slide in Normal view.

2   On the **Slide Show** menu, click **Custom Animation**.

3   Click the text, and in the **Custom Animation** task pane, click **Add Effect**.

4   Choose the animation options you want to apply.

1   Display the slide.

2   In the **Custom Animation** task pane, click the down arrow to the right of the animated item in the **Animation Order** list, and then click **Effect Options**.

3   Click the **Text Animation** tab, choose the animation order, and then click **OK**.

1   Click the **Slide Sorter View** button.

2   On the **Slide Show** menu, click **Slide Transition**.

3   Under **Apply to selected slides**, scroll down, and then click the transition effect you want to apply.

1   On the **Slide Show** menu, click **Slide Transition**.

2   Click the down arrow to the right of the **Sound** box, and then click the sound you want to apply.

1   Display the slide into which you want to insert sound.

2   On the **Insert** menu, point to **Movies and Sounds**, and then click **Sound from Clip Organizer**.

3 In the **Clip Art** task pane, scroll down the **Results** list, and then click the sound you want to insert.

4 Choose whether you want the sound to play automatically in the slide show or when clicked.

189 **To insert a movie clip**

1 Display the slide into which you want to insert the movie.

2 On the **Insert** menu, point to **Movies and Sounds,** and then click **Movie from Clip Organizer**.

3 In the **Clip Art** task pane, scroll down the **Results** list, and then click the movie clip you want to add.

189 **To insert a movie from a file**

1 Display the slide into which you want to insert the movie.

2 On the **Insert** menu, point to **Movies and Sound,** and then click **Movie from File.**

3 Navigate to the folder in which the movie file is stored ,and then double-click the file.

189 **To play a movie in a slide**

● Double-click the movie object.

189 **To modify a movie's animation settings**

1 Display the slide that contains the movie.

2 Right-click the movie object, and then click **Edit Movie Object.**

3 In the **Movie Options** dialog box, select the movie play options and the total playing time of the movie.

4 Click **OK** to close the **Movie Options** dialog box.

194 **To record a narration**

1 On the **Slide Show** menu, click **Record Narration.**

2 Click **OK.**

3 Use the rehearsed slide timings, or click to advance through the slide show and add voice narration (your own explanation of the slides) as you go.

4 Right-click anywhere on the screen, and then click **Pause Narration.**

5 Right-click anywhere on the screen, and then click **Resume Narration.**

6 Right-click anywhere on the screen, and then click **End Show.**

7 Click **Save.**

201 **To delete all comments in a slide**

● On the Reviewing toolbar, click the down arrow to the right of the **Delete Comment** button, and then click **Delete All Markers on the Current Slide**.

201 **To accept changes**

1 Click the small box in the slide to display the marker.

2 Select the check boxes for the changes you want to apply or unapply.

3 On the Reviewing toolbar, click the **Apply** or **Unapply** button.

205 **To password protect a file**

1 On the **Tools** menu, click **Options**.

2 Click the **Security** tab to display security options.

3 In the **Password to modify** box, type a password.

4 Click **OK** to close the **Options** dialog box.

5 In the **Confirm Password** dialog box, in the **Reenter password to modify** box, type the password, and then click **OK**.

205 **To open a password-protected file as read-only**

1 Double-click the protected file.

2 In the **Password** dialog box, click **Read Only**.

210 **To send a presentation for review by using e-mail**

1 On the **File** menu, point to **Send To**, and then click **Mail Recipient (for Review)**.

2 Click in the **To:** box, if necessary, and then type the recipient's e-mail address.

3 Click in the message area below the text *Please review the attached document*, and if necessary, type an additional note.

4 On the Message toolbar, click the **Send** button.

212 **To merge documents**

1 On the **View** menu, point to **Toolbars**, and then click **Reviewing**, if necessary.

2 On the **Tools** menu, click **Compare and Merge Presentations**.

3 Navigate to the folder that contains the file, click the file, and then click **Merge**.

4 Click **Continue**.

Chapter 12   **Printing Presentations**

  To add a footer to a presentation

1   On the **View** menu, click **Header and Footer**.

2   Select the **Footer** check box, and then type the footer text.

3   Select any options you want to apply to the footer, and then click **Apply** to apply the footer to the selected slide, or click **Apply to All** to apply the footer to all slides in the presentation.

  To add a header to a presentation

1   On the **View** menu, click **Header and Footer**.

2   Click the **Notes and Handouts** tab.

3   Click in the **Header** box, and then type the header text.

4   Select any options you want to apply to the header, and then click **Apply** to apply the header to the selected slide, or click **Apply to All** to apply the header to all slides in the presentation.

  To view a presentation in print preview

●   On the Standard toolbar, click the **Print Preview** button.

  To preview a color presentation in black and white

●   On the Print Preview toolbar, click the down arrow to the right of the **Options** button, point to **Color/Grayscale**, and then click **Color (On Black and White Printer)**.

  To change the print settings

1   On the **File** menu, click **Print**.

2   In the **Printer** area, click the down arrow to the right of the **Name** box, and click the printer to which you want to send the presentation.

3   Click **Properties**.

4   In the **Properties** dialog box, specify the print settings you want.

5   In the **Print** dialog box, click **OK** to print the presentation with the selected print settings.

  To change the slide size setting

1   On the **File** menu, click **Page Setup**.

2   Click the down arrow to the right of the **Slides sized for** box, and then click the slide size you want.

3   Click **OK**.

228 **To switch to a different printer**

1   On the **File** menu, click **Print**.

2   In the **Printer** area, click the down arrow to the right of the **Name** box, and click the printer to which you want to send the presentation.

3   Click **Properties**, and in the **Properties** dialog box, specify the printer settings you want.

4   In the **Print** dialog box, click **OK** to print the presentation on the selected printer.

228 **To print a presentation**

1   On the **File** menu, click **Print**.

2   Click the down arrow to the right of the **Print what** box, and then click the part of the presentation you want to print.

3   Select any other print options you want to apply, and then click **OK**.

Chapter 13 **Setting Up and Delivering Slide Shows**

Page 238 **To prepare a presentation for use on another computer using Package for CD**

1   On the **File** menu, click **Package for CD**.

2   In the **Name the CD** box, type the name of your presentation, and click **Options**.

3   Select the **Embedded TrueType fonts** check box, and click **OK**.

4   Click **Copy to Folder**, click **Browse**, navigate to the folder that contains the presentation, and click **Select**.

5   When you return to the **Copy to Folder** dialog box, click **OK**, and then click **Close** to close the **Package for CD** dialog box.

241 **To start a slide show with a particular slide**

●   Select the slide in Normal or Slide Sorter view, and then click the **Slide Show** button.

241 **To move to the next slide or previous slide**

1   Press the ⮕ key or the ⬅ key.

2   Click the **Next** button or the **Previous** button on the popup toolbar that appears when you move the mouse during a slide show.

3   Right-click the screen, and click **Next** or **Previous** on the shortcut menu.

241 **To jump to a slide that is out of sequence or hidden**

    1   Click the **Navigation** button on the popup toolbar that appears when you move the mouse during a slide show, click **Go to Slide,** and click the slide on the submenu.

    2   Right-click the screen, click **Go to Slide,** and then click the slide on the submenu.

241 **To end a slide show at any time**

    1   Press Esc.

    2   Click the **Navigation** button on the popup toolbar, and click **End Show.**

    3   Right-click the screen, and click **End Show** on the shortcut menu.

241 **To mark up a slide using the pen tool**

    1   Click a slide, and then click the **Slide Show** button.

    2   Right-click anywhere on the screen, click **Pointer Options** on the shortcut menu, click **Felt Tip Pen,** and then make your mark.

241 **To remove marks on a slide**

    ●   Right-click anywhere on the screen, click **Pointer Options,** and then click **Erase All Ink on Slide.**

241 **To change the color of the pen tool**

    1   On the popup toolbar, click the **Pointer** arrow, and then click **Ink Color.**

    2   On the **Ink Color** palette, click any color box.

245 **To deliver a slide show on one monitor and use Presenter view on another:**

    1   Open the PowerPoint presentation you want to set up.

    2   On the **Slide Show** menu, click **Set Up Show.**

    3   In the **Set Up Show** dialog box's **Multiple monitors** area, click the down arrow to the right of the **Display slide show on** box, and click the name of the monitor you want to use to project the slide show.

    4   Select the **Show Presenter View** check box, and click **OK.**

    5   Click **Slide Show** button to start the slide show, using the navigation tools in Presenter view to deliver the presentation.

246 **To change the order of slides in a list**

    ●   Select a slide, and in the **Define Custom Show** dialog box click the up arrow or the down arrow to the right of the **Slides in custom show** box.

246 To hide a slide

● In Slide Sorter view, select a slide and then click the **Hide Slide** button on the Slide Sorter toolbar.

250 To manually set slide timings

1 Click the **Slide Sorter View** button, and then click a slide.

2 On the **Slide Show** menu, click **Slide Transition.**

3 In the **Advance slide** area, select the **Automatically after** check box, and then click the up arrow twice to the timing you want.

4 Click **Slide Show**.

5 At the bottom of the **Slide Transition** task pane, click the **Apply to All Slides** button.

250 To set slide timings automatically while rehearsing your slide show

1 Click Slide 1, and then on the Slide Sorter toolbar, click the **Rehearse Timings** button.

2 Wait the length of time you want to spend on that slide, and then click the **Next** button.

3 Work your way slowly through the slide show, clicking **Next** to display each bullet point on each slide and then move to the next slide.

4 If you want to repeat the rehearsal for a particular slide, click the **Repeat** button on the Rehearsal toolbar to reset the Slide Time for that slide to 0.00.00.

5 Click **Yes** at the end of the slide show when the message box displays the elapsed time for the presentation and asks whether you want to apply the recorded slide timings.

254 To set up a self-running slide show

1 Open the presentation, and then on the **Slide Show** menu, click **Set Up Show**.

2 In the **Set Up Show** dialog box's **Show type** area, select the **Browsed at a kiosk (full screen)** option.

3 Click **OK**.

4 To test the show, move to Slide 1, and click the **Slide Show** button.

5 Press Esc to stop the slide show.

6 On the **File** menu, click **Save As** and navigate to the folder where you want to store the self-running presentation.

7 Click the down arrow to the right of the **Save as type** box, and click **PowerPoint Show** in the drop-down list.

8 In the **File name** box, assign a name to the self-running version of the show, and click **Save**.

Chapter 14   Creating Web Presentations

To create a summary slide or home page

1 Click the **Slide Sorter View** button.

2 On the **Edit** menu, click **Select All** to select all of the slides in the presentation.

3 On the Slide Sorter toolbar, click the **Summary Slide** button.

To create a hyperlink

1 Select the text or object you want to use as a hyperlink.

2 On the **Slide Show** menu, click **Action Settings**.

3 Select the **Hyperlink to** option.

4 Click the down arrow to the right of the **Hyperlink to** box, and then click the item to which you want to link.

5 Specify any other necessary hyperlink information, and click **OK**.

To insert a home Page Action button

1 On the **View** menu, point to **Master**, and click **Slide Master**.

2 On the **Slide Show** menu, point to **Action Buttons**. The **Action Buttons** submenu appears.

3 Click the **Action Buttons: Home** button in the top row, second column.

4 Position the cross-hair pointer in the lower-right corner of the slide.

5 Drag the pointer to make the **Home** button appear.

6 In the **Action Settings** dialog box, select any effects you want to apply to the action button, and then click **OK**.

7 On the Slide Master View toolbar, click **Close Master View**.

To preview a presentation as a Web page

● On the **File** menu, click **Web Page Preview**.

To save presentation graphics in PNG format

1 On the **Tools** menu, click **Options**.

2 Click the **General** tab, if necessary, and then click **Web Options**.

3   Click the **Browsers** tab.

4   Select the **Allow PNG as a graphics format** check box, if necessary.

5   Click the **General** tab.

6   Select the **Add slide navigation controls** check box (if necessary), click the down arrow to the right of the **Colors** box, and then click **Presentation colors (accent color)**.

7   Select the **Show slide animation while browsing** check box.

8   Click **OK** to close the **Web Options** dialog box, and then click **OK** to close the **Options** dialog box.

270   **To save a presentation as a Web page**

1   On the **File** menu, click **Save as Web Page**.

2   Type a name in the **File name** box.

3   Navigate to the folder in which you want to save the presentation and click **Publish**.

4   Select the **Complete presentation** option, if necessary, and then select the **All browsers listed above (creates larger files)** option.

5   Clear the **Open published Web page in browser** check box, if necessary, and then click **Publish**.

270   **To open a presentation in a Web browser**

1   On the Standard toolbar, click the **Open** button.

2   Navigate to the folder that contains the presentation.

3   In the folders and files list, click the presentation.

4   Click the down arrow to the right of the **Open** button, and then click **Open in Browser**.

276   **To create a Web presentation with the AutoContent Wizard**

1   On the Standard toolbar, click the **New** button, and then click **From AutoContent Wizard** in the **New Presentation** task pane.

2   After reading the introduction, click **Next**.

3   Select a presentation type, and then click **Next**.

4   Select the **Web presentation** option, and then click **Next**.

5   Type your presentation title, add information to the footer, if desired, and then click **Next**.

6   Click **Finish** to create a Web presentation.

Chapter 15   Customizing PowerPoint

Page 279   **To move a toolbar**

- Drag the toolbar by its move handle (the four dots at the left edge of the toolbar) to the new location.

279   **To reset menu and toolbar usage data**

1   On the **Tools** menu, click **Customize**.

2   Click the **Options** tab, if necessary.

3   Click **Reset menu and toolbar usage data**.

4   Click **Close**.

279   **To add or remove a button from a toolbar**

1   On the toolbar, click the **Toolbar Options** down arrow.

2   Point to **Add or Remove Buttons**, and then point to the name of the toolbar you want to change.

3   Click the button in the list that you want to add or remove.

279   **To create a custom toolbar**

1   On the **Tools** menu, click **Customize**.

2   Click the **Toolbars** tab, and then click **New**.

3   In the **Toolbar name** box, type a name, and then click **OK**.

4   Click the **Commands** tab to display a list of available commands in PowerPoint.

5   In the **Categories** list, click a category to display a list of commands.

6   In the **Commands** list, drag the buttons you want to the custom toolbar that you created.

7   Click **Close** to close the **Customize** dialog box.

285   **To change font defaults**

1   On the **Format** menu, click **Font**.

2   Change the font attributes to the new default style you want.

3   Select the **Default for new objects** check box, and then click **OK**.

285   **To set object attribute defaults**

1   Create the object with the new defaults you want to set.

2   On the Drawing toolbar, click **Draw**, and then click **Set AutoShape Defaults** to set the new default.

287 **To create a macro**

   1   On the **Tools** menu, point to **Macro**, and then click **Record New Macro**.

   2   In the **Macro name** box, type a name (without any spaces) for the macro, and then click **OK**.

   3   Perform the steps you want included in the macro.

   4   On the Stop Recording toolbar, click the **Stop Recording** button.

287 **To run a macro**

   1   On the **Tools** menu, point to **Macro**, and then click **Macros**.

   2   In the **Macro name** area, click the macro you want to run.

   3   Click **Run**.

290 **To load an add-in program**

   1   On the **Tools** menu, click **Add-Ins**.

   2   Click **Add New**.

   3   Click the down arrow to the right of the **Look in** box, and then click the folder where you stored your PowerPoint add-in programs.

   4   In the list of file and folder names, click a PowerPoint add-in program, and click **OK**.

   5   In the **Available add-ins** list, click the add-in that you want to load, and then click **Load**.

   6   Click **Close**.

290 **To unload an add-in program**

   1   On the **Tools** menu, click **Add-Ins**.

   2   Click the add-in that you want to unload.

   3   Click **Unload** to remove the add-in from memory but keep its name in the list, or click **Remove** to remove the add-in from the list and from the registry file.

   4   Click **Close** to close the **Add-Ins** dialog box.

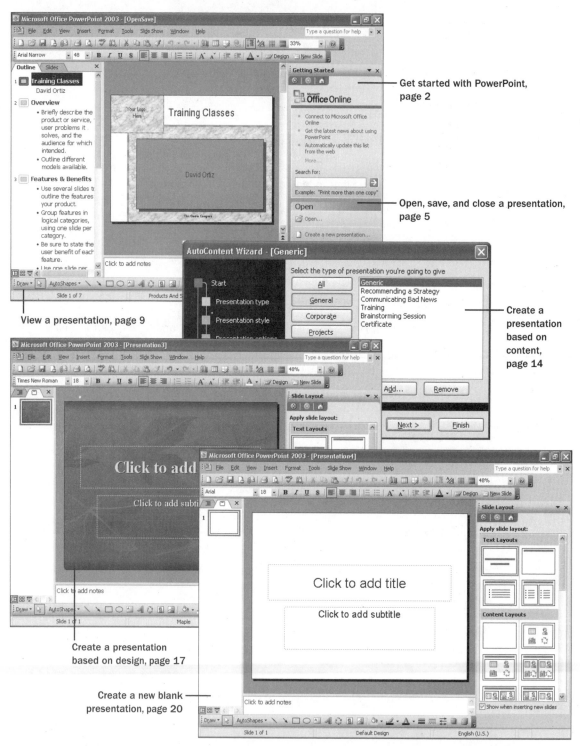

Get started with PowerPoint, page 2

Open, save, and close a presentation, page 5

View a presentation, page 9

Create a presentation based on content, page 14

Create a presentation based on design, page 17

Create a new blank presentation, page 20

Chapter 1 at a Glance

1 Creating Presentations

In this chapter you will learn to:

✔ Get started with PowerPoint.

✔ Open, save and close a presentation.

✔ View a presentation.

✔ Create a presentation based on content.

✔ Create a presentation based on design.

✔ Create a new blank presentation.

Microsoft Office PowerPoint 2003 enables you to create and organize slide shows, overhead transparencies, speaker notes, audience handouts, outlines, and more—all in a single presentation file. Whether you want to deliver training, conduct a brainstorming or business-planning session, present a progress report, manage a project, or make a marketing pitch, you can use PowerPoint's tools to help you design, create, print, share, and deliver a powerful presentation.

For example, suppose Karen Berg, the owner of a fictional business called The Garden Company, wants to improve the name recognition of her company and promote its products. As part of her promotional efforts, she wants to provide gardening classes to increase product awareness and customer skills. Karen can use PowerPoint to create a series of professional-looking slides to accomplish these purposes.

In this chapter you will familiarize yourself with PowerPoint's working environment. You will open, save, and close an existing PowerPoint presentation, and explore various ways you can view slides. Finally, you will create and save three new presentations: one from scratch, one using the help of a wizard, and one using a design template.

See Also Do you need only a quick refresher on the topics in this chapter? See the Quick Reference entries on pages xxix–xxx.

Important Before you can use the practice files in this chapter, you need to install them from the book's companion CD to their default location. See "Using the Book's CD-ROM" on page xiii for more information.

Getting Started with PowerPoint

The most common way to start PowerPoint is to use the Start button on the Windows taskbar. When you start PowerPoint, its *program window* displays the components and features common to all Microsoft Office programs, as well as some that are unique to Office 2003 and some that are unique to PowerPoint.

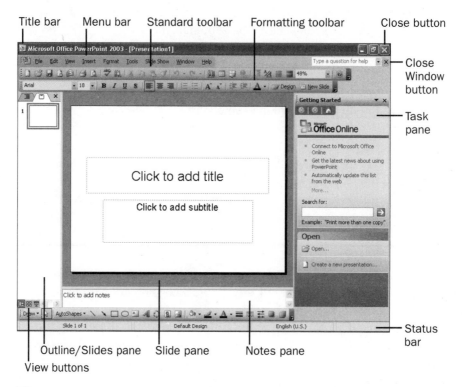

Title bar   Menu bar   Standard toolbar   Formatting toolbar   Close button

Close Window button

Task pane

Status bar

Outline/Slides pane   Slide pane   Notes pane

View buttons

Tip   What you see on your screen might not match the graphics in this book exactly. The screens in this book were captured on a monitor set to 800 x 600 resolution with 24-bit color and the Windows XP Standard color scheme. By default, the Standard and Formatting toolbars share one row, which prevents you from seeing all their buttons. To make it easier for you to find buttons, the Standard and Formatting toolbars in the graphics in this book appear on two rows. If you want to change your setting to match the screens in this book, click Customize on the Tools menu. On the Options tab, select the "Show Standard and Formatting toolbars on two rows" check box, and then click Close.

Displayed within the program window is the *presentation window*, the area in which you create slides by typing text, drawing shapes, creating graphs, and inserting objects. The *insertion point*, the blinking vertical line that appears when you click in the presentation window, indicates where text you type or an object you insert will appear.

On the right side of the program window, PowerPoint displays a *task pane* that you can use to quickly choose commands appropriate to a specific task. For example, when you first start PowerPoint, the Getting Started task pane appears with the commands you commonly use to open an existing presentation or create a new one. When you add a new slide to a presentation, the Slide Layout task pane appears, with common slide designs from which you can choose. If you want to use a task pane other than the one displayed, you can click the Other Task Panes down arrow at the right end of the task pane's title bar to display a drop-down list of the available task panes, and then click the one you want to see. You can hide the task pane to free up valuable screen space, or display it if it is hidden, by clicking Task Pane on the View menu. (This type of on/off command is called a *toggle*.) To close the task pane, click the Close button at the right end of the task pane's title bar.

Tip The task pane opens each time you start PowerPoint. If you don't want the task pane to appear when you start the program, click Options on the Tools menu, click the View tab, clear the "Startup Task Pane" check box, and click OK.

In the lower-left corner of the presentation window are view buttons that enable you to look at a presentation in different ways. By default, PowerPoint opens in *Normal view*, the main view used to write and design presentations. This view is made up of three panes:

- The *Outline/Slides pane* shows tabs that you use to alternate between seeing an outline of your slide text (Outline tab) and seeing the slides displayed as thumbnails (Slides tab).

- The *Slide pane* shows the slide selected in the Outline/Slides pane as it will appear in the presentation.

- The *Notes pane* provides a place for entering speaker notes.

You can size any of the panes by dragging the gray bars that separate them.

As with any Microsoft Windows program, you can temporarily hide the PowerPoint window with the Minimize button, and adjust the size of the window with the Restore Down/Maximize button. You can close a presentation with the Close Window button at the right end of the menu bar; and you can quit PowerPoint with the Close button at the right end of the title bar.

To find out the name of an item on the screen, you can display its *ScreenTip*. To see the name of a toolbar button, for example, you point to the button for a few seconds (this is called *hovering*), and its ScreenTip will appear.

In this exercise, you will start PowerPoint, explore various task panes, and then close the task pane.

BE SURE TO start your computer, but don't start PowerPoint yet.

1 On the taskbar, click **Start**, point to **All Programs**, point to **Microsoft Office**, and then click **Microsoft Office PowerPoint 2003**.

Tip You can also start PowerPoint by creating a shortcut icon on the Windows desktop. Simply double-click a shortcut icon to start its associated program. To create a shortcut, click the Start button, point to All Programs, point to Microsoft Office, right-click Microsoft Office PowerPoint 2003, point to Send To, and then click "Desktop (create shortcut)."

The PowerPoint window opens with a blank presentation in the presentation window and the Getting Started task pane displayed.

2 At the right end of the task pane's title bar, click the **Other Task Panes** down arrow.

A menu of available task panes appears.

3 Press the `Esc` key, or click an empty place in the presentation window.

PowerPoint closes the menu.

Close

4 Click the **Close** button at the right end of the task pane's title bar (not the one at the right end of the menu bar or the program window's title bar).

The Getting Started task pane closes, and the presentation window expands to fill the width of the program window.

5 On the **View** menu, click **Task Pane**.

Troubleshooting If you don't see the Task Pane command on the View menu, it is hidden. PowerPoint personalizes your menus and toolbars to reduce the number of menu commands and toolbar buttons you see on the screen. When you click a menu name on the menu bar, a short menu appears, containing only the commands you use most often. To make the complete menu appear, you can hover over the menu name for a second or two, double-click the menu name, or point to the chevrons (the double arrows) at the bottom of the short menu.

The Getting Started task pane opens, and the presentation window contracts to make room for it.

Opening, Saving and Closing a Presentation

Microsoft Office Specialist

If you click Open on the File menu after you start PowerPoint for the first time, the contents of the My Documents folder are displayed by default in the Open dialog box. If the file you want to open is stored in another folder, you can use the Up One Level button to move upward in your hard disk's folder structure, or you can click the down arrow to the right of the "Look in" box and then click folders and subfolders until the one you want is displayed. You can use the *Places bar* to quickly move to another location on your computer (or network, if you are connected to one). The Places bar provides easy access to locations commonly used to store files.

Places bar   Up One Level button

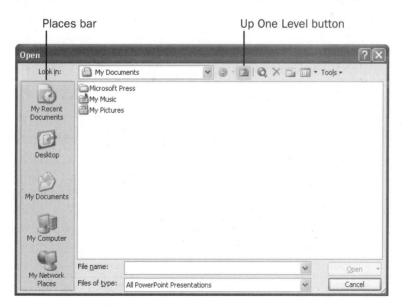

Tip If you can't locate a file but you have some information about the file, such as part of the filename, the slide title, or summary property information, you can use PowerPoint's Basic Search task pane to locate the file. For more information, search on *About finding files* in Help.

When you create a new presentation, it exists only in your computer's temporary memory until you save it. To save your work, you must give the presentation a name and store it on your computer's hard disk. The first time you save a presentation, you click the Save button on the Standard toolbar or click Save As on the File menu to open the Save As dialog box, where you assign a name and storage location. If you want to create a new folder to store the file in, you can quickly do that in the Save As dialog box by clicking the Create New Folder button on the dialog box's toolbar. To save the file in a different folder or on a different hard disk, click the down arrow to the right of the "Save in" box and navigate to that folder or disk.

Create New Folder button

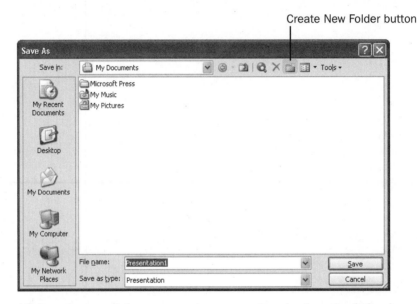

After you've saved the presentation once using the Save As dialog box, you can save new changes simply by clicking the Save button. The new version of the presentation then overwrites the previous version.

If you want to keep both the new version and the previous version, you click Save As on the File menu and use the Save As dialog box to save the new version with a different name. You can save the new file in the same folder as the old file, in a different folder (or subfolder), or on a different hard disk. (You cannot store two files with the same name in the same folder.)

In this exercise, you will start PowerPoint and open an existing presentation. You will then save the presentation with a new name in a folder that you create. Finally, you will close the presentation.

USE the *OpenSave* presentation in the practice file folder for this topic. This practice file is located in the *My Documents\Microsoft Press\PowerPoint 2003 SBS\CreatingPresent\Opening* folder and can also be accessed by clicking *Start/All Programs/Microsoft Press/PowerPoint 2003 Step by Step.*

1 On the **File** menu, click **Open**.

PowerPoint displays the Open dialog box, which is where you specify the name and location of the presentation you want to open.

2 If My Documents is not displayed in the **Look in** box, click **My Documents** on the Places bar.

3 Double-click the *Microsoft Press* folder, double-click the *PowerPoint 2003 SBS* folder, double-click the *CreatingPresent* folder, and then double-click the *Opening* folder.

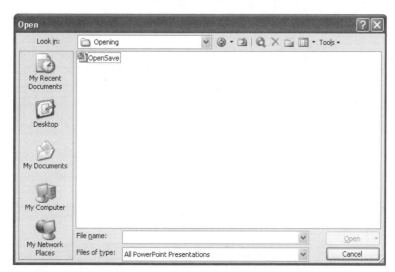

4 Click the *OpenSave* file to select it, and click **Open**.

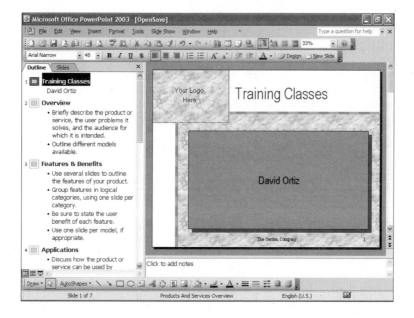

5   On the **File** menu, click **Save As**.

The Save As dialog box appears, displaying the contents of the folder you last used in the Save As or Open dialog box.

Troubleshooting   If the Opening folder is not displayed in the "Save in" box, click the My Documents icon on the Places bar, and then repeat step 3 to navigate to the Opening folder.

Create
New Folder

6   Click the **Create New Folder** button to create a subfolder of the *Opening* folder.

The New Folder dialog box appears.

7   Type **MyPresentation**, and click **OK**.

MyPresentation is now the current folder in the Save As dialog box.

8   In the **File name** box at the bottom of the **Save As** dialog box, type NewPresentation.

The new version of the presentation will be stored in the MyPresentation folder with the name NewPresentation.

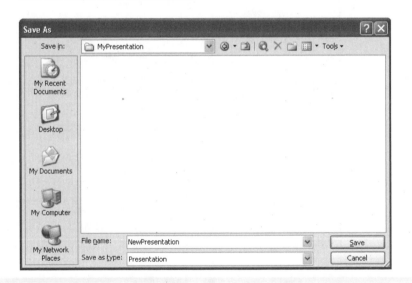

Troubleshooting   Programs that run on the Windows operating system use file name extensions to identify different types of files. For example, PowerPoint presentation files are assigned the extension *.ppt*. If you are used to typing the file name extension when you save a file, be aware that Windows XP programs do not display these extensions by default, and you shouldn't type them in the Save As dialog box. PowerPoint automatically saves the file with whatever extension is associated with the type of file selected in the "Save as type" box at the bottom of the dialog box.

9   Click **Save.**

PowerPoint saves a new version of the OpenSave presentation as NewPresentation in the MyPresentation folder. It closes the OpenSave file, which is still stored in the Opening folder, and opens the new file in the presentation window, as indicated by the NewPresentation file name in the PowerPoint title bar.

Close Window

10   Close the NewPresentation file by clicking the **Close Window** button at the right end of the menu bar.

Viewing a Presentation

Microsoft Office Specialist

PowerPoint has four views to help you create, organize, and display presentations:

- In *Normal view,* you can work with a presentation in three ways: as a text outline or set of slide miniatures (called *thumbnails*) in the Outline/Slides pane; as a slide in the Slide pane; and as speaker notes in the Notes pane.

- In *Slide Sorter view,* you can preview an entire presentation as thumbnails—as if you were looking at photographic slides on a light board—and easily reorder the slides. If titles are hard to read in this view, you can hide the slide formatting by holding down the ⌐Alt⌐ key and the mouse button.

- In *Notes Page view,* you can add fancy speaker notes. Although you can add speaker notes in Normal view's Notes pane, you must be in Notes Page view if you want to add graphics to your notes.

- In *Slide Show view,* you can display slides as an electronic presentation, with the slides filling the entire screen. At any time during the development of a presentation, you can quickly and easily review the slides for accuracy and flow as an audience will see them.

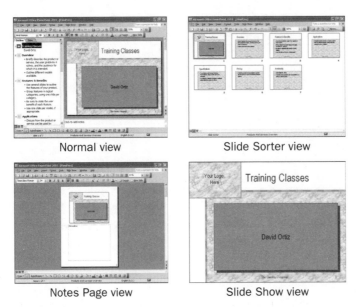

Normal view

Slide Sorter view

Notes Page view

Slide Show view

You switch from one view to another by using commands on the View menu or by clicking the view buttons in the lower-left corner of the presentation window. (There is no view button to switch to Notes Page view; you must click Notes Page on the View menu.)

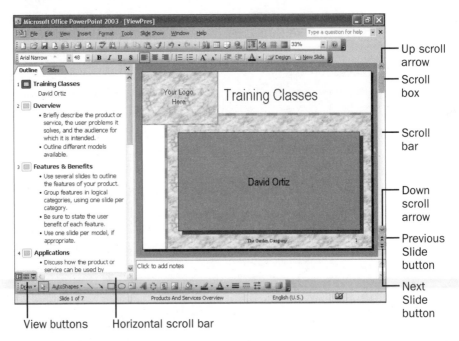

Up scroll arrow

Scroll box

Scroll bar

Down scroll arrow

Previous Slide button

Next Slide button

View buttons   Horizontal scroll bar

You can browse through the slides in a presentation in three ways: You can click the scroll arrows to scroll line by line, click above or below the scroll box to scroll window by window, or drag the scroll box to move immediately to a specific slide. To view the previous and next slides in the Slide pane, you can click the Next Slide and Previous Slide buttons, which are located at the bottom of the vertical scroll bar. You can also press the Page Up or Page Down key to scroll window by window.

In this exercise, you will switch to different PowerPoint views and then display slides in a slide show. You will also browse through the presentation by using the scroll bars and the Next Slide and Previous Slide buttons to move around in the Outline/Slides pane and to move from slide to slide in the Slide pane.

USE the *ViewPres* presentation in the practice file folder for this topic. This practice file is located in the *My Documents\Microsoft Press\PowerPoint 2003 SBS\CreatingPresent\Viewing* folder and can also be accessed by clicking *Start/All Programs/Microsoft Press/PowerPoint 2003 Step by Step*.
OPEN the *ViewPres* presentation.

1 In the **Outline/Slides** pane, click the slide icon adjacent to the *Features and Benefits* heading.

Slide 3 of the presentation is now shown in the adjacent Slide pane.

2 In the **Outline/Slides** pane, click the **Slides** tab.

The pane switches from showing an outline of the text of the presentation to showing thumbnails of the slides. Slide 3 is still selected in the Outline/Slides pane and is displayed in the Slide pane.

Outline tab

Slides tab

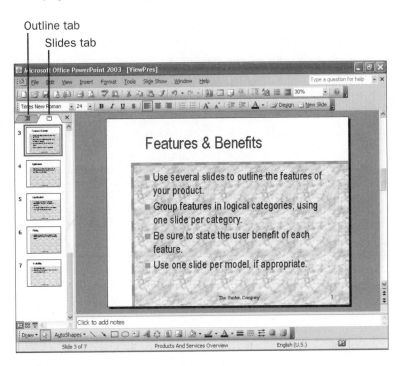

3 In the **Outline/Slides** pane, drag the scroll box to the top of the scroll bar, and click the thumbnail for the first slide.

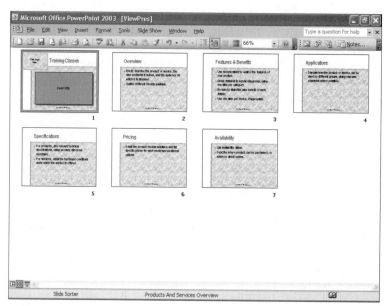

Slide
Sorter View

4 In the lower-left corner of the presentation window, click the **Slide Sorter View** button.

The Outline/Slide and Notes panes close, the Slide pane expands, and all the slides now appear as thumbnails. Slide 1 is surrounded by a dark border, indicating that the slide is selected.

5 Hold down the ⌈Alt⌋ key, point to any slide, and hold down the mouse button.

The slide's formatting disappears so that the title is easier to read.

6 Release the ⌈Alt⌋ key and the mouse button, and then double-click **Slide 1**.

PowerPoint displays the presentation in Normal view, with Slide 1 active.

Slide Show

7 In the lower-left corner of the presentation window, click the **Slide Show** button.

The program window disappears, and the first slide in the presentation is displayed full-screen.

8 Without moving your mouse, click its button to advance to the next slide.

Tip To end a slide show before you reach the last slide, press ⌈Esc⌋.

9 Continue clicking your mouse button to advance through the presentation one slide at a time.

After the last slide in the presentation, PowerPoint displays a black screen.

Tip When you run a slide show, the black screen appears by default. To change this setting, click Options on the Tools menu, click the View tab, clear the "End with black slide" check box, and click OK.

10 Click the black screen to return to Normal view.

11 In the **Outline/Slides** pane, click the **Outline** tab, and then click the down scroll arrow a few times to scroll the hidden text into view.

12 In the **Outline/Slides** pane, drag the scroll box to the end of the scroll bar.

The end of the outline appears.

13 In the **Slide** pane, click below the scroll box in the scroll bar.

The next slide appears in the Slide pane, and on the Outline tab, the text moves to display that slide's title at the top of the pane.

Previous Slide

14 At the bottom of the **Slide** pane's scroll bar, click the **Previous Slide** button.

The previous slide appears in the Slide pane and the text on the Outline tab moves again.

Next Slide

15 In the **Slide** pane, click the **Next Slide** button repeatedly until you reach the end of the presentation.

16 In the **Slide** pane's scroll bar, drag the scroll box until you see *Slide 3 of 7* in the slide indicator box, but don't release the mouse button yet.

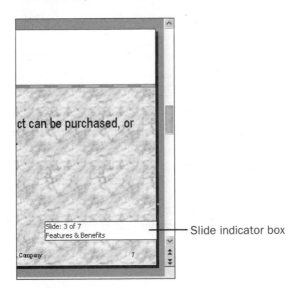
Slide indicator box

The slide indicator box tells you the slide number and title of the slide to which the scroll box is pointing. In the scroll bar, the scroll box indicates the relative position of the slide in the presentation.

17 Release the mouse button.

The Slide pane displays the third slide, and the left end of the status bar indicates that you are viewing *Slide 3 of 7*.

CLOSE the *ViewPres* presentation.

Creating a Presentation Based on Content

Microsoft Office Specialist

When you want to create a new presentation, the *AutoContent Wizard* can save you time by helping you organize and write the presentation's text. The wizard takes you through a step-by-step process, prompting you for presentation information, including the general topic of the presentation you want to give, the way you will deliver it, and the content for the *title slide*, which is the first slide in the presentation. When you finish, the wizard provides a suggested outline that you can modify.

Choosing the Best Method to Start a Presentation

The New Presentation task pane provides four options for creating a new presentation:

■ Click "Blank presentation" if you have content ready and a design in mind. After you click this option, the Slide Layout task pane appears with predesigned slide layouts from which you can choose a layout suitable for the slide you want to create.

■ Click "From design template" if you have content ready but need help with the look of the presentation. Each template provides predefined slide colors and text styles from which you can choose. After you click this option, the Slide Design task pane appears, in which you can choose a template.

■ Click "From AutoContent wizard" if you need help with both the presentation's content and its look. The AutoContent Wizard prompts you for a presentation title and information about the presentation and lets you choose a presentation style and type. PowerPoint then provides a basic outline to help you organize the content into a professional presentation.

■ Click "From existing presentation" if you have an existing presentation that is close enough in either content or design that you can use it as a template for the new one. After you click this option, the New from Existing Presentation dialog box appears, so that you can browse to the file you want through the "Look in" box.

■ Click "Photo Album" if you want to create an album of photographs or a portfolio of other graphics images.

In this exercise, you will use the AutoContent Wizard to create a presentation, and then you will save the results.

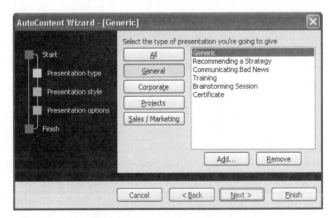

New

1   On the Standard toolbar, click the **New** button. Then if the **New Presentation** task pane is not displayed, click the **Other Task Panes** down arrow at the right end of the task pane's title bar, and click **New Presentation** in the drop-down list.

2   In the **New Presentation** task pane, click **From AutoContent wizard**.

The AutoContent Wizard displays its Start page. On the left side of the page is a "roadmap" of the pages with the active page indicated by a green box.

3   Read the introduction, and then click **Next**.

The box next to *Presentation type* turns green to indicate that this is now the current page. The second page prompts you to select a presentation type. To help you identify presentation types quickly, the wizard organizes presentations by category.

4   Click the **Sales / Marketing** button.

Presentations in the sales and marketing category appear in the list on the right side of the page.

5   In the list, click **Product/Services Overview**, and click **Next**.

The wizard prompts you to specify how you will display the presentation.

6   With the **On-screen presentation** option selected, click **Next**.

The wizard prompts you to enter information for the title slide and for footer information to be included on each slide.

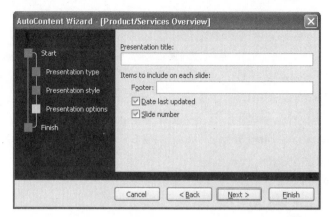

7 Click the **Presentation title** box, type Training Classes, and press the `Tab` key to move the insertion point to the Footer box.

8 In the **Footer** box, type The Garden Company.

9 Clear the **Date last updated** check box to hide the date on each slide.

10 Leave the **Slide number** check box selected so that the slide number will be displayed on each slide, and click **Next**.

11 Click **Finish**.

The PowerPoint presentation window appears in Normal view with content provided by the wizard in outline form on the Outline/Slides pane and the title slide in the Slide pane. The name on the title slide is the name of the registered PowerPoint user.

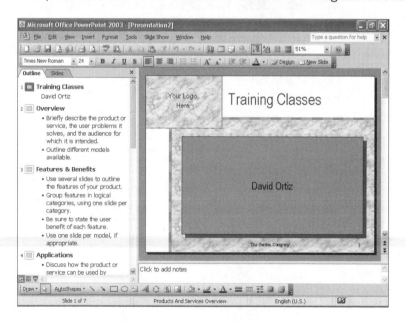

Save

12 On the Standard toolbar, click the **Save** button.

PowerPoint displays the Save As dialog box and suggests the title of the first slide as the name of the file.

13 In the **File name** box, replace the selected name with **AutoContent**.

14 On the Places bar, click **My Documents**. Then double-click the *Microsoft Press* folder, double-click the *PowerPoint 2003 SBS* folder, and double-click the *CreatingPresent* folder.

The contents of the CreatingPresent folder are displayed.

Create
New Folder

15 Click the **Create New Folder** button, type **NewAuto** as the name of the folder, and click **OK**.

16 Click **Save**, or press the [Enter] key to save the AutoContent presentation in the NewAuto folder.

The title bar now displays AutoContent as the name of the current file.

CLOSE the *AutoContent* presentation.

Creating a Presentation Based on Design

Microsoft Office Specialist

When you don't need help with the content of a presentation but you do need help with its design, you can start a new presentation, without any sample text, based on a *design template*. A design template is a blank presentation with a professionally designed format and color scheme to which you can add slides. You can use one of the design templates that come with PowerPoint, or you can create your own.

After you select a design template, you can choose the layout for each slide, such as a slide with a graph, and then type the text and add any other elements you want. You select a layout by clicking it in the Slide Layout task pane.

In this exercise, you will start a new presentation with a design template and then choose a slide layout.

1 Close any open presentations, and then display the task pane by clicking **Task Pane** on the **View** menu. If the **New Presentation** task pane is not displayed, click the **Other Task Panes** down arrow to the right of the task pane's title bar, and click **New Presentation** in the drop-down list.

2 In the **New Presentation** task pane, click **From design template**.

A blank presentation opens, and the Slide Design task pane appears, with thumbnails of a variety of design templates.

Tip The templates available in the Slide Design task pane are the same ones used by the AutoContent Wizard.

3 In the **Slide Design** task pane, point to a design template.

The name of the design template appears as a ScreenTip, and a down arrow appears on the right side of the design icon.

Troubleshooting Don't worry if your thumbnails are much larger than the ones shown here.

4 In the **Slide Design** task pane, click the down arrow to the right of the design template you are pointing to.

A menu appears with commands you can apply to the design template.

5 If **Show Large Previews** does not have a check mark beside it, click **Show Large Previews**.

The size of the design template thumbnails increases to make it easier to see the designs.

6 In the **Slide Design** task pane, drag the scroll box about half way down the vertical scroll bar until you see the Maple design, and then click **Maple**.

A title slide with the Maple design appears in the Slide pane.

7 At the right end of the task pane's title bar, click the **Other Task Panes** down arrow, and then click **Slide Layout**.

The Slide Layout task pane appears, with thumbnails of layouts you can apply to the selected slide. The default Title Slide layout is currently applied.

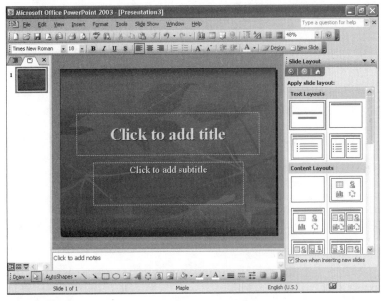

8 In the **Slide Layout** task pane, point to different slide layouts to see their ScreenTips.

9 In the **Text Layouts** area of the **Slide Layout** task pane, click the **Title Only** thumbnail.

PowerPoint applies the Title Only layout to the selected slide.

10 In the **Text Layouts** area of the **Slide Layout** task pane, click the **Title Slide** thumbnail.

PowerPoint applies the Title Slide layout to the selected slide.

Close

11 Click the **Close** button at the right end of the task pane.

The task pane closes.

Close Window

12 Click the **Close Window** button at the right end of the menu bar, and click **No** when you are asked if you want to save the file.

Creating a New Blank Presentation

If you want to create the text and design of a presentation from scratch, you can work with a new blank presentation. When you first start PowerPoint, a blank presentation appears in the presentation window. If you are already working in PowerPoint, you can click New on the File menu to display a new blank presentation.

In this exercise, you will create a blank presentation and then save it.

1 If the **New Presentation** task pane is not displayed, click the **Other Task Panes** down arrow at the right end of the task pane's title bar, and click **New Presentation** in the drop-down list.

> **Troubleshooting** If the task pane is not open, click Task Pane on the View menu.

2 In the **New Presentation** task pane, click **Blank presentation**.

New

You can also click the New button on the Standard toolbar. PowerPoint displays a blank presentation with the default Title Slide layout. The Slide Layout task pane appears, with thumbnails of the available slide layouts.

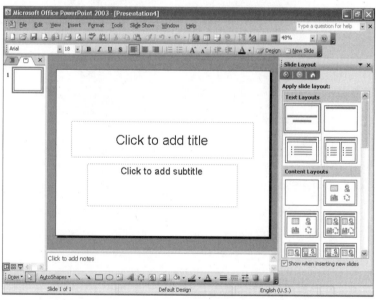

Close

3 On the title bar of the **Slide Layout** task pane, click the **Close** button.

4 On the **File** menu, click **Save As**.

The Save As dialog box appears.

5 Browse to the *My Documents\Microsoft Press\PowerPoint 2003 SBS\CreatingPresent* folder.

Create New
Folder

6 Click the **Create New Folder** button, type **NewBlank**, and click **OK**.

7 In the **File name** box, type **BlankPresentation**, and click **Save**.

PowerPoint saves the presentation with the name BlankPresentation in the NewBlank folder.

CLOSE the *BlankPresentation* presentation, and if you are not continuing on to the next chapter, quit PowerPoint.

> **Tip** You can tell PowerPoint to periodically save a presentation you are working on in case the program stops responding or you lose electrical power. PowerPoint saves the changes in a recovery file according to the time interval specified in the AutoRecover option. To turn on the AutoRecover option and specify the time interval for automatic saving, click Options on the Tools menu, click the Save tab, select the "Save AutoRecover info every" check box, specify the period of time, and then click OK.

Key Points

- PowerPoint has four views to help you create, organize, and display presentations: Normal, Slide Sorter, Notes Page, and Slide Show.

- You can choose one of three ways to scroll through the slides in a presentation: by clicking the scroll arrows to scroll line by line, by clicking above or below the scroll box to scroll window by window, or by dragging the scroll box to move immediately to a specific slide.

- You can save a presentation with a new name in an existing folder or in a new folder that you can create from within PowerPoint. You cannot store two presentations with the same name in the same folder.

- The way you create a new presentation depends on whether you need help coming up with the content or the design. If you need help with the content, you can use the AutoContent Wizard. If you have content ready but need help with the look, you can use a design template. If you have content ready and have a design in mind, you can create a blank presentation.

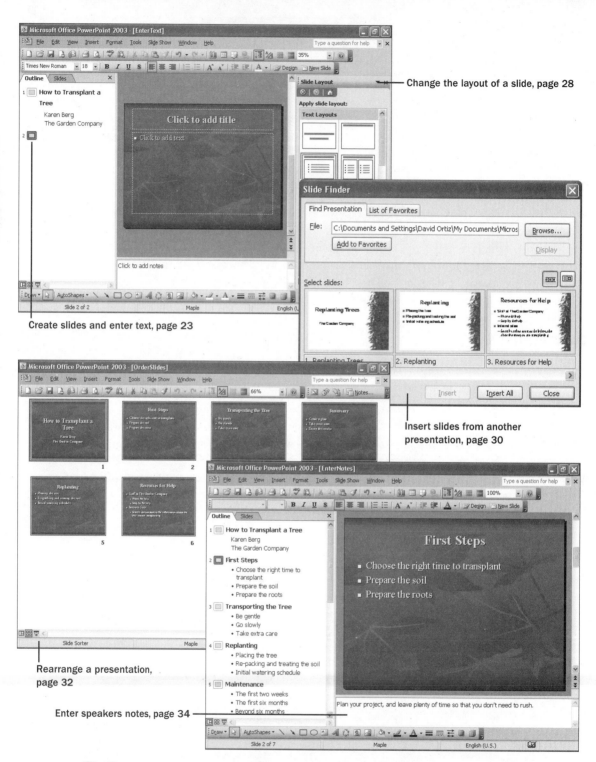

Change the layout of a slide, page 28

Create slides and enter text, page 23

Insert slides from another presentation, page 30

Rearrange a presentation, page 32

Enter speakers notes, page 34

Chapter 2 at a Glance

2 Working with Slides

In this chapter you will learn to:

✔ Create slides and enter text.

✔ Change the layout of a slide.

✔ Insert slides from another presentation.

✔ Rearrange a presentation.

✔ Enter speaker notes.

To work efficiently with Microsoft Office PowerPoint 2003, you need to know how to build a presentation by adding slides and entering text. You can add slides by using commands or simply by typing on the Outline tab of the Outline/Slides pane in Normal view. After adding a slide, you can change its layout by simply clicking a representation in the Slide Layout task pane. You can then customize the slide with your own text, using familiar word-processing techniques. After you have assembled a group of slides, you can turn your attention to their organization, and if you are planning on delivering the presentation to a live audience, you can jot down notes to guide your talk as you work, rather than waiting until the end of the development process.

In this chapter, you will enter text in a slide, create a new slide, change the slide's layout, insert slides from another presentation, rearrange slides, and enter speaker notes.

See Also Do you need only a quick refresher on the topics in this chapter? See the Quick Reference entries on pages xxx–xxxi.

Important Before you can use the practice files in this chapter, you need to install them from the book's companion CD to their default location. See "Using the Book's CD-ROM" on page xiii for more information.

Creating Slides and Entering Text

Microsoft Office Specialist

There are two ways to quickly and easily add new slides to a presentation:

■ Click the New Slide button on the Formatting toolbar.

■ Click the New Slide command on the Insert menu.

When you use either of these methods, a new slide with the default layout is inserted into the presentation immediately after the current slide, and the Slide Layout task pane opens so that you can change the default layout if you want. You can also create new slides by pressing keyboard shortcuts while you are entering text on the Outline tab of the Outline/Slides pane, as follows:

- Press Enter if the insertion point is at the right end of a slide title.
- Press Ctrl+Enter if the insertion point is at the right end of a bulleted item.
- Press Shift+Tab if the insertion point is at the left end of a bulleted item.

When you create a slide with a layout that includes text, the slide is displayed in the Slide pane with one or more boxes called *text placeholders*. After you enter text in a placeholder, the placeholder becomes a *text object*. An *object* is a discrete element of a slide that can be positioned and sized independently of other objects. In this case, the object is a box containing text.

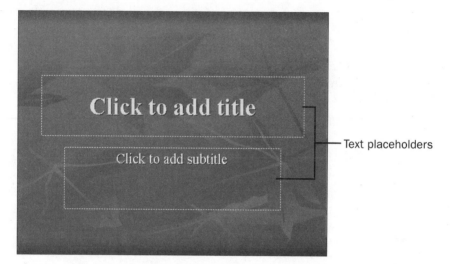

Text placeholders

You can enter and organize text either in the Slide pane or on the Outline tab of the Outline/Slides pane. As you type, the text appears in both places. On the Outline tab, a slide icon appears next to the title for each slide, and subordinate paragraphs appear below the title, indented and preceded by a bullet. In the Slide pane, how the text is displayed will depend on which layout is applied to the slide.

In this exercise, you will enter a tile and subtitle on an existing slide. You'll create a new slide and enter its title text in the Slide pane, and then you'll create more slides and enter titles and bulleted items on the Outline tab.

BE SURE TO start PowerPoint before beginning this exercise.

USE the *EnterText* presentation in the practice file folder for this topic. This practice file is located in the *My Documents\Microsoft Press\PowerPoint 2003 SBS\WorkingSlide\EnteringText* folder and can also be accessed by clicking *Start/All Programs/Microsoft Press/PowerPoint 2003 Step by Step.*

OPEN the *EnterText* presentation.

1 In the **Slide** pane, click the **Click to add title** text placeholder.

A selection box surrounds the placeholder, and a blinking insertion point appears in the center of the box, indicating that the text you type will be centered in text object.

2 Type **How to Transplant a Tree**.

Do not type a period at the end of title names or bulleted items.

Tip If you make a typing error, press Backspace to delete the mistake, and then type the correct text. For more information about editing text, see Chapter 4, "Working with Slide Text."

3 In the **Outline/Slides** pane, click the **Outline** tab and notice that the text you typed also appears there.

4 Click the **Click to add subtitle** text placeholder.

The title text object is deselected, and the subtitle object is selected.

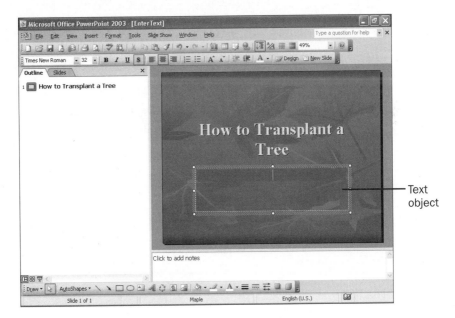

Text object

5   Type **Karen Berg**, and then press Enter to move the insertion to the next line.

6   Type **The Garden Company**.

7   On the Formatting toolbar, click the **New Slide** button.

PowerPoint creates a new slide with the default slide layout (a title and bulleted list) and opens the Slide Layout task pane. The Outline tab now displays an icon for a second slide, and the status bar displays *Slide 2 of 2*.

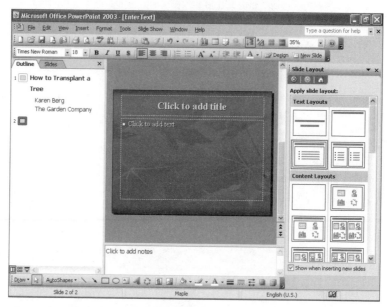

8   Without clicking anywhere, type **First Steps**.

Tip   If you start typing on an empty slide without first having selected a place-holder, PowerPoint enters the text into the title object.

The text appears both in the Slide pane and on the Outline tab. You can work directly in either place to enter your ideas.

Close

9   At the right end of the task pane's title bar, click the **Close** button.

10   On the **Outline** tab, click to the right of Slide 2's title.

A blinking insertion point appears.

11 Press [Enter].

PowerPoint adds a new slide icon on the Outline tab.

12 Press the [Tab] key.

On the Outline tab, the slide icon changes to a bullet on Slide 2.

13 Type **Choose the right time to transplant**, and press [Enter].

PowerPoint adds a new bullet at the same level.

14 Type **Prepare the soil**, and press [Enter].

15 Type **Prepare the roots**, and press [Enter].

16 Press [Shift]+[Tab].

This keyboard shortcut turns a bulleted item into a new slide.

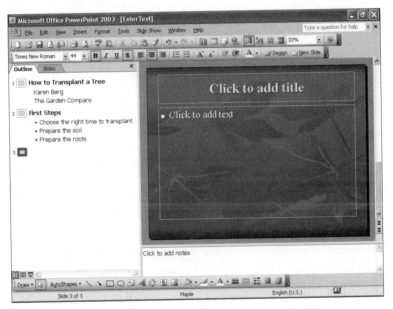

17 Type **Transporting the Tree**, press [Enter], and then press [Tab].

PowerPoint creates a new bullet for Slide 3.

18 Type **Be gentle**, and then press [Enter].

A new bullet appears.

19 Type Go slowly, press [Enter], and then type Take extra care.

20 Press [Ctrl]+[Enter].

This keyboard shortcut creates a new slide instead of another bullet.

21 Type Summary, press [Enter], and then press [Tab].

22 Type Create a plan, and press [Enter].

23 Type Take your time, and press [Enter].

24 Type Enjoy the results.

25 On the Standard toolbar, click the **Save** button to save the presentation.

Save

CLOSE the *EnterText* presentation.

Changing the Layout of a Slide

Microsoft Office Specialist

You can change the layout of an existing slide by selecting the slide and clicking a different layout thumbnail in the Slide Layout task pane. If you make changes to the layout of a slide—such as sizing or moving a placeholder—but then decide you would rather use the original layout, you can reapply the layout without losing text you have already entered, by clicking a command on the layout thumbnail's drop-down list.

When you manually alter the layout or the types of items on a slide, PowerPoint uses an *automatic layout behavior* to apply a slide layout that matches your changes.

In this exercise, you will reapply a layout to a slide, and then you'll apply a different layout.

USE the *ChangeLayout* presentation in the practice file folder for this topic. This practice file is located in the *My Documents\Microsoft Press\PowerPoint 2003 SBS\WorkingSlide\Changing* folder and can also be accessed by clicking *Start/All Programs/Microsoft Press/PowerPoint 2003 Step by Step*.
OPEN the *ChangeLayout* presentation.

1 In the vertical scroll bar to the right of the **Slide** pane, drag the scroll box to Slide 4.

2 Click anywhere in the bulleted list, and point to the text object's frame (but not to a handle). Then drag the object to the bottom of the slide.

3 On the **Format** menu, click **Slide Layout**.

The Slide Layout task pane opens with the current slide layout thumbnail selected.

4 Point to the current thumbnail, and click the down arrow that appears to its right.

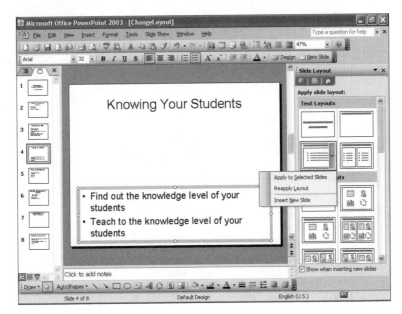

5 On the menu, click **Reapply Layout**.

PowerPoint moves the title object back to its original position on the slide.

6 In the **Slide Layout** task pane, scroll down until you reach the **Text and Content Layouts** area.

7 In the **Text and Content Layouts** area, click the **Title, Text, and Content** slide layout.

The layout of Slide 4 changes so that the bulleted list occupies the left half of the screen and a content placeholder occupies the right half. You can now insert a table, diagram or organization chart, clip art or picture, or a media clip as the content object.

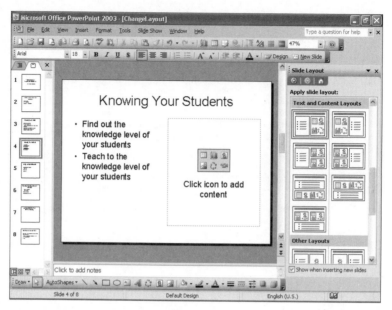

8   Close the **Slide Layout** task pane.

Save

9   On the Standard toolbar, click the **Save** button to save the presentation.

CLOSE the *ChangeLayout* presentation.

Inserting Slides from Another Presentation

You can save time while creating a presentation by using slides that you or someone else has already created. When you insert slides from one presentation into another, the slides conform to the color and design of the current presentation, so you don't have to make many changes.

In this exercise, you will insert slides from one presentation into another.

USE the *InsertSlide* and *SlideInsert* presentations in the practice file folder for this topic. These practice files are located in the *My Documents\Microsoft Press\PowerPoint 2003 SBS\WorkingSlide\Inserting* folder and can also be accessed by clicking *Start/All Programs/Microsoft Press/PowerPoint 2003 Step by Step*.
OPEN the *InsertSlide* presentation.

1   On the **Outline** tab, click to the right of the last bulleted item in Slide 4.

2   On the **Insert** menu, click **Slides from Files**.

Troubleshooting   Remember, if you don't see the Slide from Files command on the short View menu, hover over the menu name, double-click the menu name, or point to the chevrons (the double arrows) at the bottom of the short menu to expand the menu.

The Slide Finder dialog box appears.

3   On the **Find Presentation** tab, click the **Browse** button.

The Browse dialog box appears.

4   Check that My Documents appears in the **Look in** box. (If it doesn't, click the **My Documents** icon on the Places bar.) Then double-click the *Microsoft Press*, *PowerPoint 2003 SBS*, *WorkingSlide*, and *Inserting* folders.

5   Click the *SlideInsert* file, and then click **Open**.

The Slide Finder dialog box reappears.

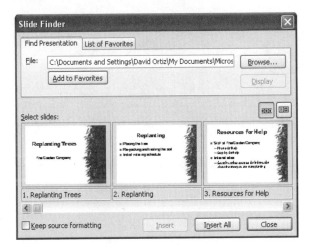

6   Click Slide 2, click Slide 3, click the right scroll arrow, and then click Slide 4 to select the slides you want to insert.

Tip   If you use one or more slides in several presentations, you can click "Add to Favorites" to save the selected slides on the List of Favorites tab in the Slide Finder dialog box.

7   Click the **Insert** button.

PowerPoint inserts the slides after the current slide.

8 Click **Close** to close the **Slide Finder** dialog box.

The text of the inserted slides appears on the Outline tab, and the last slide inserted appears in the Slide pane.

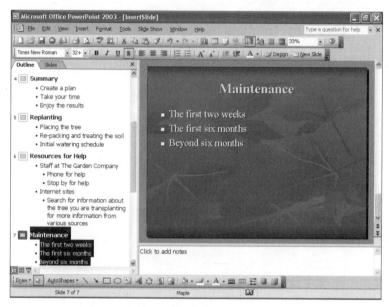

Save

9 On the Standard toolbar, click the **Save** button to save the presentation.

CLOSE the *InsertSlide* presentation.

Rearranging a Presentation

Microsoft Office Specialist

After you have created several slides, whether by adding them and entering text or by inserting them from another presentation, you might need to rearrange the order of your slides to make them most effectively communicate your message. Rearranging a presentation is best done in Slide Sorter view, where you can drag slides from one location to another.

In this exercise, you'll rearrange slides in Slide Sorter view.

USE the *OrderSlides* presentation in the practice file folder for this topic. This practice file is located in the *My Documents\Microsoft Press\PowerPoint 2003 SBS\WorkingSlide\Rearranging* folder and can also be accessed by clicking *Start/All Programs/Microsoft Press/PowerPoint 2003 Step by Step.*
OPEN the *OrderSlides* presentation.

Slide Sorter
View

1   In the lower-left corner of the Outline/Slides pane, click the **Slide Sorter View** button.

PowerPoint displays the presentation as a set of thumbnails and opens the Slide Sorter toolbar above the presentation window.

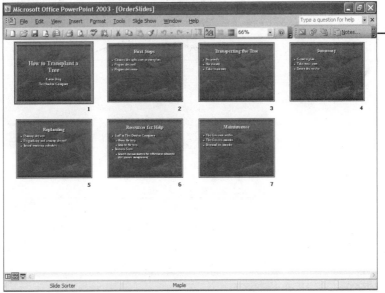

Slide
Sorter
toolbar

2   Drag Slide 4 ("Summary") to the empty space after Slide 7 ("Maintenance").

When you release the mouse button, Slide 4 moves to its new position, and PowerPoint repositions and renumbers the other slides in the presentation.

Tip   In Slide Sorter view, you can also move slides from one open presentation to another. Open the presentations, switch to Slide Sorter view in each presentation window, and click Arrange All on the Window menu. Then drag the slides from one presentation window to another.

3   Drag Slide 5 ("Resources for Help") between Slides 6 and 7.

4 Double-click Slide 2.

PowerPoint returns to the previous view—in this case, Normal view—with Slide 2 active.

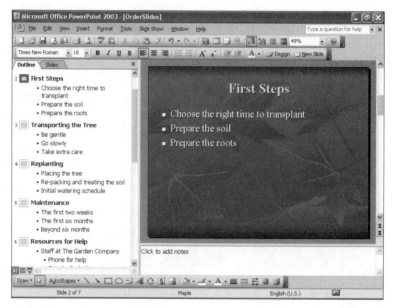

Save

5 On the Standard toolbar, click the **Save** button to save the presentation.

CLOSE the *OrderSlides* presentation.

Entering Speaker Notes

If you will be delivering your presentation before a live audience, you will probably need some speaker notes to guide you. Each slide in a PowerPoint presentation has a corresponding notes page. As you create each slide, you can enter notes that relate to the slide's content on this page. You do this in the Notes pane.

You enter and change text in the Notes pane the same way you do in the Slide pane and on the Outline tab. You simply click the Notes pane and begin typing. If you want to include something other than text in your speaker notes, you must switch to Notes Page view by clicking Notes Page on the View menu. You also switch to Notes Page view if you want to review all the notes at once.

In this exercise, you will enter text in the Notes pane, switch to Notes Page view, and move from page to page.

USE the *EnterNotes* presentation in the practice file folder for this topic. This practice file is located in the *My Documents\Microsoft Press\PowerPoint 2003 SBS\WorkingSlide\EnteringNotes* folder and can also be accessed by clicking *Start/All Programs/Microsoft Press/PowerPoint 2003 Step by Step*.
OPEN the *EnterNotes* presentation.

Next Slide

1 At the bottom of the vertical scroll bar to the right of the Slide pane, click the **Next Slide** button.

2 In Slide 2's **Notes** pane, click the **Click to add notes** text placeholder.

The notes placeholder text disappears, and a blinking insertion point appears.

3 Type Plan your project, and leave plenty of time so that you don't need to rush.

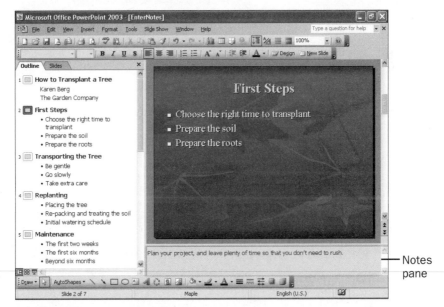

Notes pane

4 On the **View** menu, click **Notes Page**.

Slide 2 is displayed in Notes Page view, with the view percentage set so that the page will fit in the window.

Zoom

5 On the Standard toolbar, click the down arrow to the right of the **Zoom** box, and then click **75%**.

You can now read the notes more easily.

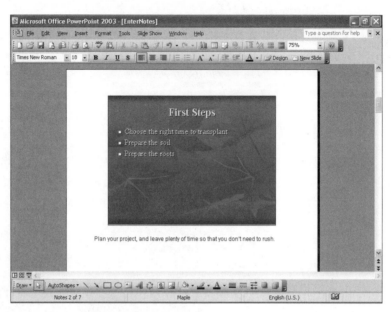

6 Click the **Next Slide** button.

The status bar displays *Notes 3 of 7*.

7 On Slide 3, click the **Click to add text** placeholder.

8 Type It is important to have a large enough vehicle to transport the tree and the soil and other supplies you will need.

9 On the Standard toolbar, click the down arrow to the right of the **Zoom** box, and click **Fit**.

The entire notes page appears in the window.

Normal View

10 Click the **Normal View** button.

The note you entered in Notes Page view appears in the Notes pane in Normal view.

Save

11 On the Standard toolbar, click the **Save** button to save the presentation.

CLOSE the *EnterNotes* presentation, and if you are not continuing on to the next chapter, quit PowerPoint.

Key Points

- You can enter text in either the Slide pane or on the Outline tab of the Outline/Slides pane. As you type, the text appears in both locations.

- You can quickly and easily add new slides to a presentation by either clicking the New Slide button on the Formatting toolbar or by clicking the New Slide command on the Insert menu.

- You can change the current layout of a slide by selecting a new layout from the Slide Layout task pane. You can also reapply the original slide layout without losing any slide content.

- You can insert slides from one presentation into another. The inserted slides conform to the design of the presentation into which they are inserted.

- You can rearrange a presentation in Slide Sorter view by dragging slides from one location to another.

- You can enter speaker notes that appear on separate notes pages.

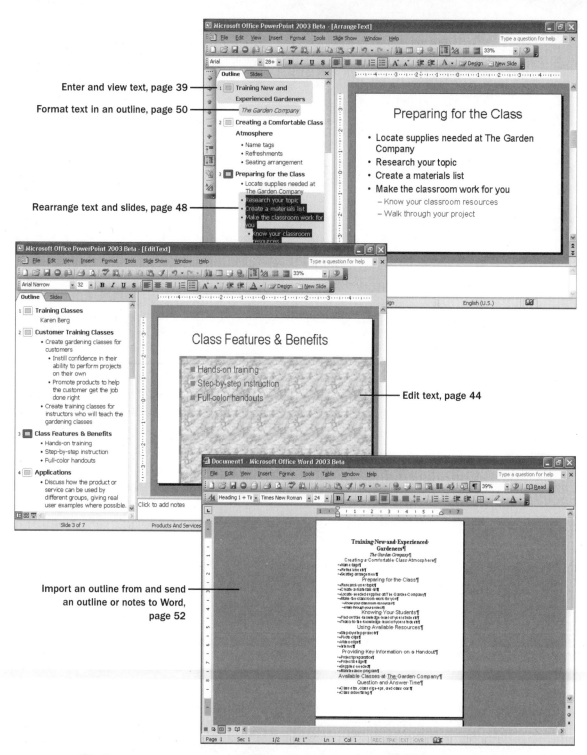

Enter and view text, page 39

Format text in an outline, page 50

Rearrange text and slides, page 48

Edit text, page 44

Import an outline from and send an outline or notes to Word, page 52

Chapter 3 at a Glance

3 Working with Outlines

In this chapter you will learn to:

✔ Enter and view text.

✔ Edit text.

✔ Rearrange text and slides.

✔ Format text in an outline.

✔ Import an outline from Word.

✔ Send an outline or notes to Word.

Before you create a presentation, you'll need to gather your thoughts, either by holding ideas in your head, jotting them down on paper, or storing them electronically. No matter how you undertake this preparation, when it's time to create the presentation, Microsoft Office PowerPoint 2003 provides you with the editing and outlining tools you need to quickly organize text on slides and rearrange slides within a presentation.

If the information you want to use already exists in another Microsoft Office System program, such as Microsoft Office Word 2003, you can easily import it and then work with it in PowerPoint to create a coherent presentation. If you want to use the text from a PowerPoint presentation in another Office program, you can just as easily export it.

In this chapter, you'll enter and edit text on the Outline tab of the Outline/Slides pane. You'll delete and rearrange text and slides, format text, and insert additional information from a Word document. When you are satisfied with the presentation's outline, you'll save it in formats that can be used by Word and other programs.

See Also Do you need only a quick refresher on the topics in this chapter? See the Quick Reference entries on pages xxxi–xxxii.

Important Before you can use the practice files in this chapter, you need to install them from the book's companion CD to their default location. See "Using the Book's CD-ROM" on page xiii for more information.

Entering and Viewing Text

Microsoft Office Specialist

PowerPoint makes it easy to view the entire content of your presentation at a glance, using the Outline tab of the Outline/Slides pane in Normal view. You can collapse the display on this tab to view only the slide titles, and you can expand the display to view the content of one or more slides, so that you can focus on certain parts.

In Normal view, you can select and edit text, and create slides and bulleted items by increasing or decreasing their indent. When you increase the indent of a slide title, or *demote* it, the title becomes a bulleted item. Demoting a bulleted item makes it a sub-item. When you decrease the indent of a bulleted item, or *promote* it, the item becomes a slide title. Promoting a sub-item makes it a bulleted item. You can quickly perform these tasks using the Outlining toolbar.

With the formatting options available in PowerPoint, you can format the text in a variety of ways. However, if the text is hard to read on the Outline tab, you can hide the formatting in the outline. The formatting information isn't lost; it's just not shown on the Outline tab. When you print an outline, the text is printed with the formatting intact.

To see more or less of the text on the screen, you can expand or reduce the zoom percentage of the presentation by using the Zoom box on the Standard toolbar, or the Zoom command on the View menu. This affects only the view on your screen; it doesn't affect the size of the text on your presentation.

Tip The standard zoom percentages are 25%, 33%, 50%, 66%, 75%, and 100%. You can also use 150%, 200%, 300%, and 400%, which are helpful for working on graphics or other objects. If you need to set a nonstandard percentage, you can type it in the Zoom box on the Standard toolbar. To scale the view so that the presentation is sized to fit your monitor, click the Fit view.

In this exercise, you will enter text on the Outline tab of the Outline/Slides pane. You will then change the indents of various paragraphs, change the zoom percentage, and collapse and expand the outline.

BE SURE TO start PowerPoint before beginning this exercise.
USE the *TextOutline* presentation in the practice file folder for this topic. This practice file is located in the *My Documents\Microsoft Press\PowerPoint 2003 SBS\WorkingOutline\Entering* folder and can also be accessed by clicking *Start/All Programs/Microsoft Press/PowerPoint 2003 Step by Step*.
OPEN the *TextOutline* presentation.

1 In the **Outline/Slides** pane, click the **Outline** tab.

2 On the **View** menu, point to **Toolbars,** and then click **Outlining**. If the Drawing toolbar is visible, turn it off.

3 On the **Outline** tab, click to the right of the icon for Slide 1.

The Slide 1 icon is selected in the outline and the blinking insertion point indicates where the text you type will appear.

4 Type Training New and Experienced Gardeners.

The text appears both on the Outline tab and as the title of the slide in the Slide pane.

Outlining toolbar

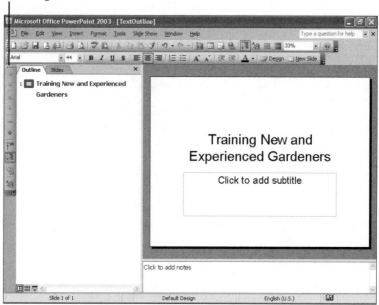

Tip If the Outline tab is not wide enough to display the outline text, you can drag the right border of the pane to the right to expand the Outline/Slides pane. This reduces the size of the Slide and Notes panes.

Demote

5 Press Enter to add a new slide, and then on the Outlining toolbar, click the **Demote** button.

The insertion point shifts to the right to start a new paragraph on the title slide, below the title. (You can also press the Tab key to demote a paragraph.)

6 Type The Garden Company, and press Enter.

The new paragraph becomes this title slide's sub-title.

7 Type Creating a Comfortable Class Atmosphere (don't press Enter).

Promote

8 On the Outlining toolbar, click the **Promote** button.

The text shifts to the left to create a title for a new slide, and a slide icon appears next to the title.

9 Press Enter, and type **Name tags**.

10 On the Outlining toolbar, click the **Demote** button.

The text shifts to the right to create a bulleted item under Slide 2's title.

11 Press Enter, and type **Refreshments**.

12 Press Enter, and type **Seating arrangement**.

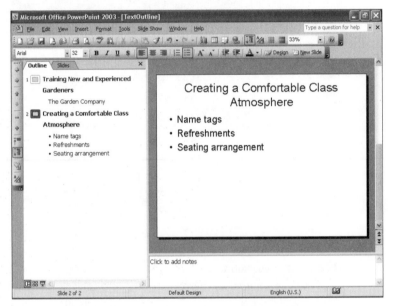

85% ▾
Zoom

13 On the Standard toolbar, click the down arrow to the right of the **Zoom** box, and click **25%**.

The zoom percentage for the Outline tab decreases from 33% to 25%.

14 On the Standard toolbar, click the **Zoom** box (not the down arrow) to select the current zoom percentage.

15 Type **33**, and press Enter.

The percentage changes to 33%.

16 On the **Outline** tab, click the Slide 2 title.

Collapse

17 On the Outlining toolbar, click the **Collapse** button.

The Slide 2 outline collapses to show only the title, while the Slide 1 outline remains expanded.

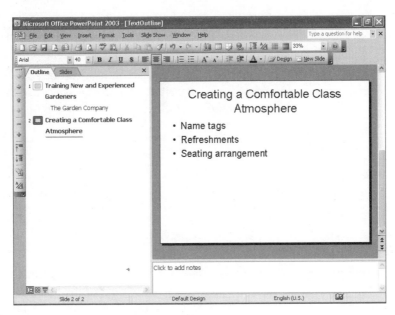

Collapse All

18 On the Outlining toolbar, click the **Collapse All** button.

Only the titles of both slides are visible.

19 Click the Slide 1 title.

Expand

20 On the Outlining toolbar, click the **Expand** button.

The Slide 1 outline expands to show its subtitle again.

Expand All

21 On the Outlining toolbar, click the **Expand All** button.

Now all the text in the outline is visible.

Show
Formatting

22 On the Outlining toolbar, click the **Show Formatting** button a couple of times, pausing between clicks to note the change in the text on the **Outline** tab.

The Show Formatting button is a *toggle* command. Notice that when you click it and then click it again, the text in the Outline tab switches between plain and formatted text.

Save

23 On the Standard toolbar, click the **Save** button to save the presentation.

CLOSE the *TextOutline* presentation.

Editing Text

You can edit text in the Slide pane or on the Outline tab of the Outline/Slides pane. A typical slide contains a title, called *title text*, and a list of items, called *bullet points*. Items called *subpoints* might be indented below the bullet points. In the Slide pane, text appears in text-object boxes, and on the Outline tab, text appears in bulleted outline form.

When you *hover* over text on the Outline tab or in a text object on the slide, the pointer changes to an I-beam. When you click text, a blinking insertion point appears where you clicked to indicate where text will appear when you type.

Before you can edit or format existing text, you have to *select* it. Selected text appears highlighted on the screen. You can select specific items as follows:

- To select a word, double-click it. The word and the space following it are selected. Punctuation following a word is not selected.

- To select all the text on a slide, click its slide icon on the Outline tab.

- To select a bullet point, click its bullet.

You can select adjacent words, lines, or paragraphs by dragging through them. Or you can position the insertion point at the beginning of the text you want to select, hold down the `Shift` key, and either press an arrow key to select characters one at a time or click at the end of the text you want to select.

To delete text, you select it and press either the `Del` key or the `Backspace` key. To replace text, you select it and type the new text.

Tip PowerPoint's spell-checking feature indicates a possible spelling error with a red wavy underline. You can right-click a word with a red wavy line to display a shortcut menu with a list of possible spellings, and then click the correct spelling. You can turn off or modify this feature by clicking Options on the Tools menu and changing the settings on the Spelling and Style tab.

If you change your mind about a change you have made, you can reverse it by clicking the Undo button. The number of actions you can undo is set to 20, but you can change that number by clicking Options on the Tools menu, clicking the Edit tab, and changing the "Maximum number of undos" option. If you undo an action in error, you can click the Redo button to restore the action. You can undo or redo actions only in the order in which you performed them—that is, you cannot reverse your fourth previous action without first reversing the three actions that followed it. To undo a number of actions at the same time, you can click the down arrow to the right of the Undo button and then click the earliest action you want to undo in the drop-down list.

In this exercise, you will edit text on the Outline tab of the Outline/Slides pane, and undo and redo actions that you recently performed.

USE the *EditText* presentation in the practice file folder for this topic. This practice file is located in the *My Documents\Microsoft Press\PowerPoint 2003 SBS\WorkingOutline\Editing* folder and can also be accessed by clicking *Start/All Programs/Microsoft Press/PowerPoint 2003 Step by Step*.
OPEN the *EditText* presentation.

1 On the **Outline** tab of the **Outline/Slides** pane, double-click the word *Overview* in Slide 2 to select the title.

2 Type Customer Training Classes.

Notice that what you type replaces the selection. Notice also that the text changes in the Slide pane. (If you make a mistake while typing, press [Backspace] to delete the error and then type the correction.)

3 On the **Outline** tab, position the pointer on or slightly to the left of the first bullet on Slide 2, and when the pointer changes to a four-headed arrow, click once to select the entire bullet point.

4 Type Create gardening classes for customers to instill confidence in their ability to perform projects on their own and promote products to help the customer get the job done right (no period).

5 Click the second bullet on Slide 2, and type Create training classes for instructors who will teach the gardening classes (again, no period).

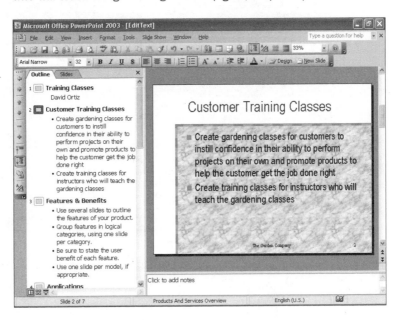

Undo

6 On the Standard toolbar, click the **Undo** button to reverse your last action.

7 On the Standard toolbar, click the down arrow to the right of the **Undo** button.

The Undo list appears, displaying the first two items as *Typing*.

8 Click the second **Typing** item in the list.

The first bullet and title in Slide 2 reverts to the original text, which was created by the AutoContent Wizard.

Redo

9 On the Standard toolbar, click the **Redo** button to restore the title text in Slide 2.

10 On the Standard toolbar, click the down arrow to the right of the **Redo** button, and then click the second **Typing** item in the list to restore the bullet points.

11 In the first bullet point on Slide 2, click at the right end of the word *customers*, and press Enter.

Word breaks the bullet point into two.

12 Press the Tab key to demote the new bullet point to a sub-point. Then delete *to*, and change *instill* to *Instill*.

13 Click at the right end of the word *own*, press Enter, delete *and*, and change *promote* to *Promote*.

Slide 2 now has two bullet points, one with two sub-points.

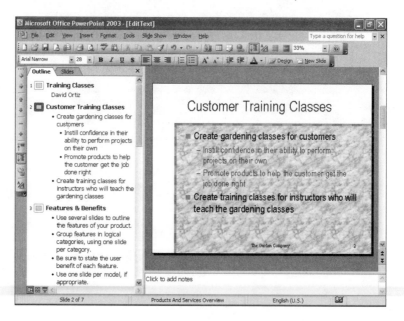

14 Click Slide 3's title, press Home to move the insertion point to the beginning of the text, type **Class**, and then press Space .

15 In Slide 3, click the bullet to the left of the first bullet point, and type **Hands-on training** (no period).

16 Click the second bullet, type **Step-by-step instruction**, and then press Enter .

A new bullet appears. It will be gray until you add text.

17 Type **Full-color handouts**.

18 Click the next bullet to select the text of the bullet point, and press the Del key.

The bullet point is deleted.

19 Repeat the last step to delete the last bullet point, and then press Backspace twice to remove the gray bullet.

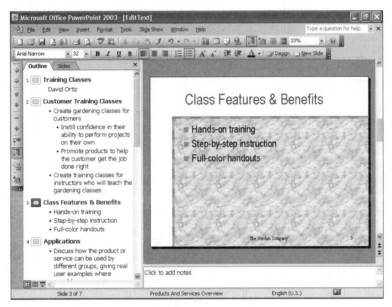

20 Click Slide 4's icon, and then press Del .

The entire *Applications* slide is deleted. PowerPoint renumbers the slides, and the *Specifications* slide is now Slide 4.

21 On the **Edit** menu, click **Delete Slide** to delete the *Specifications* slide.

3 Working with Outlines

22 Right-click the new Slide 4, and click **Delete Slide** from the shortcut menu.

23 Repeat the previous step to delete Slide 4 again.

The presentation now contains only three slides.

Save

24 On the Standard toolbar, click the **Save** button to save the presentation.

CLOSE the *EditText* presentation.

Rearranging Text and Slides

Microsoft Office Specialist

On the Outline tab of the Outline/Slides pane, you can rearrange the text on one or more slides in a presentation. After selecting the item you want to move, you can click the Move Up button or the Move Down button on the Outlining toolbar, or you can drag the selected item to the desired location.

See Also For information about different ways to select text and slides, see "Editing Text" in this chapter.

To move selected words and phrases, you can use the same techniques you would use in a word processor, such as Microsoft Office Word 2003.

In this exercise, you will use different methods to rearrange slides, bullet points, and words.

USE the *ArrangeText* presentation in the practice file folder for this topic. This practice file is located in the *My Documents\Microsoft Press\PowerPoint 2003 SBS\WorkingOutline\Arranging* folder and can also be accessed by clicking *Start/All Programs/Microsoft Press/PowerPoint 2003 Step by Step.*
OPEN the *ArrangeText* presentation.

1 In Slide 3, double-click the word *needed*, and then drag it to the left of the word *supplies* on the same line.

As you drag, a gray insertion point shows where PowerPoint will place the word. When you release the mouse button, the word *needed* moves to its new position to the left of *supplies*.

2 Drag the scroll box until Slide 5 is at the top of the **Outline** tab.

3 Click the icon for Slide 5, point to the icon, and drag it down until the black indicator bar sits above Slide 7.

When you release the mouse button, PowerPoint renumbers the slides.

48

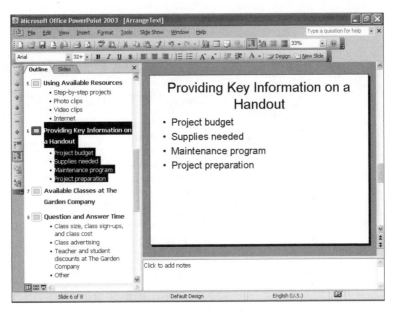

4   In Slide 6, click the bullet to the left of the *Project preparation* bullet point.

Move Up

5   On the Outlining toolbar, click the **Move Up** button three times.

The *Project preparation* bullet point is now the first one on the slide.

6   Scroll up to Slide 3, and click the first bullet to select the *Research your topic* bullet point.

7   Hold down the `Shift` key, and click the bullet for the *Walk through your project* sub-point.

All the bullet points and sub-points between the two clicks are selected.

Tip   You can also select multiple paragraphs by dragging through them. Click where you want the selection to begin, and drag down to where you want the selection to end. When you release the mouse button, PowerPoint selects everything between the first click and the end point of the drag action.

Move Down

8   On the Outlining toolbar, click the **Move Down** button.

The entire selection moves down in the slide, and what was the last bullet point is now the first.

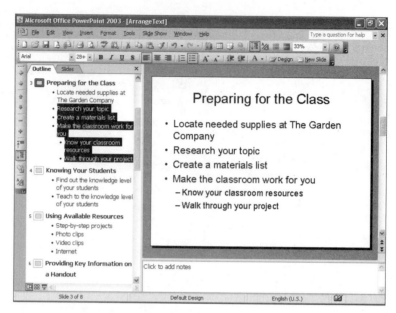

9 Click in the middle of the word *Locate* in the first bullet point in Slide 3.

10 Drag to the right and down through the text of the bullet point.

Even though you started the selection in the middle of the word *Locate*, PowerPoint selects the entire word because the Automatic Word Selection feature is turned on.

Tip To turn off the Automatic Word Selection command, on the Tools menu, click Options, click the Edit tab, and then clear the "When selecting, automatically select entire word" check box.

11 On the Outlining toolbar, click the **Move Down** button twice, until the bullet point sits below *Create a materials list* in the slide.

Save

12 On the Standard toolbar, click the **Save** button to save the presentation.

CLOSE the *ArrangeText* presentation.
BE SURE TO turn off the Outlining and Drawing toolbars.

Formatting Text in an Outline

Microsoft Office Specialist

After you finish entering and moving text on the Outline tab, you can change the look of the text by applying character formatting. Most formatting changes are not visible on the Outline tab, but they do show up in the adjacent Slide pane. As a result, you can use the quick selection and navigation techniques available on the Outline tab while monitoring the results of your formatting changes on the slides.

To format text, you first select it, and then apply the specific formatting that you want, using the buttons on the Formatting toolbar. The Formatting toolbar includes buttons to change the font type, color and size, and to apply bold, italic, and underline styles.

In this exercise, you will change the style, font, size, and color of text in an outline.

USE the *FormatText* presentation in the practice file folder for this topic. This practice file is located in the *My Documents\Microsoft Press\PowerPoint 2003 SBS\WorkingOutline\Formatting* folder and can also be accessed by clicking *Start/All Programs/Microsoft Press/PowerPoint 2003 Step by Step*.
OPEN the *FormatText* presentation.

1 If Slide 1's title is not selected on the **Outline** tab of the **Outline/Slides** pane, drag through it to select it.

Bold

2 On the Formatting toolbar, click the **Bold** button.

PowerPoint changes the style of the selected text to bold in the Slide pane but not the Outline/Slides pane.

Font Color

3 On the Formatting toolbar, click the down arrow to the right of the **Font Color** button, and then click the **Bright Green** box at the right end of the color palette.

Again, the change can be seen only in the Slide pane.

Italic

4 Triple-click *The Garden Company*, and on the Formatting toolbar, click the **Italic** button.

This time the change is visible in both panes.

Font Size

5 With the subtitle still selected, on the Formatting toolbar, click the down arrow to the right of the **Font Size** box, and click **36** in the drop-down list.

6 Double-click in the blank area to the right of the word *Gardeners* to select the entire title without selecting the subtitle.

Take a moment to experiment with double-clicking at the right end of a title until you get the hang of just where to point to select the entire title.

Increase
Font Size

7 On the Formatting toolbar, click the **Increase Font Size** button.

The title font size changes from 44 points to 48 points. Size changes are implemented only in the Slide pane.

8 On the Formatting toolbar, click the down arrow to the right of the **Font** box, scroll down the font list, and then click **Times New Roman**.

In the Slide pane, the title's font changes from Arial to Times New Roman, but in the Outline/Slides pane, the font is unchanged.

9 Select Slide 1's subtitle, click the down arrow to the right of the **Font** box again, and then click **Times New Roman**.

Tip PowerPoint places recently used fonts at the top of the font list, separated from the rest of the list by a double line, so you don't have to scroll down the long list of fonts to find your favorites.

10 On the **Outline** tab, click a blank area to deselect the text in the outline.

Only the italic formatting is visible on the Outline tab.

Save

11 On the Standard toolbar, click the **Save** button to save the presentation.

CLOSE the *FormatText* presentation.

Importing an Outline from Word

Microsoft Office Specialist

You can insert text from another program into a PowerPoint presentation. The text can be in Word format (*.doc*), *Rich Text Format (RTF)* (*.rtf*), or plain text (*.txt*). You can also insert a Web document in HTML format into a presentation.

When you insert a Word or Rich Text Format document, PowerPoint creates an outline of slide titles and bullet points based on heading styles in the inserted document. When you insert text from a plain text document, paragraphs not preceded by tabs become slide titles, and paragraphs preceded by tabs become bullet points. When you insert the text from an HTML file, it appears within a text box on the slide.

In this exercise, you will insert a Word outline into a presentation.

USE the *InsertOutline* presentation and the *Outline* document in the practice file folder for this topic. These practice files are located in the *My Documents\Microsoft Press\PowerPoint 2003 SBS\WorkingOutline \Importing* folder and can also be accessed by clicking *Start/All Programs/Microsoft Press/PowerPoint 2003 Step by Step.*
OPEN the *InsertOutline* presentation.

1   In Slide 3 on the **Outline** tab of the **Outline/Slides** pane, click the blank area to the right of the *Full color handouts* bullet point.

2   On the **Insert** menu, click **Slides from Outline** (not Slides from Files).

The Insert Outline dialog box appears.

3   Navigate to the *My Documents\Microsoft Press\PowerPoint 2003 SBS\WorkingOutline \Importing* folder.

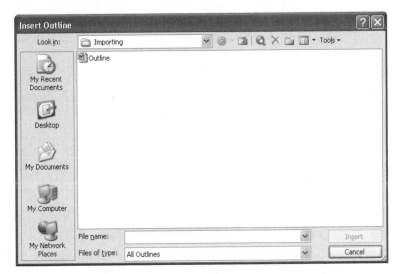

4   Click **Outline**, and then click **Insert**.

PowerPoint inserts the Word outline into the presentation.

Tip   If a message tells you that you need to install a converter, insert the Microsoft Office 2003 installation CD-ROM, and then click OK to install it.

5   On the **Outline** tab, click a blank area to deselect the text, and scroll down to see Slides 4 through 7.

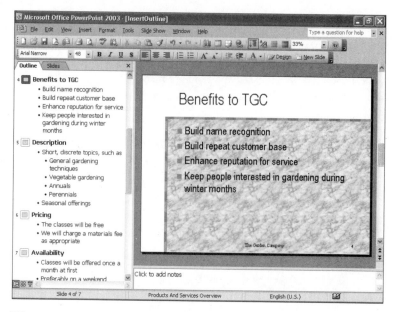

Tip You can start a new presentation from a Word outline using the Open command. On the Standard toolbar, click the Open button, click the down arrow to the right of the "Files of type" box, click All Files, and then double-click the outline file you want to use to start the presentation.

Save

6 On the Standard toolbar, click the **Save** button to save the presentation.

CLOSE the *InsertOutline* presentation.

Sending an Outline or Notes to Word

Microsoft Office Specialist

You can export a presentation outline or speaker notes directly from PowerPoint into a Word document. PowerPoint starts Word and sends or copies the outline or notes pages in the presentation to a blank Word document. (Obviously, you must have Word installed on your computer to be able to do this.)

When you want to use the text from a presentation in another program, you can save the presentation text in Rich Text Format (RTF). Saving an outline in RTF saves any formatting applied to the presentation text in such a way that it is retained when you open it in another program. Many programs, including Word for Macintosh and older versions of PowerPoint, can import outlines saved in RTF.

In this exercise, you will send a presentation outline to Word, and then save the Word document.

USE the *SendOutline* presentation in the practice file folder for this topic. This practice file is located in the *My Documents\Microsoft Press\PowerPoint 2003 SBS\WorkingOutline\Exporting* folder and can also be accessed by clicking *Start/All Programs/Microsoft Press/PowerPoint 2003 Step by Step*.
OPEN the *SendOutline* presentation.

1 On the **File** menu, point to **Send To**, and then click **Microsoft Office Word**.

The Send To Microsoft Office Word dialog box appears with five page layout options and two pasting options.

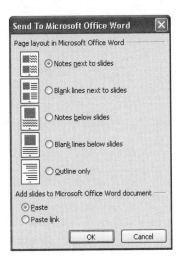

Important The "Page layout in Microsoft Office Word" options determine the way the information will look when you open it in Word. The "Add slides to Microsoft Office Word document" options determine whether the information is simply pasted into the Word document or whether a link is maintained between the pasted information and the original slides. If you select the "Paste link" option and then make changes to the original slides, those changes will be reflected in the Word document the next time you open it.

2 Select the **Outline only** option, and then click **OK**.

PowerPoint starts Word and inserts the presentation outline into a blank Word document.

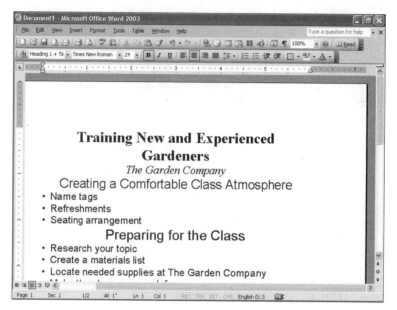

Don't worry if your outline is displayed at a different zoom percentage from ours.

3 On Word's **File** menu, click **Save As**.

The Save As dialog box appears.

4 In the **File name** box, type **PPTOutline**.

Tip The setting in the "Save as type" box determines the format in which Office programs save the file and the extension that will be appended to the file name to identify the format. You don't have to type the extension.

5 Navigate to the *My Documents\Microsoft Press\PowerPoint 2003 SBS\WorkingOutline \Exporting* folder, and click **Save**.

Word saves the presentation outline in a document called *PPTOutline* in the designated folder.

6 On Word's **File** menu, click **Exit**.

Word closes, and PowerPoint appears.

7 On the **File** menu, click **Save As**.

The Save As dialog box appears.

8 In the **File name** box, type **RTFOutline**.

9 Click the down arrow to the right of the **Save as type** box, and click **Outline/RTF** in the drop-down list.

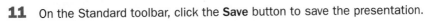

10 If necessary, navigate to the *My Documents\Microsoft Press\PowerPoint 2003 SBS \WorkingOutline\Exporting* folder, and then click **Save**.

PowerPoint saves the presentation's outline in RTF format in a document called *Outline.rtf* in the designated folder. (You don't need to type the *.rtf*; PowerPoint supplies it for you.)

11 On the Standard toolbar, click the **Save** button to save the presentation.

Save

CLOSE the *SendOutline* presentation, and if you are not continuing on to the next chapter, quit PowerPoint.

Key Points

- On the Outline tab, you can quickly enter the text of a presentation, demoting slides to bullet points and promoting bullet points to slides as necessary.

- You can collapse and expand a presentation's outline to see as much or a little detail as you want.

- You can easily edit text on the Outline tab. If you make a mistake, you can reverse an editing action by clicking the Undo button. You can click the Redo button to restore the undone action.

- You can rearrange the text on slides and the slides themselves by using the Move Up and Move Down buttons on the Outlining toolbar, or by dragging selected text or slides to the desired location.

- You can apply formatting to selected text on the Outline tab and see the results in the Slide pane. To format text, you can use the buttons on the Formatting toolbar.

- You can insert text created in other programs into the Outline tab. Acceptable formats include Word format (*.doc*), Rich Text Format (*.rtf*), and plain text (*.txt*).

- You can export a presentation outline or speaker notes directly from PowerPoint directly to Word. You can also save a presentation in various formats so that it can be used in other programs.

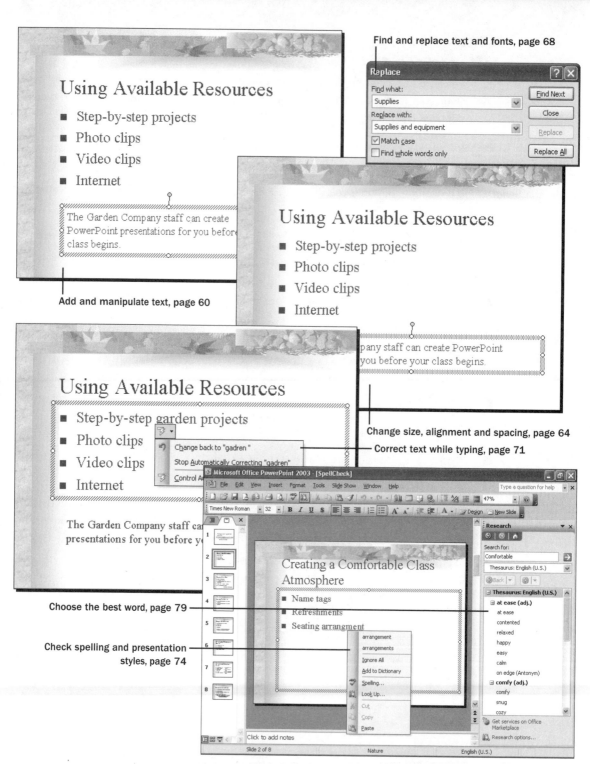

Find and replace text and fonts, page 68

Add and manipulate text, page 60

Change size, alignment and spacing, page 64

Correct text while typing, page 71

Choose the best word, page 79

Check spelling and presentation styles, page 74

4 Working with Slide Text

In this chapter you will learn to:

✔ Add and manipulate text.

✔ Change size, alignment, and spacing.

✔ Find and replace text and fonts.

✔ Correct text while typing.

✔ Check spelling and presentation styles.

✔ Choose the best word.

In Microsoft Office PowerPoint 2003, you can add text directly to the slides of a presentation and then modify the text to fine-tune your message. You have complete control over the placement and position of slide text. With PowerPoint, you have several alternatives for placing text in *text objects* on your slides:

■ Text placeholders for entering slide titles and subtitles

■ Text labels for short notes and phrases

■ Word processing boxes for longer text.

You can also place text inside objects such as circles, rectangles, or stars.

In this chapter, you will create several kinds of text objects. You will also edit text, change its appearance, find and replace words and phrases, and replace fonts. You will watch PowerPoint correct errors as you type them, check spelling, check presentation styles, and use the Thesaurus to find the word that best suits your presentation.

See Also   Do you need only a quick refresher on the topics in this chapter? See the Quick Reference entries on pages xxxii–xxxiii.

Important   Before you can use the practice files in this chapter, you need to install them from the book's companion CD to their default location. See "Using the Book's CD-ROM" on page xiii for more information.

Adding and Manipulating Text

In PowerPoint, it's easy to add and edit text from both the Slide pane and the Outline/Slides pane. In the Slide Pane, you can enter titles, bullet items, and supplemental text. To change the title or bullet items, or create new ones, you can view them without the supplemental text on the Outline tab of the Outline/Slides pane, and make changes from there as well.

Text appears on slides in objects, boxes that contain text and that are handled as a unit—for example, a title is one text object, and a bulleted list is another. Before you can manipulate a text object, you first need to select it in one of two ways:

- Clicking anywhere in the text in the text object displays a *slanted-line selection box* around the text object. You can then edit the text—for example, you can add, delete, or correct words and punctuation.

The Garden Company —— Slanted-line selection box

- Clicking the edge of a slanted-line selection box selects the entire object and displays a *dotted selection box* around the text object. You can then manipulate the object as a unit—for example, you can size the object, move it, or copy it as a whole.

The Garden Company —— Dotted selection box

To deselect an object, you click a blank area of the slide.

The white circles at each corner of either type of selection box are *sizing handles*, which you can use to size the object.

When a text object is surrounded by a dotted selection box, you can move or copy the text object anywhere on the slide. Dragging is the most efficient way to move a text object within a single slide, and you can copy it just as easily by holding down the [Ctrl] key while you drag it.

When you want to include other types of text on a slide—for example, annotations or minor points that do not belong in a list—you can create a text box using the Text Box button on the Drawing toolbar. There are two types of text boxes:

- A *text label* is used for text that does not wrap to a second line within the text box, such as a short note or phrase. You simply click the Text Box button, click the slide where you want to place the label, and then type the text.

■   A *word processing box* is used for text that wraps within the text box, such as longer notes or sentences. You can create a word processing box by using the Text Box tool to drag a text box of the appropriate size, and then typing the text.

After you have created a text label or word processing box, you can change one into the other by changing the word-wrap and fit-text options in the Format Text Box dialog box. You can also change a text label into a word processing box by dragging one of the corner sizing handles.

In this exercise, you will select and deselect a text object, move a text object by dragging its selection box, add text in a text object, and then create a text label and a word processing box.

BE SURE TO start PowerPoint before beginning this exercise.
USE the *AddText* presentation in the practice file folder for this topic. This practice file is located in the *My Documents\Microsoft Press\PowerPoint 2003 SBS\WorkingText\Adding* folder and can also be accessed by clicking *Start/All Programs/Microsoft Press/PowerPoint 2003 Step by Step*.
OPEN the *AddText* presentation.

1   On Slide 1, click the subtitle.

The text within the text object is selected, as indicated by the blinking insertion point and the slanted-line selection box.

2   Point to the selection box, and when the pointer changes to a four-headed arrow, click the mouse button once.

The text object is selected as a unit, as indicated by the dotted selection box.

Tip   You can select an object as a unit with just one click. Position the pointer above or below the object until it changes to a four-headed arrow, and then click. The dotted selection box appears to show that the entire object is selected.

3   Click outside the selection box in a blank area of the slide to deselect the object.

Next Slide

4   In the **Slide** pane, click the **Next Slide** button at the bottom of the vertical scroll bar twice.

Slide 3 is now displayed.

5   Double-click *TGC* in the bulleted list, and type The Garden Company.

6   Click a blank area of the slide to deselect the object.

Text Box

7   If necessary, display the Drawing toolbar. Then click the **Text Box** button, and point below the last bullet on the slide.

The pointer appears as an upside-down T.

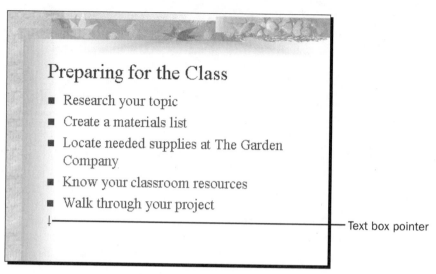

Text box pointer

8 Click the slide to create a text box.

A small, empty text box appears with a blinking insertion point inside it.

9 Type **See Slide 5 for available resources**.

If you wanted to rotate the object, you could drag the green rotating handle above the text box.

10 Click the slanted-line selection box (don't click a handle).

The slanted-line selection box changes to a dotted selection box.

11 Point to the dotted selection box (not to a handle), and drag the box to the right.

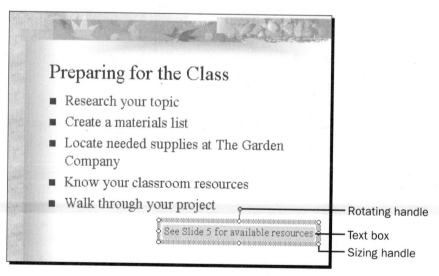

Rotating handle

Text box

Sizing handle

Tip If you look carefully, you can see the text label in the slide's thumbnail on the Slides tab of the Outline\Slides pane. However, the text label does not appear on the Outline tab. Only text entered in a title or bullet point object appears on the Outline tab.

12 Click a blank area of the slide to deselect the text box.

13 Move to Slide 5, and on the Drawing toolbar, click the **Text Box** button.

14 Point below the last bullet, and drag to create a box that extends the width of the slide's title.

No matter what height you make the box, it snaps to a standard size when you release the mouse button. It is surrounded by a slanted-line selection box and contains a blinking insertion point.

15 Type **The Garden Company staff can create PowerPoint presentations for you before your class begins.**

The width of the box does not change, but as the words wrap, the box's height increases to accommodate the complete entry.

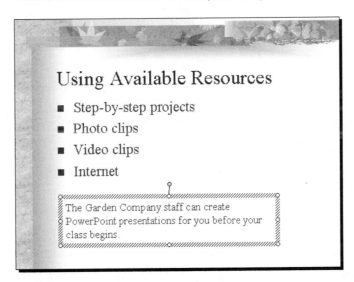

16 Click a blank area of the slide to deselect the text box.

17 On the Standard toolbar, click the **Save** button to save the presentation.

Save

CLOSE the *AddText* presentation.

Changing Size, Alignment, and Spacing

Microsoft Office Specialist

A text object can be adjusted to accommodate the text it holds, and text can be wrapped to fit within an object of a certain size.

To size an object to fit a given amount of text, you can either manually size it or you can use the "Resize AutoShape to fit text" option on the Text Box tab in the Format AutoShape dialog box.

To control the way text is aligned within an object, you can select the object and click one of the following alignment buttons on the Formatting toolbar:

■ The Align Left button aligns text evenly along the left edge of the object and is useful for paragraph text.

■ The Align Right button aligns text evenly along the right edge of the object and is useful for text labels.

■ The Center button aligns text in the middle of the object and is useful for titles and headings.

You can also select an object and adjust the space between lines of text by using the Line Spacing command on the Format menu. You can adjust the space before and after paragraphs by clicking the Increase Paragraph Spacing or Decrease Paragraph Spacing button on the Formatting toolbar.

In this exercise, you will adjust a text object and a text placeholder, change the alignment of text in a text object, decrease paragraph spacing, and adjust line spacing.

USE the *AlignText* presentation in the practice file folder for this topic. This practice file is located in the *My Documents\Microsoft Press\PowerPoint 2003 SBS\WorkingText\Aligning* folder and can also be accessed by clicking *Start/All Programs/Microsoft Press/PowerPoint 2003 Step by Step*.
OPEN the *AlignText* presentation.

1   On the **Slides** tab of the **Outline\Slides** pane, click Slide 5.

2   Click the text at the bottom of the slide, and then click the slanted-line selection box to select the entire text box.

The text box is surrounded by a dotted selection box.

3   Point to the right-middle handle, and when the pointer changes to a two-headed arrow, drag the handle to the right to extend the text box about an inch.

The text wraps to fit the wider text object.

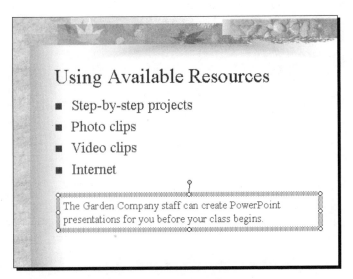

4 On the **Format** menu, click **Text Box**.

Troubleshooting This command is available only if a text box is selected. If you don't see the command, reselect the text box at the bottom of Slide 5.

The Format Text Box dialog box appears.

5 Click the **Text Box** tab, and clear the **Word wrap text in AutoShape** check box.

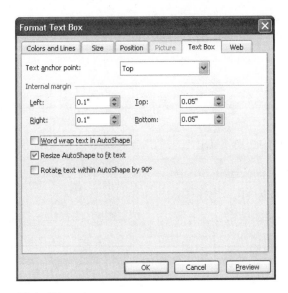

6 Click **OK**.

The word processing box changes to a text label and stretches in one long line beyond the slide boundary.

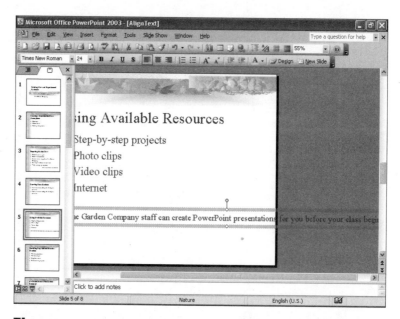

Tip You can convert a text label to a word processing box by dragging a sizing handle to reduce the width of the text box. The text inside the box wraps to fit the new dimensions of the text box.

Undo

7 On the Standard toolbar, click the **Undo** button to restore the word processing box.

8 Point to the left of the bullet points on Slide 5, and when the pointer changes to a four-headed arrow, click to select the bullet point text object.

The dotted selection box indicates that the text object is larger than it needs to be.

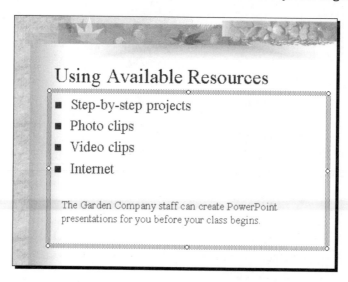

9 On the **Format** menu, click **Placeholder**.

The Format AutoShape dialog box appears.

Tip The command on the Format menu changes depending on the type of object selected. As you saw in step 4, if a text box is selected, the command on the Format menu is Text Box, and the Format Text Box dialog box appears when you click the command.

10 Click the **Text Box** tab, select the **Resize AutoShape to fit text** check box, and click **OK**.

The object adjusts to fit the size of the text.

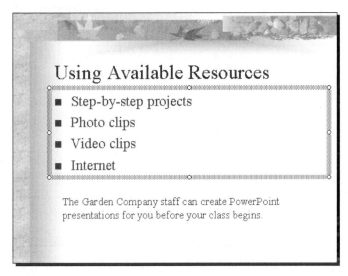

11 Click a blank area of the slide to deselect the object, and then move to Slide 8.

12 Click the text in the word processing box at the bottom of the slide, and on the Formatting toolbar, click the **Center** button.

The text in the text object is centered in the text box.

Center

13 On the **Format** menu, click **Line Spacing**.

The Line Spacing dialog box appears.

14 In the **Before paragraph** box, click the up arrow until the setting is **1**.

Tip You can also click the Increase Paragraph Spacing button on the Formatting toolbar to increase the space before paragraphs. If this button is not available on the Formatting toolbar, click the Toolbar Options button at the right end of the toolbar, point to Add or Remove Buttons and then Formatting to display a list of additional Formatting buttons, click the Increase Paragraph Spacing button to place it on the toolbar, and then click a blank area of the slide to deselect the menu.

15   In the **Line Spacing** box, click the up arrow until the setting is **1.5**.

16   Click the **Preview** button.

The paragraph spacing and line spacing of the word processing box at the bottom of the slide have both increased.

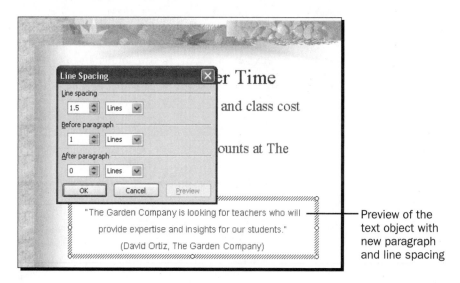

Preview of the text object with new paragraph and line spacing

Tip   You can manipulate a title or bulleted list object the same way you manipulate a text label or word processing box.

17   Click **Cancel** to close the **Line Spacing** dialog box without making any changes.

18   On the Standard toolbar, click the **Save** button to save the presentation.

Save

CLOSE the *AlignText* presentation.

Finding and Replacing Text and Fonts

Microsoft Office Specialist

You can locate and change specific text in a presentation by using the Find and Replace commands on the Edit. You use the Find tab of the Find and Replace dialog box to locate each occurrence of the text you are looking for, and you use the Replace tab to locate the text and replace it with something else. You can change all occurrences of the text with the click of a button, or only specific occurrences.

The Find and Replace commands include options for more detailed searches:

■   To search for whole words, you select the "Find whole words only" check box. For example, if the text you are searching for is *plan*, PowerPoint skips over *plant*.

■ To search for a word or phrase that exactly matches the *case*, or capitalization, you specify, you select the "Match case" check box. For example, if you are searching for *IRS*, PowerPoint skips over *firs*.

In addition to finding and replacing text, you can also find and replace a font in a presentation. With the Replace Fonts command, you can replace every instance of one font with another.

In this exercise, you will use the Replace command to find and replace a word, and then you'll use the Replace Fonts command to find and replace a font.

USE the *ReplaceText* presentation in the practice file folder for this topic. This practice file is located in the *My Documents\Microsoft Press\PowerPoint 2003 SBS\WorkingText\Finding* folder and can also be accessed by clicking *Start/All Programs/Microsoft Press/PowerPoint 2003 Step by Step*.
OPEN the *ReplaceText* presentation.

1 On the **Edit** menu, click **Replace**.

The Replace dialog box appears.

2 In the **Find what** box, type Supplies, and press [Tab].

3 In the **Replace with** box, type Supplies and equipment.

4 Select the **Match case** check box to find the text in the **Find what** box exactly as you typed it.

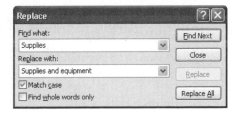

5 Click **Find Next**.

PowerPoint finds and selects the word *Supplies* on Slide 6.

Tip If the Replace dialog box covers up the selected text, move the dialog box out of the way by dragging its title bar.

6 Click **Replace**.

PowerPoint replaces *Supplies* with *Supplies and equipment*. An alert box tells you that PowerPoint has finished searching the presentation.

7 Click **OK**, and then click **Close** to close the **Replace** dialog box.

8 Click a blank area of the slide to deselect the text object on Slide 6.

9 On the **Format** menu, click **Replace Fonts**.

The Replace Font dialog box appears.

10 Click the down arrow to the right of the **Replace** box, and click **Arial** in the drop-down list.

11 Click the down arrow to the right of the **With** box, scroll down the drop-down list, and click **Impact**.

12 Click **Replace**.

Throughout the presentation, the text formatted with the Arial font changes to the Impact font.

13 Click **Close** to close the **Replace Font** dialog box.

14 Move to Slide 8.

At the bottom of the slide, the note in the word processing box is now displayed in the Impact font.

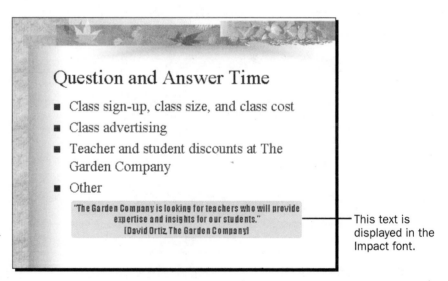

15 On the Standard toolbar, click the **Save** button to save the presentation.

Save

CLOSE the *ReplaceText* presentation.

Correcting Text While Typing

As you type text in a presentation, you might be aware that you have made a typographical error, but when you look at the text, the mistake isn't there. PowerPoint uses a feature called *AutoCorrect* to correct common capitalization and spelling errors as you type them. For example, if you type *teh* instead of *the* or *WHen* instead of *When*, AutoCorrect corrects the entry.

When you point to a word that AutoCorrect has changed, the AutoCorrect Options button appears, enabling you to control text correction. You can change the text back to its original spelling, or you can stop AutoCorrect from automatically making corrections. You can also display the AutoCorrect dialog box and make changes to the AutoCorrect settings.

You can customize AutoCorrect to recognize misspellings you routinely type or to ignore text you do not want AutoCorrect to change. You can also create your own AutoCorrect entries to automate the typing of frequently used text. For example, people at The Garden Company could customize AutoCorrect to enter the name of the company when they type only *tgc*.

In addition to using AutoCorrect to correct text as you type, PowerPoint uses the AutoFit feature to size text to fit its object. For example, if you type more text than will fit in a title's text object, AutoFit shrinks the font's size until it all fits. The AutoFit Options button, which appears near the text the first time its size is changed, gives you control over automatic sizing. For example, you can stop sizing text for the current text object while retaining your global AutoFit settings. You can also display the AutoCorrect dialog box and change the AutoFit settings there.

In this exercise, you will add an AutoCorrect entry, use AutoCorrect to fix a misspelled word, and then use AutoFit to make the size of text fit its object.

USE the *CorrectText* presentation in the practice file folder for this topic. This practice file is located in the *My Documents\Microsoft Press\PowerPoint 2003 SBS\WorkingText\Correcting* folder and can also be accessed by clicking *Start/All Programs/Microsoft Press/PowerPoint 2003 Step by Step*.
OPEN the *CorrectText* presentation.

1 On the **Tools** menu, click **AutoCorrect Options**.

The AutoCorrect dialog box appears.

2 In the **Replace** box on the **AutoCorrect** tab, type gadren, and press Tab.

3 In the **With** box, type garden, and then click **Add**.

When you type *gadren* in any presentation, PowerPoint will replace it with *garden*.

4 Click **OK** to close the **AutoCorrect** dialog box.

5 Move to Slide 5, click to the left of the word *projects*, type gadren, and press Space .

PowerPoint corrects the word *gadren* to *garden*.

AutoCorrect
Options

6 Point to *garden* to display the **AutoCorrect Options** button, and click the button.

A drop-down list of options appears.

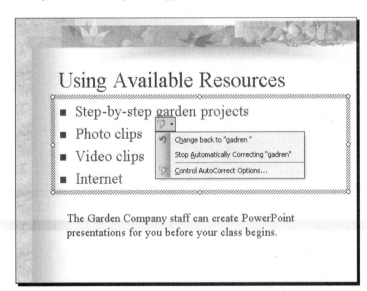

7 Click a blank area of the slide to close the **AutoCorrect Options** menu.

8 Move to Slide 7, click to the right of the word *table* in the last bullet point, and press the ⌤ Enter ⌤ key.

9 Type **Installing a new lawn.**

PowerPoint makes the text of the bullet points smaller so that they all fit in the text object. The AutoFit Options button appears to the left of the object.

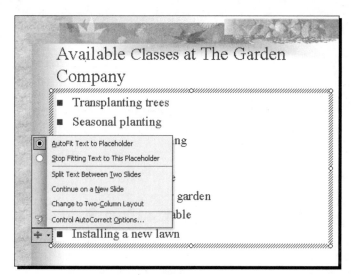

AutoFit Options

10 Click to the **AutoFit Options** button to display a list of options.

11 Click **Change to Two-Column Layout**.

Another bulleted list object appears to the right of the first one.

12 Type **Installing a sprinkler system.**

13 Select the *Bouquets from your garden*, *Building a potting table*, and *Installing a new lawn* bullet points in the bulleted list on the left.

14 Drag the selection to the left of *Installing a sprinkler system* in the bulleted list on the right.

All the bullet points in both lists increase in size.

15 Click a blank area of the slide to deselect the object.

> ## Available Classes at The Garden Company
>
> - Transplanting trees
> - Seasonal planting
> - Feeding and fertilizing
> - Pruning
> - Garden maintenance
>
> - Bouquets from your garden
> - Building a potting table
> - Installing a new lawn
> - Installing a sprinkler system

Save

16 On the Standard toolbar, click the **Save** button to save the presentation.

CLOSE the *CorrectText* presentation.

Checking Spelling and Presentation Styles

Microsoft Office Specialist

You can use two different methods to ensure that the words in your presentations are spelled correctly:

■ By default, PowerPoint's spelling checker checks the spelling of the entire presentation—all slides, outlines, notes pages, and handout pages—against its built-in dictionary. To draw attention to words that are not in its dictionary and that might be misspelled, PowerPoint underlines them with a wavy red line. When you encounter a wavy red line under a word, you can right-click the word and choose the correct spelling from the shortcut menu, or tell PowerPoint to ignore the word. To turn off this feature, you can click Options on the Tools menu and clear the "Check spelling as you type" check box on the Spelling and Style tab of the Options dialog box.

■ You can opt out of using the "Check spelling as you type" option and instead use the Spelling button on the Standard toolbar to check the entire presentation when you finish creating it. PowerPoint then works its way through the presentation, and if it encounters a word that is not in its dictionary, it displays a dialog box so that you can decide how to deal with the word.

PowerPoint includes built-in dictionaries in several languages, so you can check presentations that use languages other than English. (You can mark foreign words so that PowerPoint won't flag them as misspellings.) You can add words to PowerPoint's supplemental dictionary (called CUSTOM.DIC), or create custom dictionaries to check the spelling of unique words. You can also use dictionaries from other Microsoft programs.

PowerPoint's style checker works with the Office Assistant to help you keep the styles you use in your presentations consistent. That way, your audience can focus on content without being distracted by visual mistakes. When the Office Assistant is visible, the style checker reviews the presentation for typical errors—incorrect font size, too many fonts, too many words, inconsistent punctuation, and other readability problems. The style checker then suggests ways to improve the presentation.

In this exercise, you will correct a misspelled word, mark a foreign word, and check the spelling of an entire presentation. You will then set the style options and check the presentation style.

USE the *SpellCheck* presentation in the practice file folder for this topic. This practice file is located in the *My Documents\Microsoft Press\PowerPoint 2003 SBS\WorkingText\Spelling* folder and can also be accessed by clicking *Start/All Programs/Microsoft Press/PowerPoint 2003 Step by Step*.
OPEN the *SpellCheck* presentation.

1   Move to Slide 2, and right-click the word *arrangment*, which has a wavy red underline.

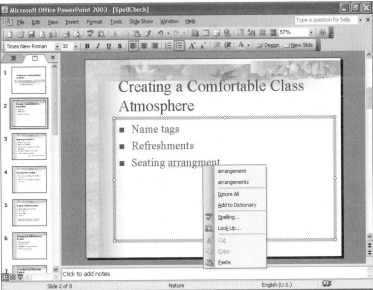

2   Click *arrangement* in the list to replace the misspelled word, and then move to Slide 8.

The French phrase *je ne sais quoi* has been flagged as a possible error.

3 Select *je ne sais quoi*, and on the **Tools** menu, click **Language**.

The Language dialog box appears.

4 Scroll down the list, click **French (France)**, click **OK**, and then click a blank area of the slide.

Behind the scenes, PowerPoint has marked the phrase as French, and the phrase no longer has wavy red underlines.

Spelling

5 Move to Slide 1, and on the Standard toolbar, click the **Spelling** button.

Troubleshooting If a message box tells you that this feature is not yet installed, click Yes to install it before proceeding.

PowerPoint begins checking the spelling in the presentation. The spelling checker stops on the word *Maintanance* and displays the Spelling dialog box.

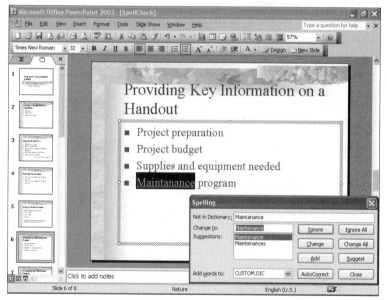

6 Click **Change**.

PowerPoint replaces *Maintanance* with the suggested *Maintenance*, and then stops on the word *Bouquays*, suggesting *Bouquets* as the correct spelling.

Tip Click the AutoCorrect button in the Spelling dialog box to add the misspelling and the correct spelling of a word to the AutoCorrect table of entries.

7   Click **Change**.

Next the spelling checker stops on *TGCGardenersOnly*. This term does not appear in the dictionary, but you know it is a proper name that is spelled correctly.

8   Click **Add**.

The term *TGCGardenersOnly* is added to the supplemental dictionary called CUSTOM.DIC. A message box tells you that PowerPoint has finished the spelling check.

Tip   If you do not want to change a word or add it to the supplemental dictionary, you can click Ignore or Ignore All. The spelling checker then ignores that word or all instances of the word in the presentation in subsequent spell checking sessions.

9   Click **OK**.

10 Move to Slide 1, and on the **Tools** menu, click **Options**.

The Options dialog box appears.

11 Click the **Spelling and Style** tab, select the **Check style** check box, and then click **Style Options**.

Troubleshooting   If PowerPoint prompts you to turn on the Office Assistant, click Enable Assistant, and then click Yes if you are prompted to install this feature.

The Style Options dialog box appears.

12 Select the **Slide title punctuation** check box. Then click the down arrow to the right of the adjacent box, and click **Paragraphs do not have punctuation**.

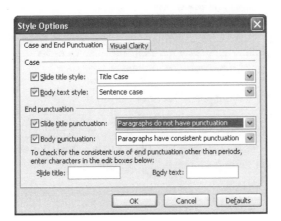

13   Click **OK** to close the **Style Options** dialog box, and then click **OK** again to close the **Options** dialog box.

14   Click the title of Slide 1, and then click the light bulb icon that appears.

The Office Assistant appears to tell you that the title of this slide does not conform to the rule that all words should have initial capital letters (title case).

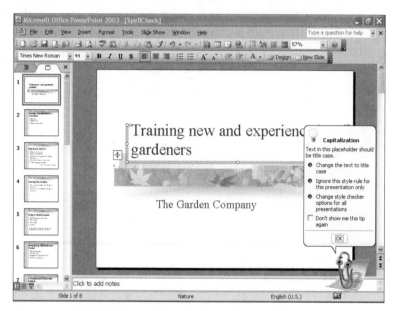

15   Select the **Change the text to title case** option.

PowerPoint capitalizes all the words of the title.

Tip   If you make a decision about a style tip, the Office Assistant might not display that tip again unless you reset the tips. To reset the tips, right-click the Office Assistant, click Options, click "Reset my tips," and click OK.

Save

16   On the Standard toolbar, click the **Save** button to save the presentation.

BE SURE TO click Options on the Tools menu and clear the "Check style" check box on the Spelling and Style tab if you don't want PowerPoint to continue giving style suggestions.
CLOSE the *SpellCheck* presentation.

Changing Capitalization

You can change the case of selected text by using the Change Case command on the Format menu. Options include sentence case, title case, uppercase, lowercase, or toggle case, which changes uppercase to lowercase and vice versa.

To change the text case:

1 Select the text you want to change.

2 On the **Format** menu, click **Change Case**.

The Change Case dialog box appears with the Sentence case option set as the default.

3 Click the option you want to apply to the selected text.

4 Click **OK**.

Choosing the Best Word

New in Office 2003
Thesaurus and Research task pane

Language is often contextual—the language you use in a presentation to club members is different from the language you use in a business presentation. To make sure you are using words that best convey your meaning in any given context, you can use PowerPoint's *Thesaurus* to look up alternative words, or synonyms, for a selected word. To use the Thesaurus, you select the word you want to look up, and on the Tools menu, click Thesaurus. The Research task pane appears, displaying a list of synonyms with equivalent meanings.

In this exercise, you will access the Thesaurus and replace a word with a more appropriate one.

USE the *Thesaurus* presentation in the practice file folder for this topic. This practice file is located in the *My Documents\Microsoft Press\PowerPoint 2003 SBS\WorkingText\Choosing* folder and can also be accessed by clicking *Start/All Programs/Microsoft Press/PowerPoint 2003 Step by Step*.
OPEN the *Thesaurus* presentation.

1 Move to Slide 2, and double-click the word *Comfortable* in the title.

2 On the **Tools** menu, click **Thesaurus**.

The Research task pane appears, listing synonyms for the word *comfortable*.

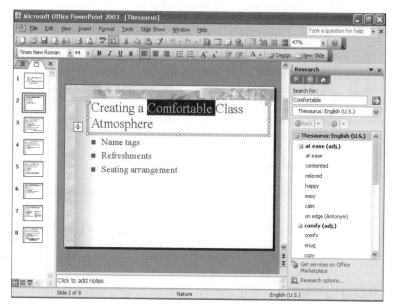

3 Click the minus sign to the left of *comfy* to bring more of the synonym list into view.

4 Point to the word *relaxed*, click the down arrow that appears to the right, and click **Insert** on the drop-down menu.

You can also simply click the word to insert it. Word replaces *Comfortable* with *Relaxed*, mirroring the existing punctuation.

Save

5 On the Standard toolbar, click the **Save** button to save the document.

CLOSE the *Thesaurus* presentation and the Research task pane, and if you are not continuing on to the next chapter, quit PowerPoint.

Key Points

- When you click the text in a text object, it is surrounded by a slanted-line selection box, which indicates that you can edit and format the text. When you click the slanted-line selection box, the text is surrounded by a dotted selection box, which indicates that you can manipulate the object as a unit.

- In addition to titles and bullet points or other paragraphs, you can create two types of text boxes: text labels, and word processing boxes. The first is a single line of text, and the second is a note that wraps in a box. You can change one into the other by changing the word-wrap and fit-text options in the Format Text Box dialog box.

■ You can align text to the left or right, or you can center it in a text object. You can also adjust the text object to fit the amount of text it contains.

■ You can use the Find and Replace commands on the Edit menu to locate and change text. You can also replace one font with another throughout a presentation with the Replace Font command.

■ PowerPoint uses AutoCorrect to correct common capitalization and spelling errors as you type. It uses AutoFit to ensure that the text you type fits in its object. The AutoCorrect Options and AutoFit Options buttons give you control over whether text is corrected and sized.

■ PowerPoint's spelling checker checks the spelling of slides, outlines, notes pages, and handout pages. You can mark foreign words and add words to a dictionary so that they don't get flagged as misspellings.

■ You can use PowerPoint's Thesaurus to look up synonyms for a selected word and insert a new word into the presentation.

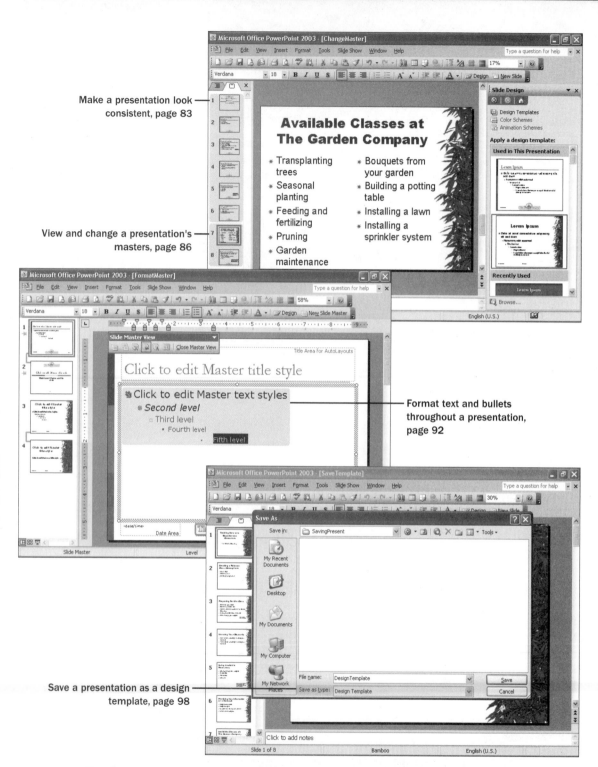

Make a presentation look consistent, page 83

View and change a presentation's masters, page 86

Format text and bullets throughout a presentation, page 92

Save a presentation as a design template, page 98

Chapter 5 at a Glance

5 Applying and Modifying Design Templates

In this chapter you will learn to:

✔ Make a presentation look consistent.

✔ View and change a presentation's masters.

✔ Format text and bullets throughout a presentation.

✔ Save a presentation as a design template.

Microsoft Office PowerPoint 2003 comes with a wide variety of professionally designed *templates*—sets of colors, text formats, and graphics that can help you achieve the look that you want for your presentations. You can use one of these predefined templates to create a new presentation, or you can apply a template to an existing presentation.

When you apply a template to a presentation, the slides take on the characteristics of the template so that a uniform design is maintained throughout the presentation. PowerPoint templates use *masters*—design patterns for slides, handouts, and speaker notes. When you create a slide, for example, it assumes the design of its corresponding master. You can then customize the slide's text, graphics, and other elements.

In this chapter, you will apply a PowerPoint template to a presentation, view various masters, change the display of the master objects, modify and format the master text, and save a presentation as a template.

See Also Do you need only a quick refresher on the topics in this chapter? See the Quick Reference entries on page xxxiv.

Important Before you can use the practice files in this chapter, you need to install them from the book's companion CD to their default location. See "Using the Book's CD-ROM" on page xiii for more information.

Making a Presentation Look Consistent

Microsoft Office Specialist

When you apply a template to a presentation, PowerPoint copies the information from the masters in the template to the corresponding masters in the presentation. All slides in a presentation then acquire the look of the template. You can use one of the many templates that come with PowerPoint, or you can create your own from existing presentations.

Reapplying a Slide Layout

If you make changes to the layout of a slide but then decide you would rather use the original slide layout, you can reapply the original slide layout to that slide.

To reapply a slide layout:

1 Display the slide to which you want to reapply a slide layout.

2 On the **Format** menu, click **Slide Layout** to display the **Slide Layout** task pane.

3 Point to the slide layout you want to reapply, and click the down arrow that appears.

4 On the drop-down menu, click **Reapply Layout**.

PowerPoint reapplies the slide layout.

See Also For more information about slide layouts, see "Creating a Presentation Based on Design" in Chapter 1.

You can apply different templates throughout the development process until you find the look that you like best. To apply a template to an existing presentation, you open the presentation and then use the Slide Design task pane to locate and select the template that you want.

In this exercise, you will apply a template to an existing presentation.

BE SURE TO start PowerPoint before beginning this exercise.
USE the *AddTemplate* presentation and *ApplyTemplate* template in the practice file folder for this topic. These practice files are located in the *My Documents\Microsoft Press\PowerPoint 2003 SBS\ApplyingDesign \MakingLook* folder and can also be accessed by clicking *Start/All Programs/Microsoft Press/PowerPoint 2003 Step by Step*.
OPEN the *AddTemplate* presentation.

Slide Design

1 On the Formatting toolbar, click the **Slide Design** button.

The Slide Design task pane opens.

2 With **Design Templates** active in the **Slide Design** task pane, click **Browse** at the bottom of the pane.

The Apply Design Template dialog box appears.

3   On the Places bar, click the **My Documents** icon. Then navigate to the *Microsoft Press \PowerPoint 2003 SBS\ApplyingDesign\MakingLook* folder, and click *ApplyTemplate*.

A preview of the template's design is shown in the box on the right.

4   Click **Apply**.

PowerPoint applies the information from the ApplyTemplate design template to the masters in the presentation. The text style and format, colors, and background objects change to match those of the template, but the content remains the same.

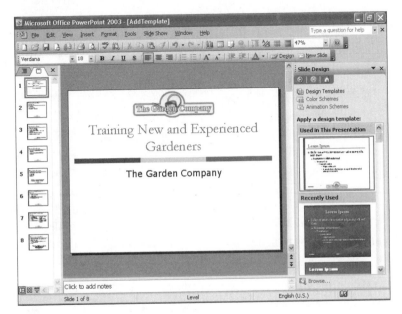

Tip   If the template thumbnails in your "Apply a design template" list are a lot smaller than ours, don't worry. If you want to display larger thumbnails, right-click a template, and click Show Large Previews on the shortcut menu.

5   Close the **Slide Design** task pane.

6   On the Standard toolbar, click the **Save** button to save the presentation.

Save

CLOSE the *AddTemplate* presentation.

Viewing and Changing a Presentation's Masters

*Microsoft
Office
Specialist*

By default, PowerPoint presentations have four *masters*:

■ The *Slide Master* controls the look of the slides in the presentation. All the Slide Master's characteristics (background color, text color, font, and font size) appear on all slides. When you make a change to these characteristics of the Slide Master, all the slides reflect the change. For example, if you want to include your company logo or the date on every slide, you can place it on the Slide Master.

■ The *Title Master* controls the look of title slides. In other words, changing the Title Master affects only slides to which you have applied a title slide layout.

■ The *Handout Master* controls the look of student handouts.

■ The *Notes Pages Master* controls the look of speaker notes.

Of these, the Slide Master and Title Master are the most important because almost all presentations use them, and together they comprise the slide-title master pair.

Masters contain text placeholders for title text, paragraph text or bullet points, date and time, footer information, and slide numbers. (They might also contain placeholders for graphics.) Text placeholders control text formatting. If you want to make a change—to the content, size, position, or format of a text object—that shows in all the slides throughout your presentation, you change the corresponding text placeholder on the Slide Master or Title Master. For example, if you change the format of the title text placeholder on the Slide Master to italic, the title of each slide changes to italic.

Tip   If you want to override the settings on the Slide Master for a particular slide, you can use commands on the Format menu. For example, you can delete a background graphic on a slide by using the Background command.

You make changes to the masters in *Slide Master view*. If you need more than one basic slide or title design for a presentation, or if you want to apply more than one template to a presentation, you can add an additional Slide Master or Title Master by using buttons on the Master toolbar, which appears when you switch to Slide Master view. This toolbar contains buttons to insert, delete, rename, duplicate, and preserve masters. (When you preserve a master, you protect it from being inadvertently deleted.) Clicking the Close Master View button on the Master toolbar returns you to the view you were in before you switched to Slide Master view.

Tip   You can control whether a presentation can have multiple masters or whether it should be restricted to one slide-title master pair. To change the multiple master setting, click Options on the Tools menu, and then click the Edit tab. In the "Disable new features" area, make sure the "Multiple masters" check box is cleared if you want to allow more than one master, or disable the feature by selecting its check box, thereby restricting the presentation to using one set of masters.

In this exercise, you will view the Title Master and the Slide Master in Slide Master view, switch between them, preserve the original masters, insert a second slide-title master pair, and view the Handout Master and Notes Master. You will also remove the footer from the Title Master and edit the placeholders on the Slide Master.

USE the *ChangeMaster* presentation in the practice file folder for this topic. This practice file is located in the *My Documents\Microsoft Press\PowerPoint 2003 SBS\ApplyingDesign\ViewingMaster* folder and can also be accessed *Start/All Programs/Microsoft Press/PowerPoint 2003 Step by Step*.
OPEN the *ChangeMaster* presentation.

1   With Slide 1 displayed in Normal view, point to **Master** on the **View** menu, and click **Slide Master**.

You are now in Slide Master view. (You cannot click a view button in the lower-left corner for Master views as you can for other views.) The pane on the left shows slide miniatures of the Slide Master and Title Master, with Slide 2—the Title Master—selected. The Title Master appears in the Slide pane to the right, and the Slide Master View toolbar is displayed.

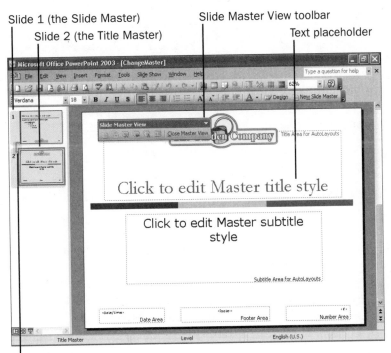

Slide 1 (the Slide Master)
Slide 2 (the Title Master)
Slide Master View toolbar
Text placeholder

The two slides are connected to show that they are a slide-title master pair.

Tip   If a Title Master does not appear when you switch to Slide Master view, the presentation you are working on doesn't have a title slide. You can create a Title Master by clicking New Title Master on the Insert menu.

2 In the left pane, click Slide 1.

The Slide Master slide is displayed in the pane on the right.

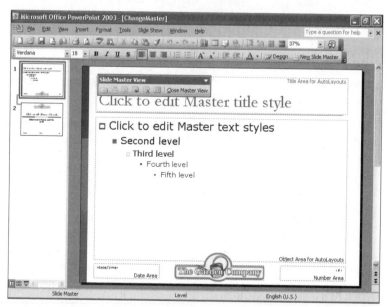

Preserve
Master

3 On the Slide Master View toolbar, click the **Preserve Master** button.

In the left pane, a gray thumbtack appears next to each thumbnail, indicating that PowerPoint will not delete these masters unless you specifically tell it to.

Tip While designing a presentation, you might work with multiple masters. If PowerPoint detects that a master is not applied to any of the slides in a presentation, it might delete the master, assuming you don't want to use it. Clicking the Preserve Master button on the Slide Master View toolbar prevents this from happening. You can still change the master, and if you decide you no longer need it, you can delete it.

Insert New
Slide Master

4 On the Slide Master View toolbar, click the **Insert New Slide Master** button.

In the left pane, a new Slide 3 with a generic slide design appears below Slide 2.

Insert New
Title Master

5 On the Slide Master View toolbar, click the **Insert New Title Master** button.

Slide 4 appears below Slide 3, with a generic title slide design. The two new masters are connected to show that they are a slide-title master pair, and they both have gray thumbtacks.

6 On the Slide Master View toolbar, click the **Preserve Master** button to turn it off.

PowerPoint asks whether you want to delete these masters because they are currently not used by any slides.

7 Click **No**.

The gray thumbtacks disappear from Slides 3 and 4, meaning that these masters are no longer preserved.

Slide Design

8 On the Formatting toolbar, click the **Slide Design** button.

The Slide Design task pane opens with the Design Templates option active.

9 At the bottom of the **Slide Design** task pane, click **Browse**. Then click the **My Documents** icon on the Places bar, navigate to the *Microsoft Press \PowerPoint 2003 SBS\ApplyingDesign\ViewingMaster* folder, and double-click *Bamboo*.

The Bamboo design template is applied to both the new masters.

10 Close the **Slide Design** task pane.

11 On the **View** menu, point to **Master**, and then click **Handout Master**.

The Handout Master appears, and the Handout Master View toolbar is displayed.

Show
positioning
of 3-per-page
handouts

12 On the Handout Master View toolbar, click the **Show positioning of 3-per-page handouts** button.

The master changes to show three handouts per page. (We've moved the toolbar for a better view.)

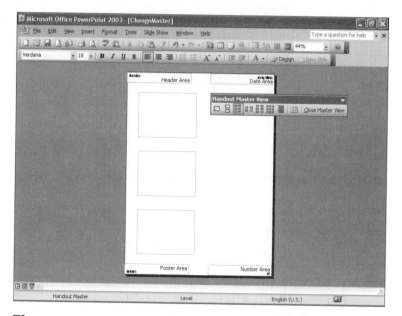

Tip Using the Handout Master View toolbar, you can show the positioning of one, two, three, four, six, or nine slides per page.

13 On the **View** menu, point to **Master**, and then click **Notes Master**.

The Notes Master appears, showing the positions of the slide image and speaker notes on the notes pages. The Notes Master View toolbar is displayed.

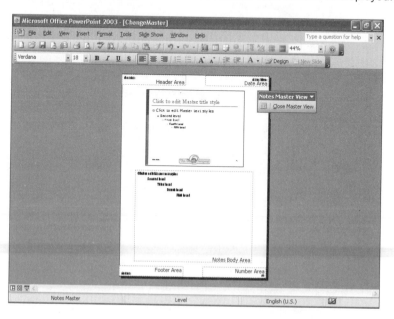

14 On the Notes Master View toolbar, click the **Close Master View** button.

PowerPoint returns to Slide 1 of the presentation in Normal view.

> **Tip** You can also switch back to Normal view by clicking the Normal View button in the lower-left corner of the window.

15 Move to Slide 7, and display the **Slide Design** task pane.

16 In the **Used in This Presentation** area at the top of the **Apply a design template** list, point to the **Bamboo** design template, click the down arrow that appears, and then click **Apply to Selected Slides**.

PowerPoint applies the Bamboo design template to Slide 7 only.

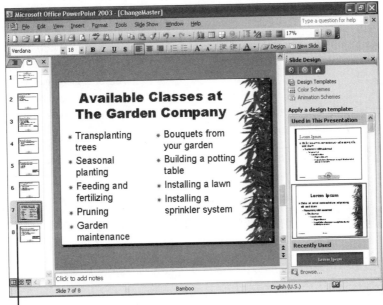

The Bamboo design template is applied only to Slide 7.

17 Close the **Slide Design** task pane.

18 On the **View** menu, click **Header and Footer**.

The Header and Footer dialog box appears.

19 In the **Include on slide** area, select the **Slide number** check box and the **Don't show on title slide** check box.

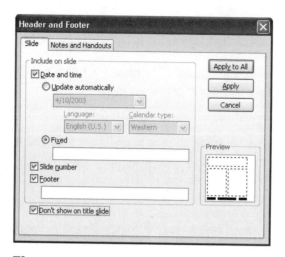

Tip   In addition to hiding objects on masters, you can hide them on individual slides. For example, you might want to hide a background object, such as the date and time, header and footer, slide number, or a graphic, so that it doesn't appear on a particular slide. Display the slide, and click Background on the Format menu to display the Background dialog box. Then select the "Omit background graphics from master" check box, and click Apply.

20   Click **Apply to All** to close the **Header and Footer** dialog box, and then in the **Slides** pane, click Slide 1.

The footer information is no longer displayed on Slide 1 (the title slide).

21   Click the **Next Slide** button to display Slide 2.

Next Slide

The footer information is still displayed on the other slides.

22   On the Standard toolbar, click the **Save** button to save the presentation.

Save

CLOSE the *ChangeMaster* presentation.

Formatting Text and Bullets Throughout a Presentation

Microsoft Office Specialist

Formatting the placeholders in Slide Master view makes text objects consistent across all slides in a presentation. The master placeholders determine the style and position of those text objects—the title, bulleted text, date and time, slide number, and footer. You can format the master placeholders to look any way you want.

In addition to formatting the text, you can customize the bullets for individual bullet points or for all the bullet points in an object. You can change a bullet's font, style, and color, and you can replace it with picture or a number. You can also control the distance between a bullet and its text in much the same way you control indents in Word, by moving indent markers on a ruler, as follows:

- The *First Line Indent marker*—the upper triangle—controls the first line of the paragraph.

- The *Hanging Indent marker*—the lower triangle—controls the left edge of the remaining lines of the paragraph.

- The *Left Indent marker*—the small square—controls how far the entire paragraph sits from the edge of the text object.

Hanging Indent marker

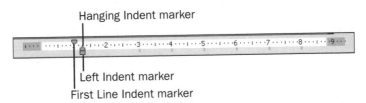

Left Indent marker
First Line Indent marker

By default, the markers of each bullet level are set so that the first line of each paragraph starts further to the left than the remaining lines, which "hang" below it. This setting is called a *hanging indent*. To adjust the relationship between the first and remaining lines, you drag the First Line Indent and Hanging Indent markers to the left or right on the ruler. To adjust the distance of the text from the edge of the text object, you drag the Left Indent marker.

In this exercise, you will format a text placeholder on the Slide Master and format bullets with a different symbol and a picture. You will then display the ruler and adjust the indent markers.

USE the *FormatMaster* presentation in the practice file folder for this topic. This practice file is located in the *My Documents\Microsoft Press\PowerPoint 2003 SBS\ApplyingDesign\FormattingText* folder and can also be accessed by clicking *Start/All Programs/Microsoft Press/PowerPoint 2003 Step by Step*.
OPEN the *FormatMaster* presentation.

1 On the **View** menu, point to **Master**, and then click **Slide Master** to switch to Slide Master view.

2 If Slide 1—the Slide Master—is not displayed, click Slide 1 in the left pane, and then click the **Number Area** placeholder to select that text object.

3 On the Formatting toolbar, click the down arrow to the right of the **Font Size** box, and click **18**.

18 ▾
Font Size

4 Click a blank area outside the text placeholder to deselect it.

Tip If you delete a placeholder and then want to restore it, you can click the Undo button if you notice the deletion before you do anything else. If it's too late to use the Undo button, click Master Layout on the Format menu, select the appropriate placeholder check box, and click OK.

5 Click *Second level* to select the text.

Troubleshooting You can also click to the right of the text to select it. But if you click the bullet to the left, PowerPoint selects that level and all the levels below it.

6 On the Formatting toolbar, click the **Italic** button.

The *Second level* text changes to italic.

7 Click a blank area outside the text placeholder to deselect it.

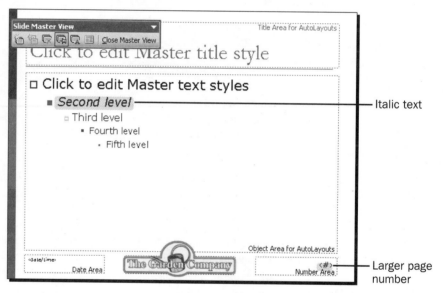

8 In the same text placeholder, click *Click to edit Master text styles*.

The first-level bullet point in the text placeholder is selected.

9 On the **Format** menu, click **Bullets and Numbering**.

The Bullets and Numbering dialog box appears.

10 Increase the size of the bullet by clicking the up arrow to the right of the **Size** box until the setting is **100**.

Tip   You can change the bullet color, adjust its size in relation to the text of the bullet point, change the symbol (by selecting a predefined symbol or by using the Picture or Customize command), or change the bullets to numbers.

11   Click **Picture**.

The Picture Bullet dialog box appears.

12   Scroll toward the bottom of the list box, and click the autumn-leaf image.

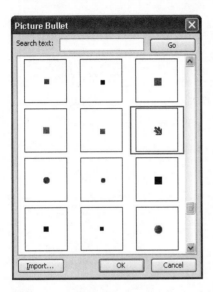

Tip   You can use a scanned photograph or other image that is suitable for a bullet. Open the Picture Bullet dialog box, click Import, and in the Add Clips to Organizer dialog box, find and select the image you want to import, and click Add. The image then appears as one of the choices in the Picture Bullet dialog box.

13   Click **OK**.

The bullet image for the first-level bullet points is now a leaf.

14   Right-click *Second level* in the text placeholder, and click **Bullets and Numbering** on the shortcut menu.

15   In the **Bullets and Numbering** dialog box, click **Customize**.

The Symbol dialog box appears.

16   With **Wingdings** selected in the **Font** box, scroll down the symbol list, and click the eight-pointed star symbol in the last column of the ninth row.

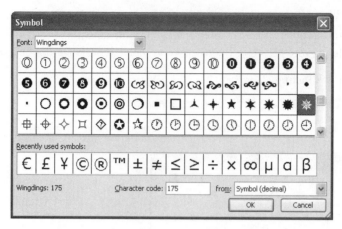

17 Click **OK** to return to the **Bullets and Numbering** dialog box.

18 Click the up arrow to the right of the **Size** box until the setting is **85**, and click **OK**.

The *Second level* bullet is a fancy star.

19 Click **Ruler** on the **View** menu.

Horizontal and vertical rulers appear along the top and left edges of the Slide pane. On the horizontal ruler are five sets of indent markers—one for each level in the bulleted list.

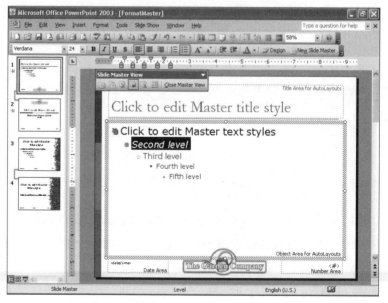

20 Click *Fifth level* to select the text.

Left Indent marker

21 Drag the fifth-level **Left Indent** marker (the square) to the right to the 4-inch mark on the ruler.

The First Line Indent marker and the Hanging Indent marker move with the Left Indent marker, maintaining the distance of the bullet from the bullet point.

Important If you drag an indent marker to the position of another indent marker, the marker you are dragging pushes the other marker in the direction you are dragging until you release the mouse button. When adjusting indents, it is best to start with the lowest level indent so that you have room to work.

First Line Indent marker

22 Drag the fifth-level **First Line Indent** marker (the down-pointing triangle) to the 3-inch mark on the ruler.

Troubleshooting If you have trouble positioning the indent markers, remember that you can always click the Undo button on the Standard toolbar and try again.

Hanging Indent marker

23 Drag the fifth-level **Hanging Indent** marker (the up-pointing triangle) to the 3 $^1/_2$-inch mark on the ruler.

The bullet point text moves closer to its bullet.

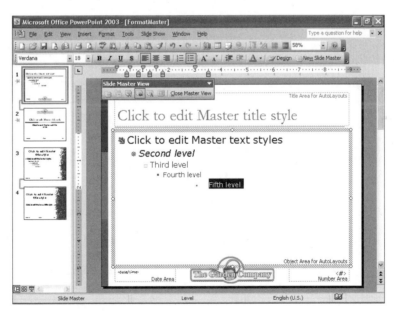

Close Master View

24 On the **View** menu, click **Ruler** to turn off the rulers. Then on the Slide Master View toolbar, click the **Close Master View** button.

You return to Slide 1 in Normal view.

Next Slide

25 Click the **Next Slide** button to move to Slide 2.

The bullets on Slide 2 are now leaves, reflecting the change you made to the Slide Master.

Save

26 On the Standard toolbar, click the **Save** button to save the presentation.

CLOSE the *FormatMaster* presentation.

Saving a Presentation as a Design Template

Microsoft Office Specialist

If you spend a lot of time customizing the masters of a particular presentation and you think you might want to use the new design for future presentations, you can save the presentation as a new design template. For example, The Garden Company might customize the slide-title master pair of a presentation to include the company's logo and contact information; use a custom, nature-related background and leaf-shaped bullets; and format text in various shades of green. If they want all company presentations to have the same distinctive look, they can save the presentation as a design template. It will then be included as a choice in the Slide Design task pane for future PowerPoint presentations.

In this exercise, you will save a presentation as a design template.

USE the *SaveTemplate* presentation in the practice file folder for this topic. This practice file is located in the *My Documents\Microsoft Press\PowerPoint 2003 SBS\ApplyingDesign\SavingPresent* folder and can also be accessed by clicking *Start/All Programs/Microsoft Press/PowerPoint 2003 Step by Step*.
OPEN the *SaveTemplate* file.

1 On the **File** menu, click **Save As**.

The Save As dialog box appears.

2 In the **File name** box, type DesignTemplate.

3 Click the down arrow to the right of the **Save as type** box, and click **Design Template** in the drop-down list.

PowerPoint displays the default Templates folder.

Important Design templates have to be stored in the default Templates folder in order for them to show up automatically in the Slide Design task pane. If you store a template somewhere else, as you do in this exercise, you can click Browse at the bottom of the pane, navigate to the folder where the template is stored, and double-click the template to make it available.

4   On the Places bar, click the **My Documents** icon, and then navigate to the *Microsoft Press\PowerPoint 2003 SBS\ApplyingDesign\SavingPresent* folder.

5   Click **Save**.

PowerPoint saves the template in the specified folder.

CLOSE the *DesignTemplate* template, and if you are not continuing on to the next chapter, quit PowerPoint.

Smart Tags

**New in
Office 2003**
Smart tags

If you frequently use certain types of information, such as the date and time, names, street addresses, or telephone numbers, in PowerPoint presentations, you can turn on the smart tag feature so that PowerPoint will recognize the information. On the Tools menu, click AutoCorrect Options. click the Smart Tags tab, select the "Label text with smart tags" check box, and click OK. PowerPoint then displays a dotted line under the text to indicate that it has been flagged with a smart tag. Pointing to the underlined text displays the Smart Tag Actions button. You can click this button to display a menu of options for performing common tasks associated with that type of information.

Key Points

■   You can apply different templates until you find the look that you like best. You can use one of the many templates that come with PowerPoint, or you can create your own from an existing presentation.

■   A template has four masters: the Slide Master, the Title Master, the Handout Master, and the Notes Page Master. Changing the Slide Master changes the look of all the slides in the presentation.

■   You can change the look of the text in a presentation by formatting the text placeholders on the masters. You can customize the bullets in a presentation for individual bullet points, or customize entire text objects.

■   After you have set up a presentation to look the way you want, you can save it as a design template that you can apply to other presentations.

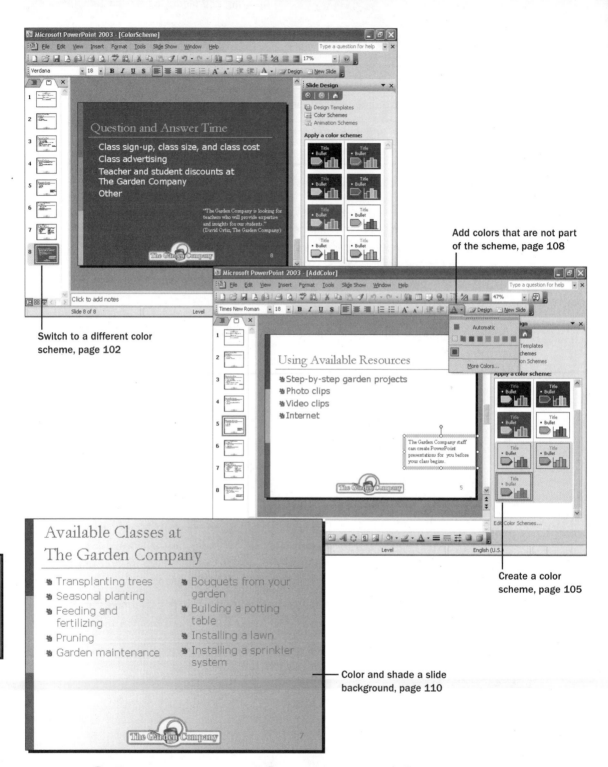

Switch to a different color
scheme, page 102

Add colors that are not part
of the scheme, page 108

Create a color
scheme, page 105

Color and shade a slide
background, page 110

Chapter 6 at a Glance

6 Changing Presentation Colors

In this chapter you will learn to:

✔ Switch to a different color scheme.

✔ Create a color scheme.

✔ Add colors that are not part of the scheme.

✔ Color and shade a slide background.

Every presentation you create with Microsoft Office PowerPoint 2003, even a blank one, has a set of colors associated with it. This *color scheme* consists of eight complementary colors designed to be used for the various elements of a slide—background, text, lines, shadows, fills, and accents.

You are not limited to using the colors in a presentation's color scheme, but because they have been selected by professional designers based on good design principles, using them does ensure that your slides will be pleasing to the eye. If you have experience working with color or have a natural talent for combining colors, you can experiment with colors and schemes until you find a combination that produces an aesthetically pleasing design.

In this chapter, you will view and choose a color scheme, change a scheme's colors, create a new color scheme, and add additional colors. You will also add first a colored background and then a textured background to a slide.

See Also Do you need only a quick refresher on the topics in this chapter? See the Quick Reference entries on pages xxxiv–xxxv.

 Important Before you can use the practice files in this chapter, you need to install them from the book's companion CD to their default location. See "Using the Book's CD-ROM" on page xiii for more information.

Switching to a Different Color Scheme

Microsoft Office Specialist

Understanding color schemes can help you create professional-looking presentations that use an appropriate balance of color. Every presentation uses at least one color scheme. A presentation with more than one set of slide masters can have more than one color scheme. A color scheme can be the default color scheme applied to a template, or it can be a set of custom colors that you choose.

See Also   For more information about slide masters, see "Viewing and Changing a Presentation's Masters" in Chapter 5.

To view a presentation's color scheme, you click Color Schemes in the Slide Design task pane. The Slide Design task pane displays all the color schemes that you can apply to the presentation, with the presentation's current color scheme surrounded by a selection rectangle. To change the colors in a scheme, you click Edit Color Schemes at the bottom of the task pane and then use the Edit Color Scheme dialog box. You can also choose a different color scheme or create your own color scheme by using this dialog box. After you decide which colors you want, you can apply the color scheme to one or all of the slides in a presentation.

Each PowerPoint color scheme consists of a palette of eight colors. These colors appear on the drop-down palette when you click the down arrow to the right of the Fill Color or Font Color button on the Drawing toolbar. These eight colors correspond to the following elements in a presentation:

- The Background color is used for the "canvas" of the slide. All other colors must show up against it.

- The "Text and lines" color must contrast with the background color so that the text shows up clearly.

- The Shadows color is generally a darker shade of the background so that it produces a shadowed effect behind objects.

- The "Title text" color must also contrast with the background color because the slide titles need to stand out.

- The Fill color is used to fill objects and must contrast with both the background color and the color used for text and lines.

- The primary Accent color is designed to complement the colors of other objects in the presentation.

■ The "Accent and hyperlink" color is designed to complement the colors of other objects and is also used to draw attention to hyperlinks.

■ The "Accent and followed hyperlink" color is designed to complement the colors of other objects and is also used to mark visited hyperlinks.

In this exercise, you will examine the current color scheme of a presentation and then choose another color scheme.

BE SURE TO start PowerPoint before beginning this exercise.
USE the *ColorScheme* presentation in the practice file folder for this topic. This practice file is located in the *My Documents\Microsoft Press\PowerPoint 2003 SBS\ChangingColor\SwitchingScheme* folder and can also be accessed by clicking *Start/All Programs/Microsoft Press/PowerPoint 2003 Step by Step*.
OPEN the *ColorScheme* presentation.

Slide Design

1 Move to Slide 8, and on the Formatting toolbar, click the **Slide Design** button to open the **Slide Design** task pane.

2 In the **Slide Design** task pane, click **Color Schemes**.

The task pane displays a preview of the color scheme currently used by the Slide Master—which is identified by the selection box around it—and the other available color schemes.

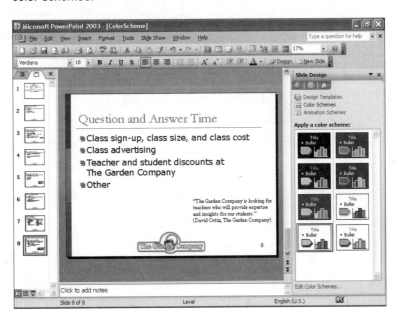

Troubleshooting If you see only a couple of color schemes in one column in the "Apply a color scheme" area of the task pane, your task pane is set to show large previews. If you want your screen to look like ours, right-click any preview, and then click Show Large Previews on the shortcut menu to deselect it.

3 If your screen shows large previews, scroll to the top of the **Apply a color scheme** box to see what schemes are available.

4 Point to the color scheme with the grayish green background, click the down arrow that appears, and then click **Apply to Selected Slides**.

The colors on Slide 8 change to those of the new color scheme. The colors on the other slides remain the same.

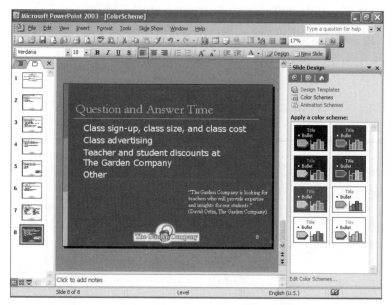

5 Close the **Slide Design** task pane.

Save

6 On the Standard toolbar, click the **Save** button to save the presentation.

CLOSE the *ColorScheme* presentation.

Creating a Color Scheme

Microsoft Office Specialist

You can modify any or all of the colors within a color scheme to create your own color combinations, and you can apply your color scheme changes to one slide or to an entire presentation. For example, The Garden Company might want to create a customized color scheme that complements the company's logo while emphasizing the natural theme of the store throughout an entire presentation.

To change colors, you open the Edit Color Scheme dialog box from the Color Schemes section of the Slide Design task pane, and then use the Change Color feature available on the Custom tab. You can select colors from a standard color palette or specify a color based on *RGB (Red, Green, and Blue) values*. Because a large percentage of the visible spectrum can be represented by mixing red, green, and blue, specifying RGB values is an easy way of identifying the specific shade of the specific color that you want PowerPoint to use.

You can create a new color scheme by altering an existing color scheme. You can then add the new scheme to the list of available schemes, making it available in the Slide Design task pane and on the Standard tab of the Edit Color Scheme dialog box.

Tip You can reuse color schemes without having to re-create them. On the Slides tab, you simply select the slide with the color scheme you want to reuse, click the Format Painter button on the Standard toolbar to copy the color scheme, and then click another slide to apply the color scheme. You can also use the Format Painter button to copy a color scheme from one presentation to another.

In this exercise, you will change colors in a color scheme and add a new color scheme to the presentation's set of color schemes.

USE the *CreateScheme* presentation in the practice file folder for this topic. This practice file is located in the *My Documents\Microsoft Press\PowerPoint 2003 SBS\ChangingColor\CreatingScheme* folder and can also be accessed by clicking *Start/All Programs/Microsoft Press/PowerPoint 2003 Step by Step*.
OPEN the *CreateScheme* presentation.

Slide Design

1 On the Formatting toolbar, click the **Slide Design** button to open the **Slide Design** task pane.

2 In the **Slide Design** task pane, click **Color Schemes**.

The available color schemes appear in the task pane.

3 At the bottom of the **Slide Design** task pane, click **Edit Color Schemes**.

The Edit Color Scheme dialog box appears, showing the Custom tab. The "Scheme colors" area of this tab displays eight colored boxes that make up the presentation's current color scheme.

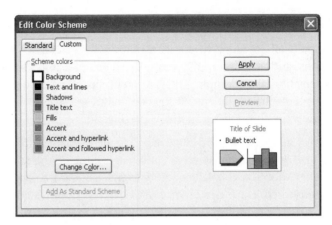

4 In the **Scheme colors** area, click the **Text and lines** color box to select the color.

5 Click **Change Color**.

The Text and Line Color dialog box appears, showing the Standard tab, which displays a color palette of standard colors from which to choose.

6 In the six-sided color palette, click the dark orange toward the middle of the lower outer edge.

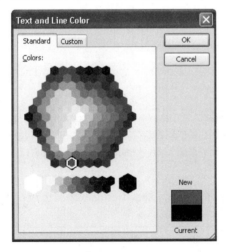

The New color and the Current color appear in the lower-right corner of the Text and Line Color dialog box.

7   Click **OK**.

The "Text and lines" color box changes to dark orange in the "Scheme colors" list.

8   Double-click the **Shadows** color box, and then click the **Custom** tab.

This tab of the Shadow Color dialog box shows the current color as a combination of red, green, and blue.

9   Using the up and down arrows, or by typing the numbers, set the **Red** value to 153, the **Green** value to 0, and the **Blue** value to 51.

The new setting produces a dark pinkish-red.

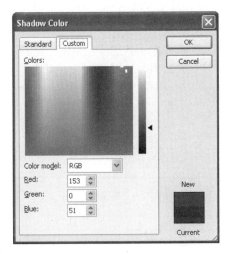

10   Click **OK**.

11   Change the **Title text** color to RGB values of 0, 128, and 0.

12   Change the remaining colors, picking shades of orange or red for **Accent** and **Accent and hyperlink**, and shades of green for **Fills** and **Accent and followed hyperlink**.

13   When you have finished, click **Add As Standard Scheme** to create a new color scheme.

The Add As Standard Scheme button becomes unavailable, indicating that the color scheme has been added to the color scheme list.

14   Click the **Standard** tab.

The new color scheme appears in the "Color schemes" box in the Edit Color Scheme dialog box, surrounded by a selection box.

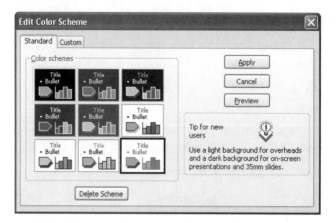

Important   If you want to delete a color scheme, you can select it on the Standard tab of the Edit Color Scheme dialog box and then click Delete Scheme. Be careful when deleting a color scheme. You cannot undo the operation and retrieve the color scheme.

15 Click **Apply**.

A new color scheme appears in the Slide Design task pane. PowerPoint applies the change to all the slides.

Close

16 In the **Slide Design** task pane, click the **Close** button.

The task pane closes.

17 On the Standard toolbar, click the **Save** button.

Save

CLOSE the *CreateScheme* presentation.

Adding Colors That Are Not Part of the Scheme

Microsoft Office Specialist

Although working with the eight colors of a harmonious color scheme enables you to create presentations with a pleasing design impact, you might want to play with a wider palette. You can add other colors to the drop-down palettes that appear when you click a toolbar button that applies color—for example, the Font Color button on the Formatting toolbar. After you have added a color to one drop-down palette, it appears on all color palettes and remains on them even if you change the color scheme applied to the presentation.

In this exercise, you will add a new color to the drop-down palettes.

USE the *AddColor* presentation in the practice file folder for this topic. This practice file is located in the *My Documents\Microsoft Press\PowerPoint 2003 SBS\ChangingColor\AddingColor* folder and can also be accessed by clicking *Start/All Programs/Microsoft Press/PowerPoint 2003 Step by Step*.
OPEN the *AddColor* presentation.

1 Move to Slide 5, and point slightly to the left of the note about creating presentations.

2 When the pointer changes to a four-headed arrow, click once to surround the text object with a dotted selection box.

Font Color

3 If necessary, display the Drawing toolbar, and then click the down arrow to the right of the **Font Color** button.

A color palette appears.

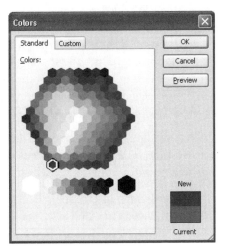

4 On the color palette, click **More Colors.**

The Colors dialog box appears.

5 In the color spectrum, click the dark brown color in the lower-left corner.

6   Click **OK**.

The text in the selected object changes to the dark brown color.

7   On the Drawing toolbar, click the down arrow to the right of the **Font Color** button.

The color that you just added appears on the second line of the palette and is now available for use throughout the presentation.

8   Click a blank area in the presentation window to close the palette.

9   On the Standard toolbar, click the **Save** button to save the presentation.

Save

CLOSE the *AddColor* presentation.

Coloring and Shading a Slide Background

Microsoft Office Specialist

In PowerPoint, you can customize the *background* of a slide by adding a color, a shade, a texture, a pattern, or even a picture.

A shaded background is a visual effect in which a solid color gradually changes from light to dark or dark to light. PowerPoint offers one-color and two-color shaded backgrounds with six styles: horizontal, vertical, diagonal up, diagonal down, from corner, and from title. For a one-color shaded background, the shading color can be adjusted lighter or darker, depending on your needs. You can also choose a preset color background, one of 24 professionally designed backgrounds in which the color shading changes direction according to the shading style selected.

If you want something fancier than shading, you can give the slide background a texture or a pattern, or you can use a picture. PowerPoint comes with several different textures, patterns, and pictures that you can apply to a presentation.

Tip   To add a picture to a slide's background, click Background on the Format menu, click the down arrow to the right of the Background box, click Fill Effects, and then click the Picture tab. Click Select Picture, navigate to the folder that contains the picture you want to use, double-click the file name, and then click OK. To apply the change to the current slide, click Apply, or to apply the change to all slides, click Apply to All.

In this exercise, you will add a shade to a slide background and then change the background from shaded to textured.

USE the *AddBackground* presentation in the practice file folder for this topic. This practice file is located in the *My Documents\Microsoft Press\PowerPoint 2003 SBS\ChangingColor\ColoringSlide* folder and can also be accessed by clicking *Start/All Programs/Microsoft Press/PowerPoint 2003 Step by Step*.
OPEN the *AddBackground* presentation.

1 Move to Slide 7, and on the **Format** menu, click **Background**.

The Background dialog box appears.

2 Below the preview in the **Background fill** box, click the down arrow to the right of the text box.

A drop-down palette appears.

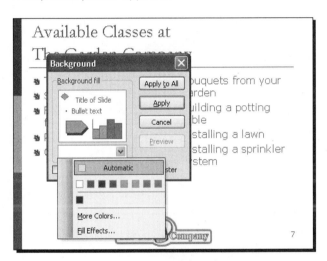

3 Click **Fill Effects** in the drop-down palette.

The Fill Effects dialog box appears, showing the Gradient tab with three color options, six shading styles, and four variants for the selected shading style. Currently, no colors or shading style are selected.

4 In the **Colors** area, select the **One color** option.

The Color 1 box appears.

5 Click the down arrow to the right of the **Color 1** box, and click the **Light Green** color box (fills) on the drop-down palette.

6 In the box below **Color 1**, drag the slide control all the way to the **Light** end of the box.

7 In the **Shading styles** area, select the **Vertical** option.

The boxes in the Variants area change to vertical styles.

8 In the **Variants** area, click the upper-right shading box.

The Sample box displays a preview of your selection.

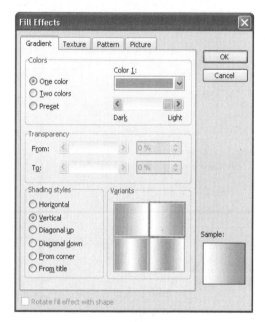

Tip For a gradient that shifts from one color to a second color, select the "Two colors" option and then pick a second color. Choosing the Preset option accesses a series of professionally designed color gradients, which range from simple to complex. The different shading styles and variants change the angle and direction of the color gradient—you can even have it emanating from the slide's title. If you're applying a gradient fill effect to a shape instead of to a slide's background, you can adjust the transparency to show what's underneath the shape, and you can decide whether the fill is static or rotates when the shape rotates.

9 Click **OK**.

10 In the **Background** dialog box, click **Apply**.

PowerPoint applies the shaded background only to the current slide.

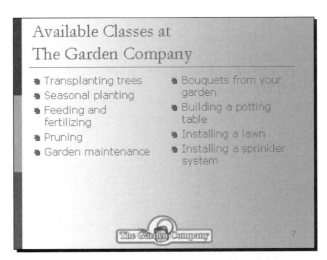

11 Move to Slide 1, and on the **Format** menu, click **Background**.

The Background dialog box appears.

12 Click the down arrow to the right of the box at the bottom of the **Background fill** area, and then click **Fill Effects**.

The Fill Effects dialog box appears.

13 Click the **Texture** tab, and click the **Papyrus** textured fill in the lower-left corner.

The name of the texture appears at the bottom of the dialog box, and the selected texture is displayed in the Sample box.

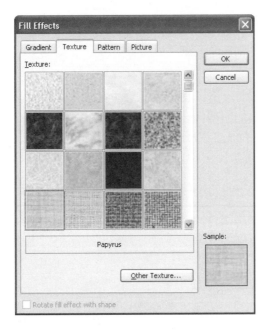

Tip   If you have a background texture or other graphic image of your own that you'd like to use as a background for slides, you can click Other Texture, browse to your file, and double-click it. PowerPoint adds your graphic to the options available on the Texture tab, and you can select and apply it just as you would any of the textures that come with PowerPoint.

14 Click **OK**, and then in the **Background** dialog box, click **Apply**.

PowerPoint applies the textured background only to the current slide.

15 On the **Format** menu, click **Background**.

The Background dialog box appears.

16 Click the down arrow to the right of the **Background fill** box, and click the **White** color box on the drop-down palette.

17 Click **Apply to All**.

PowerPoint applies the color scheme's background to all the slides in the presentation.

Save

18 On the Standard toolbar, click the **Save** button to save the presentation.

CLOSE the *AddBackground* presentation, and if you are not continuing on to the next chapter, quit PowerPoint.

114

Key Points

- You can change the colors in your color scheme, choose a different color scheme, or create your own color scheme. You can apply the color scheme to one or all the slides in a presentation.

- You can modify any or all of the colors within a color scheme to create your own color combinations. You can apply your color scheme changes to the current slide or to the entire presentation.

- In addition to the eight basic color scheme colors, you can add more colors to your presentation. Colors that you add to a specific color palette appear in all color palettes and remain there even if the color scheme changes.

- You can add a color, a shade, a texture, a pattern, or even a picture to the background of one slide or all slides. PowerPoint has several different textures, patterns, and pictures that you can apply to a presentation.

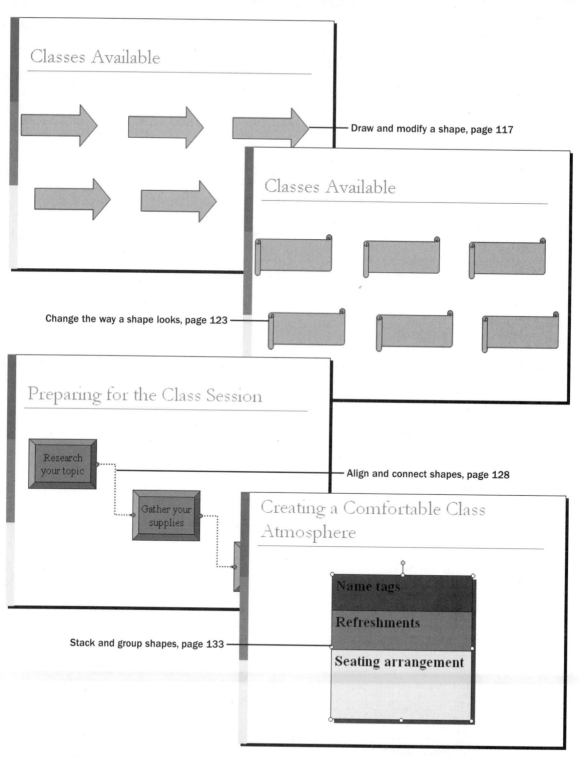

Classes Available

Draw and modify a shape, page 117

Classes Available

Change the way a shape looks, page 123

Preparing for the Class Session

Research your topic

Gather your supplies

Align and connect shapes, page 128

Creating a Comfortable Class Atmosphere

Name tags

Refreshments

Seating arrangement

Stack and group shapes, page 133

Chapter 7 at a Glance

7 Creating Shapes

In this chapter you will learn to:

✔   Draw and modify a shape.

✔   Change the way a shape looks.

✔   Align and connect shapes.

✔   Stack and group shapes.

To emphasize the key points in your presentation, you might want to include shapes in addition to text. The *shapes* you draw, like the pictures you import from other programs and the text you type, are objects that can be sized, moved, copied, and formatted in a variety of ways to suit your needs.

Microsoft Office PowerPoint 2003 provides tools for creating several types of shapes, including stars, banners, boxes, lines, circles, and squares. You can also draw free-form shapes of your own. With a little imagination, you will soon discover that there are endless ways to combine shapes to create drawings that can enhance your message. After combining shapes, you can work with shapes individually or as a group.

In this chapter, you'll draw and size shapes, copy and move them, and change the way they look. You'll also align and connect shapes, change their stacking order, and group and ungroup them.

See Also   Do you need only a quick refresher on the topics in this chapter? See the Quick Reference entries on pages xxxvi–xxxviii.

Important   Before you can use the practice files in this chapter, you need to install them from the book's companion CD to their default location. See "Using the Book's CD-ROM" on page xiii for more information.

Drawing and Modifying a Shape

Microsoft Office Specialist

To create almost any shape in PowerPoint, you use one simple technique: you select a drawing tool from the Drawing toolbar or the AutoShapes menu and then drag in the location where you want the shape to appear. The exception is free-form shapes, which are made up of multiple lines and curves. In any case, after you draw a shape, it is surrounded by a set of handles, indicating that it is selected. If it becomes deselected, you can click any visible part of it to reselect it.

The handles around a selected shape serve the following purposes:

- You can drag the white *sizing handles* to change the size of a shape.

- If a shape has a yellow diamond-shaped *adjustment handle* next to one of the sizing handles, the shape is adjustable. You can use this handle to alter the appearance of the shape without changing its size.

- You can drag the green *rotating handle* to adjust the angle of rotation of a shape.

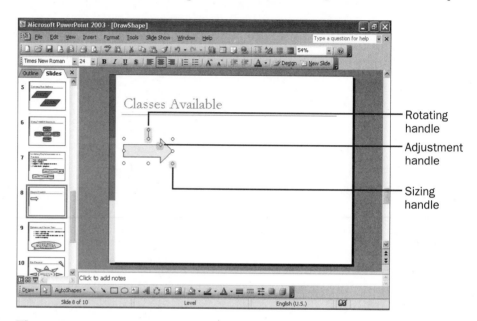

Tip   After you create a shape, you can change its orientation on the slide by rotating or flipping it. Rotating turns a shape 90 degrees to the right or left; flipping turns a shape 180 degrees horizontally or vertically. If you need a more exact rotation, which you cannot achieve in 90-degree or 180-degree increments, you can drag the green rotating handle at the top of a shape to rotate it to any position. (You can also rotate and flip any type of picture—including bitmaps.) This is useful when you want to change the orientation of a shape, such as changing the direction of an arrow. To rotate or flip a shape, select it, and on the Drawing toolbar, click the Draw button, point to Rotate or Flip, and then choose the option you want. You can also use the Free Rotate command on the Flip and Rotate submenu of the Draw menu to rotate a shape to any angle. The Free Rotate command changes the sizing handles to green rotating handles, which you can drag to rotate the shape to any position.

You can copy or cut a selected shape or multiple shapes to the *Office Clipboard* and then paste the shapes in other parts of the presentation. When you copy multiple shapes, the Clipboard task pane displays all the items, and you can then paste them elsewhere in the same presentation, in another presentation, or in any Office program, either individually or all at once.

Tip To manually open the Office Clipboard, you click Office Clipboard on the Edit menu. You can change the way the Office Clipboard works by changing options in the Clipboard task pane. To access these options, you click Options at the bottom of the Clipboard task pane.

You can also copy a shape by dragging it while holding down the [Ctrl] key or by using the Duplicate command on the Edit menu. To move a shape from one location to another, you can simply drag it without holding down the [Ctrl] key.

In this exercise, you will draw a shape using a drawing tool from the AutoShapes menu. You will then change the shape's size and adjust its shape. Finally, you will copy and move the shape and then copy multiple shapes.

BE SURE TO start PowerPoint before beginning this exercise.
USE the *DrawShape* presentation in the practice file folder for this topic. This practice file is located in the *My Documents\Microsoft Press\PowerPoint 2003 SBS\CreatingShape\DrawingShape* folder and can also be accessed by clicking *Start/All Programs/Microsoft Press/PowerPoint 2003 Step by Step*.
OPEN the *DrawShape* presentation.

1 If the Drawing toolbar is not displayed, point to **Toolbars** on the **View** menu, and then click **Drawing**.

2 Move to Slide 8, and on the Drawing toolbar, click **AutoShapes**.

Right Arrow

3 Point to **Block Arrows**, and then click the **Right Arrow** button in the first column of the first row.

In the presentation window, the pointer changes to a crosshair.

Tip If you click a drawing tool and then change your mind about creating a shape, you can turn off the tool by clicking its button on the Drawing toolbar.

4 Position the crosshair pointer on the left side of the slide, adjacent to the top of the green bar. Then hold down the [Shift] key, and drag to the left about 1 inch.

Tip   Holding down the [Shift] key while you drag maintains the proportions of the shape. Holding down the [Ctrl] key instead of [Shift] creates a proportional shape from its center outward.

The white handles around the block arrow indicate that it is selected.

5   Drag the arrow's right-middle handle until its point aligns with the capital letter *A*.

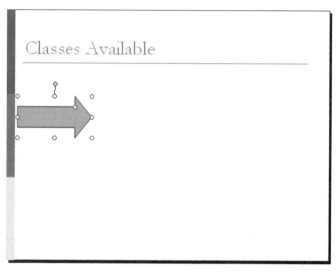

6   Point to the arrow's adjustment handle (the yellow diamond), and when the pointer changes to an arrowhead, drag to the left.

Dragging the adjustment handle changes the shape of the arrow while maintaining its size.

Undo

7   On the Standard toolbar, click the **Undo** button.

The arrow's original shape is restored.

Copy

8   With the arrow still selected, click the **Copy** button on the Standard toolbar.

A copy of the arrow is stored on the Office Clipboard.

Close

Tip   If the Office Clipboard already contains one or more items, the Clipboard task pane opens. To close it, click the Close button at the right end of its title bar.

Paste

9   On the Standard toolbar, click the **Paste** button.

A copy of the arrow is pasted on the slide, overlapping the original arrow.

120

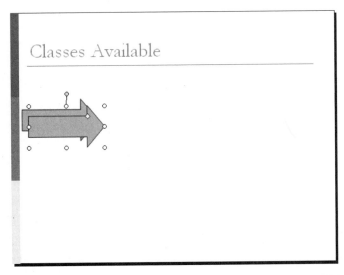

10 Drag the new arrow about half an inch to the right of the original arrow, and align the two shapes.

> **Tip** To move a shape horizontally or vertically in a straight line, hold down [Shift] while you drag the shape.

11 Point to the second arrow, hold down [Ctrl], and drag another copy of the arrow about half an inch to the right of the second one.

Three identical arrows now appear in a row.

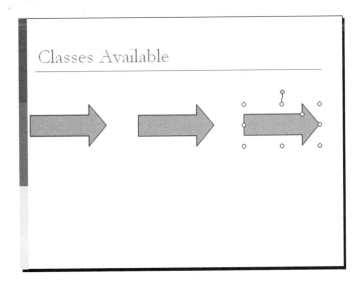

Troubleshooting If you release the mouse button too soon and need to drag the copy of the arrow a little further to the right, drag without holding down the Ctrl key. Otherwise you will create another copy of the arrow.

12 With the third arrow still selected, hold down Shift, and click the other two arrows in turn.

All the arrows are now selected.

13 Hold down Shift, and click the middle arrow again.

The shape is removed from the selection.

14 Click a blank area of the slide to deselect all the arrows.

15 Point to the left edge of the slide, just below the title. Then drag down and to the right to draw a selection box around all the arrows.

When you release the mouse button, all the shapes within the selection box are selected.

16 On the Standard toolbar, click the **Copy** button.

The Clipboard task pane opens, showing the single copied arrow and the set of three copied arrows.

Troubleshooting If the Office Clipboard doesn't appear, you can click Office Clipboard on the Edit menu to open it.

17 In the **Clipboard** task pane, click the item with the three arrows.

A copy of the three arrows is pasted onto the slide. The new arrows overlap the original arrows.

18 Point to one of the three selected arrows, and when the pointer changes to a four-headed arrow, drag the set of three arrows down and to the right.

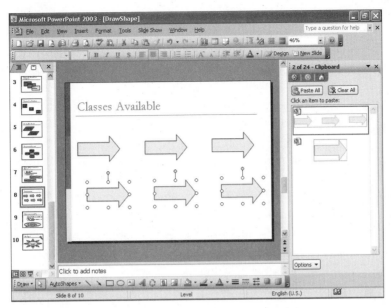

19 In the **Clipboard** task pane, click **Clear All** to remove the items from the Office Clipboard. Then close the task pane.

Save

20 On the Standard toolbar, click the **Save** button to save the presentation. If you have finished working with shapes, turn off the Drawing toolbar.

CLOSE the *DrawShape* presentation.

Changing the Way a Shape Looks

Microsoft Office Specialist

After drawing an AutoShape, you can change it by selecting it, clicking the Draw button on the Drawing toolbar, clicking Change AutoShape, and then choosing a new shape.

In addition to changing the actual shape, you can change the look of a shape by changing its *attributes*. A shape might have graphic attributes—such as fill, line, and shadow—or text attributes—such as style, font, color, embossment, and shadow. The shapes you draw usually have only a fill and a border until you apply other attributes. You can change these attributes for a single shape or for all shapes of a particular type.

You can make dramatic changes to the look of a shape by altering the following attributes:

■ You can change the line style of the border of a shape by making the border heavier or changing its color.

■ You can give a shape or its text a shadow to help create a three-dimensional appearance. You can choose the color of the shadow and its *offset*, the direction in which it falls from the shape.

123

■ You can add text to a shape. PowerPoint centers the text as you type, and the text becomes part of the shape. You can then format the text by selecting the shape and using the buttons on the Formatting toolbar to achieve the look you want, including changing the text font and color, adding a shadow effect to it, or adding an embossed effect.

■ You can change the shape to look three-dimensional by clicking the 3-D Style button on the Drawing toolbar, clicking 3-D Settings, and then choosing the 3-D effects you want from the 3-D Settings toolbar. You can change the depth of the shape and its color, rotation, angle, direction of lighting, and surface texture.

Having applied attributes to one shape, you can easily apply the same attributes to other shapes:

■ Copy the attributes of one shape to another shape by selecting the shape that has the desired attributes, clicking the Format Painter button on the Standard toolbar, and then clicking the shape to which you want the attributes copied.

■ Copy the attributes of one shape to multiple shapes by double-clicking the Format Paint button, and then clicking each shape in turn. When you have finished applying the attributes, click the Format Painter button to toggle it off, or press the Esc key.

■ If you apply attributes to a shape and then decide you want all shapes of that type to have the same attributes, you can select the shape, click the Draw button on the Drawing toolbar, and then click Set AutoShape Defaults. From then on, any shapes you draw of that type will have the new default attributes.

In this exercise, you will change a shape and then add text to it. You will modify the fill and frame, add and modify a shadow, change the text color and style, and then copy the text formatting with the Format Painter button.

USE the *ChangeShape* presentation in the practice file folder for this topic. This practice file is located in the *My Documents\Microsoft Press\PowerPoint 2003 SBS\CreatingShape\ChangingShape* folder and can also be accessed by clicking *Start/All Programs/Microsoft Press/PowerPoint 2003 Step by Step*.
OPEN the *ChangeShape* presentation.

1 If the Drawing toolbar is not displayed, point to **Toolbars** on the **View** menu, and then click **Drawing**.

2 Move to Slide 8, and click the first arrow to select it.

3 Hold down the [Shift] key, and then click each of the six arrows to add them to the selection.

Draw ▾ **4** On the Drawing toolbar, click the **Draw** button, point to **Change AutoShape**, and then point to **Stars and Banners**.

5 On the **Stars and Banners** submenu, click the **Change Shape to Horizontal Scroll** button in the second column of the fourth row.

Each arrow changes to a scroll that is the same size and has the same attributes as the original arrow.

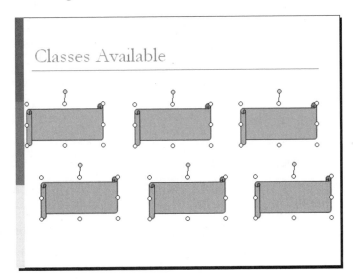

6 Click a blank area of the slide to deselect the shapes.

7 Click the upper-left scroll, and type Trees/shrubs.

When you click a shape, a slanted-line selection box appears around it, indicating that the shape is ready for you to enter or edit text.

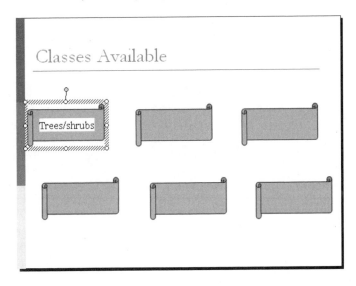

8 Click the upper-middle scroll, and type Lawn care, and then click the upper-right scroll, and type Flowers.

9 In the lower-left scroll, type Indoor plants; in the lower-middle scroll, type Transplanting; and then in the lower-right scroll, type Landscaping.

10 Click a blank area of the slide to deselect the scroll.

11 Move to Slide 10, and click one of the rays of the sun shape.

The sun shape is surrounded by a dotted selection box. (If you click the center oval of the sun, the shape is surrounded by a slanted-line selection box because that part of the shape contains text.)

Fill Color

12 On the Drawing toolbar, click the down arrow to the right of the **Fill Color** button, and click **Fill Effects**.

The Fill Effects dialog box appears.

13 Click the **Texture** tab, click the **Water Droplets** textured fill (in the first column of the fifth row), and click **OK**.

Tip You can click Other Texture to access textures stored on your hard disk. These might have been installed with Microsoft Office 2003 or another program, or you might have downloaded them from the Web.

The sun is filled with the new texture.

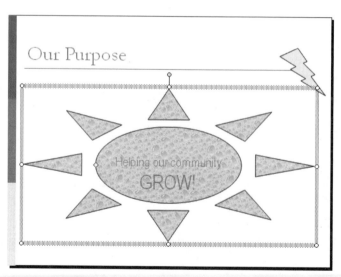

14 On the Drawing toolbar, click the down arrow to the right of the **Line Color** button, and click the **Orange** color box.

Line Color

The new line color is applied to the shape.

Shadow Style

15 On the Drawing toolbar, click the **Shadow Style** button, and then in the second column of the second row of the drop-down menu, click the **Shadow Style 6** button.

The shadow is applied to the shape.

16 On the Drawing toolbar, click the **Shadow Style** button, and then click **Shadow Settings**.

The Shadow Settings toolbar appears.

Nudge Shadow Down

17 On the **Shadow Settings** toolbar, click the **Nudge Shadow Down** button five times.

The depth of the shadow increases with each click.

Shadow Color

18 On the **Shadow Settings** toolbar, click the down arrow to the right of the **Shadow Color** button, and then click the **Orange** color box.

The shadow color changes to a semitransparent orange to coordinate with the border.

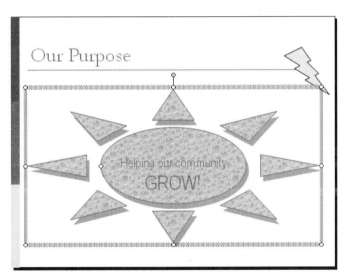

Shadow On/Off

Tip To turn off a shadow, you can either click the Shadow On/Off button on the Shadow Settings toolbar or click the Shadow button on the Drawing toolbar and then click No Shadow on the drop-down menu.

19 Close the Shadow Settings toolbar.

Font Color

20 On the Drawing toolbar, click the down arrow to the right of the **Font Color** button, and then click the **Blue** color box.

Arial
Font

21 On the Formatting toolbar, click the down arrow to the right of the **Font** button, and click **Comic Sans MS**.

The text inside the sun's oval is now displayed in blue in the Comic Sans MS font.

Format Painter

22   On the Standard toolbar, click the **Format Painter** button, and then click the lightning bolt shape.

PowerPoint applies the formats from the sun object to the lightning bolt shape.

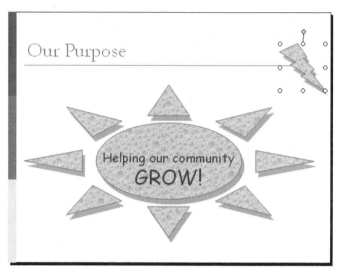

Save

23   On the Standard toolbar, click the **Save** button to save the presentation. If you have finished working with shapes, turn off the Drawing toolbar.

CLOSE the *ChangeShape* presentation.

Aligning and Connecting Shapes

Microsoft Office Specialist

After drawing shapes in rough locations on a slide, you can fine-tune their position in two ways:

- You can align shapes relative to each other by selecting them and using the Align or Distribute command. You can choose whether to align shapes vertically to the left, center, or right, or horizontally to the top, middle, or bottom.

- You can align shapes relative to a position on the slide by displaying a fixed grid across the entire slide or by displaying adjustable horizontal and vertical guidelines. You turn these on in the Grid and Guides dialog box, where you can also specify whether shapes should snap to the grid or to other shapes.

In addition to being able to position shapes precisely, you can also connect them with lines, making it easy to create flow charts and diagrams in which connected shapes indicate a hierarchy or sequence of events. When you select a connected shape, small blue handles, called *connection points*, appear. You can drag one connection point to another to change the line, or you can drag an adjustment handle to change the line's shape. After two shapes are connected, moving either shape also moves the line.

In this exercise, you will align shapes to one another and then align them to the grid and guides. You will also connect the shapes and change and format a connector line.

USE the *AlignShape* presentation in the practice file folder for this topic. This practice file is located in the *My Documents\Microsoft Press\PowerPoint 2003 SBS\CreatingShape\AligningShape* folder and can also be accessed by clicking *Start/All Programs/Microsoft Press/PowerPoint 2003 Step by Step*.
OPEN the *AlignShape* presentation.

1 If the Drawing toolbar is not displayed, point to **Toolbars** on the **View** menu, and then click **Drawing**.

2 Move to Slide 4, and select all three rectangles.

3 On the Drawing toolbar, click the **Draw** button, point to **Align or Distribute**, and then click **Align Center**.

The shapes align vertically relative to their respective centers.

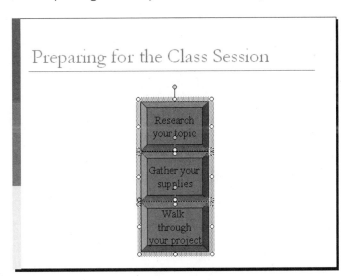

4 On the **View** menu, click **Grid and Guides**.

The Grid and Guides dialog box appears.

5 Select both the **Display grid on screen** check box and the **Display drawing guides on screen** check box.

6 Click **OK** to close the **Grid and Guides** dialog box.

A dotted-line grid appears across the slide, and two heavier dotted lines intersect in the center of the slide.

7 Point to the dotted selection box around the three shapes, hold down the [Shift] key, and drag the selected shapes to the left until their left edges touch the leftmost gridline in the white area of the slide.

Holding down the [Shift] key while you drag makes it easier to drag horizontally without nudging the selected shapes up or down.

8 Point to the vertical guide, and drag it to the left until it is aligned with the *P* in *Preparing*.

As you drag, a guide indicator shows in inches how far you are from the center of the slide.

Tip If the Guide indicator skips numbers as you drag the guides across the slide, the "Snap objects to grid" check box is selected in the Grid and Guides dialog box. When you select the "Snap objects to grid" check box, shapes snap to the grid of evenly spaced lines, helping you align the shapes.

9 Point to the dotted selection box around the three shapes, hold down [Shift], and then drag the selected shapes to the right until their left edges touch the vertical guide.

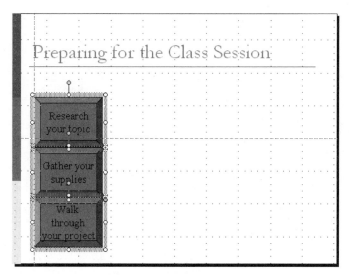

10 Point to the horizontal guide, and drag it downward until it is aligned with the bottom of the *Research your topic* shape.

11 Point to the horizontal guide again, hold down the ⌃ key, and drag a copy of the guide downward until it is aligned with the bottom of the *Gather your supplies* shape.

12 Click the middle shape, and click the slanted-line selection box to select the object. Then hold down ⌃ Shift , and drag the object's dotted selection box to the middle of the slide.

13 Repeat step 12 to drag the bottom shape to the right side of the slide.

14 On the View menu, click **Grid and Guides**, clear the **Display grid on screen** and **Display drawing guides on screen** check boxes, and click **OK**.

Elbow
Double-Arrow
Connector

15 On the Drawing toolbar, click **AutoShapes**, point to **Connectors**, and then in the third column of the second row of the drop-down menu, click the **Elbow Double-Arrow Connector** button.

16 Point to the top shape.

Blue connection points appear, and the pointer changes to a small box, called the *connection pointer*.

17 Point to the outer right-middle connection point, and drag downward to the middle shape (don't release the mouse button).

18 When connection points appear on the middle shape, click the outer left-middle one.

Red handles appear at each end of the line, indicating that the shapes are connected. A yellow, diamond-shaped adjustment handle appears in the middle of the connection line, indicating that you can adjust the line's shape.

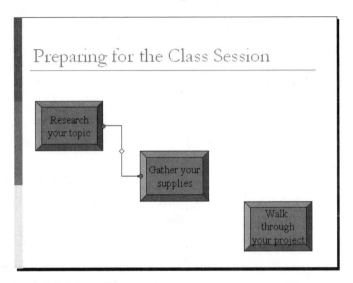

Troubleshooting   If square green handles appear at the ends of the line, the shapes are not connected. Click the Undo button to remove the line, and try drawing the connection line again.

19 On the Drawing toolbar, click **AutoShapes**, point to **Connectors**, and then click the **Elbow Double-Arrow Connector** button.

20 Draw a connection line between the outer connection point on the right side of the middle shape and the outer connection point on the left side of the bottom shape.

21 Hold down ⌗ Shift ⌗, and click the top connection line.

The two connector lines are selected.

Dash Style

22 On the Drawing toolbar, click the **Dash Style** button, and then on the menu, click the **Round Dot** line style (the second line from the top).

Line Style

23 On the Drawing toolbar, click the **Line Style** button, and then on the menu, click the **3 pt** line style.

The connector lines now have larger dots.

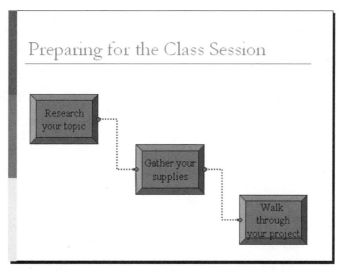

Save

24 On the Standard toolbar, click the **Save** button to save the presentation. If you have finished working with shapes, turn off the Drawing toolbar.

CLOSE the *AlignShape* presentation.

Stacking and Grouping Shapes

Microsoft Office Specialist

When shapes are placed on top of each other, they are stacked. The stacking order is determined by the order in which you draw the shapes. However, you can change the order by selecting a shape and clicking the Bring to Front, Send to Back, Bring Forward, and Send Backward commands on the Draw menu on the Drawing toolbar.

Tip   If you cannot select a shape because it is covered by others in the stack, you can press [Tab] to cycle forward or [Shift]+[Tab] to cycle backward through the stack until you select the shape you want.

Whether shapes are stacked or not, you can *group* them so that you can edit, copy, and move them as a unit. Although grouped shapes are treated as one object, each shape in the group maintains its individual attributes. You don't have to *ungroup* the objects to change an individual shape—for example, change its color. However, if you need to move or size one of the shapes in a group, you do need to first ungroup the shapes. After you have moved or sized the shape, you can regroup the same shapes by selecting one of the shapes and clicking the Regroup command.

In this exercise, you will change the stacking order of shapes and then group, ungroup, and regroup them.

USE the *StackShape* presentation in the practice file folder for this topic. This practice file is located in the *My Documents\Microsoft Press\PowerPoint 2003 SBS\CreatingShape\StackingShape* folder and can also be accessed by clicking *Start/All Programs/Microsoft Press/PowerPoint 2003 Step by Step.*
OPEN the *StackShape* presentation.

1   If the Drawing toolbar is not displayed, point to **Toolbars** on the **View** menu, and then click **Drawing**.

2   Move to Slide 3, and click the middle rectangle to select it.

Draw ▾

3   On the Drawing toolbar, click the **Draw** button, point to **Order**, and then click **Send to Back**.

The middle rectangle appears behind the other two.

4   On the Drawing toolbar, click the **Draw** button, point to **Order**, and then click **Bring to Front**.

The middle rectangle appears on top of the other shapes.

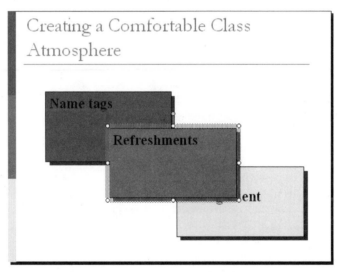

5   On the Drawing toolbar, click the **Draw button**, point to **Order**, and then click **Send Backward**.

The original stacking order is restored.

6   Click a blank area of the slide to deselect the shape, and then drag a selection box around all three shapes.

Each shape has its own dotted selection box and handles.

7 On the Drawing toolbar, click the **Draw** button, and then click **Group**.

The shapes are grouped together as one object with one set of handles around the edge of the grouped object.

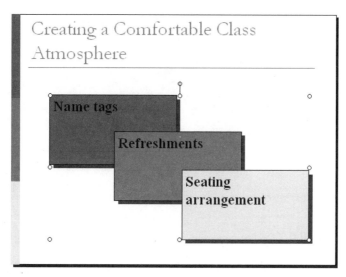

8 Click a blank area of the top rectangle.

Handles with little Xs in them surround the top rectangle to indicate that it is selected, but the white handles remain around the entire group.

Fill Color

9 On the Drawing toolbar, click the down arrow to the right of the **Fill Color** button, and then click the **Blue** color box.

The selected rectangle changes from red to blue.

10 Point to the middle rectangle, and when the pointer changes to a four-headed arrow, drag to the left until the dotted outline of the selected shapes aligns with the left end of the line below the slide title.

The entire group moves to the left. Because you pointed to the middle shape before dragging, that shape has handles with little Xs.

11 Point to the grouped object's right-middle handle, and drag to the right until the dotted outline aligns with the right end of the line below the slide title.

The sizes of all the shapes in the group change. You cannot change the size of just one shape without ungrouping.

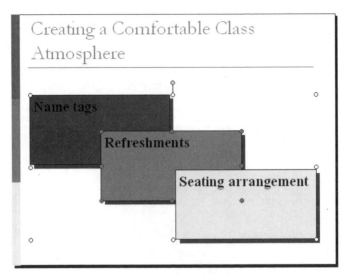

12 On the Drawing toolbar, click the **Draw** button, and then click **Ungroup**.

The object is ungrouped into individual shapes, which are all selected.

13 On the Drawing toolbar, click the **Draw** button, point to **Align and Distribute**, and then click **Align Center**.

14 On the Drawing toolbar, click the **Draw** button, and then click **Regroup**.

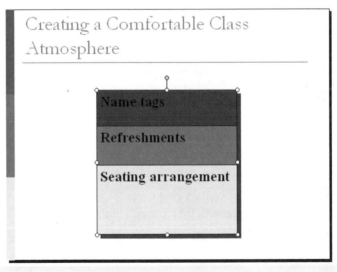

Save

15 On the Standard toolbar, click the **Save** button to save the presentation. Then turn off the Drawing toolbar.

CLOSE the *StackShape* presentation, and if you are not continuing on with the next chapter, quit PowerPoint.

Key Points

- You can create predefined AutoShapes or draw shapes of your own using the tools on the Drawing toolbar.

- You can copy a selected shape or multiple shapes to the Office Clipboard and then paste them elsewhere.

- You can change a shape's graphic attributes—fill, line, shape, and shadow—and text attributes—style, font, color, embossment, and shadow.

- You can align shapes in relation to each other or to a grid or guide, and you can connect shapes with lines. After two shapes are joined, their connection line moves if the shapes move.

- The order in which you draw shapes determines the order in which they are stacked. You can change the order at any time.

- You can group shapes and move and size them as a unit. You can change the attributes of a shape within a group without ungrouping.

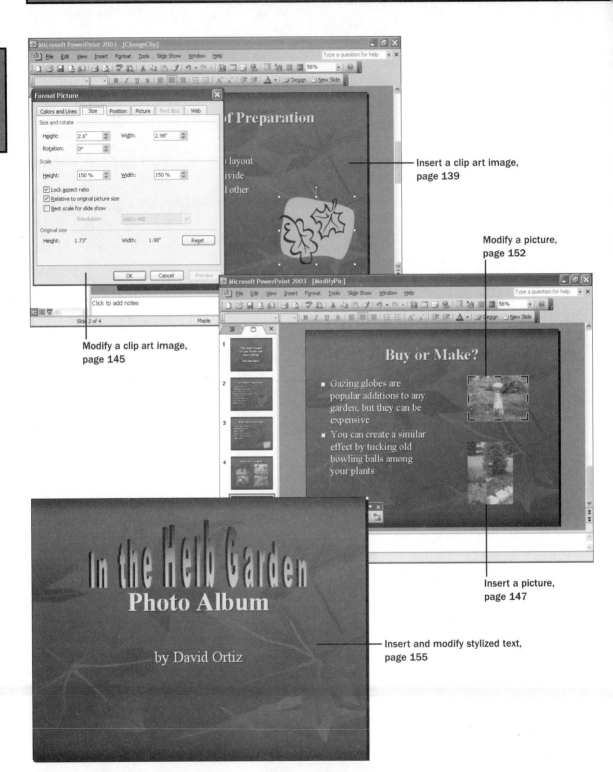

Insert a clip art image,
page 139

Modify a picture,
page 152

Modify a clip art image,
page 145

Insert a picture,
page 147

Insert and modify stylized text,
page 155

Chapter 8 at a Glance

8 Adding Graphics

In this chapter you will learn to:

✔   Insert a clip art image.

✔   Modify a clip art image.

✔   Insert a picture.

✔   Modify a picture.

✔   Insert and modify stylized text.

The general term *graphics* applies to several kinds of enhancements that you can add to slides to make your presentations more attractive or to convey information visually. Graphics can include shapes, pictures, photographs, cartoons, fancy borders and designs, and stylized text objects.

In Microsoft Office PowerPoint 2003, you can use several methods to add a graphic to a slide. The most direct way is to click a slide's content placeholder and then use the placeholder's Insert Picture button to locate and insert the graphic you want. You can also use the Picture command on the Insert menu. Having inserted the graphic, you can modify it in a variety of ways to achieve the effect you want.

In this chapter, you'll insert and modify clip art images, pictures, and stylized text created by using WordArt.

See Also   Do you need only a quick refresher on the topics in this chapter? See the Quick Reference entries on pages xxxviii–xl.

Important   Before you can use the practice files in this chapter, you need to install them from the book's companion CD to their default location. See "Using the Book's CD-ROM" on page xiii for more information.

Inserting a Clip Art Image

Microsoft Office Specialist

PowerPoint includes hundreds of professionally designed pieces of *clip art*. To add a slide with a clip art image to a presentation, you can use an AutoLayout with a content placeholder and click its Insert Clip Art button, which opens the Select Picture dialog box. You can also point to Picture on the Insert menu, and then click Clip Art or click Insert Clip Art on the Drawing toolbar to open the Clip Art task pane. In the Select Picture dialog box or the Clip Art task pane, you can search for clip art by keyword, and then simply click the image you want to insert it into the current slide.

Tip   If you click AutoShapes on the Drawing toolbar and then click More AutoShapes, PowerPoint opens the Clip Art task pane with clip art shapes displayed. You can then click a shape to add it to the current slide.

To make clip art and other media available no matter where they are actually stored, you can use the *Microsoft Clip Organizer*. This handy tool enables you to sort clip art images, pictures, sounds, and motion clips that are stored in different locations into collections. You can use the Clip Organizer to organize clip art images from The Microsoft Office System, from the Web, or from other sources. You can add images to existing collections and create new ones by clicking Add Clips to Organizer on the Clip Organizer's File menu or by clicking the Import button at the bottom of the Select Picture dialog box. To find an image, you can browse your collections or search for specific files or media types, such as movies or clip art.

Tip   To delete a clip art image from the Clip Organizer, click the down arrow to the right of the image, click "Delete from Clip Organizer," and then click Yes to confirm the deletion.

If you can't find the image you want in the Clip Organizer, you can search for additional images in *Office Online*, a clip art gallery that Microsoft maintains on its Web site. To access Office Online, you click the "Clip Art on Office Online" link at the bottom of the Clip Art task pane. This launches your Web browser and navigates to the Office Online Web page, where you can access thousands of free clip art images.

In this exercise, you will add clip art images to a couple of slides and then add an image to the Clip Organizer.

BE SURE TO start PowerPoint before beginning this exercise.
USE the *InsertArt* presentation in the practice file folder for this topic. This practice file is located in the *My Documents\Microsoft Press\PowerPoint 2003 SBS\AddingPicture\InsertingClip* folder and can also be accessed by clicking *Start/All Programs/Microsoft Press/PowerPoint 2003 Step by Step*.
OPEN the *InsertArt* presentation.

1   Move to Slide 2, click a blank area of the content placeholder, and on the **Insert** menu, point to **Picture**, and then click **Clip Art**.

The Clip Art task pane opens.

2   In the **Search for** box at the top of the task pane, type leaves, and click **Go**.

All the clip art that is identified by the keyword *leaves* is displayed.

3   Point to the stylized image of two leaves.

A ScreenTip displays the keywords associated with the image, its size in pixels and kilobytes, and its format.

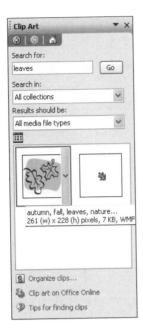

4   Click the image of the two leaves.

The image is inserted in the content placeholder, and because the image is selected, the Picture toolbar appears.

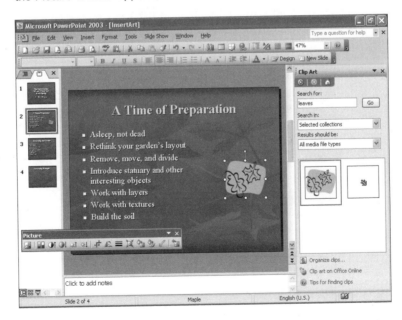

Troubleshooting If the Picture toolbar does not appear, right-click the clip art image, and then click the Show Picture Toolbar on the shortcut menu.

5 Click a blank area of the slide to deselect the image, and then close the Clip Art task pane.

6 Move to Slide 3, and click the **Insert Clip Art** button in the content placeholder.

Insert Clip Art

All the available clip art is displayed in the Select Picture dialog box.

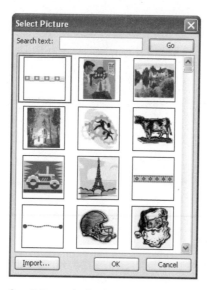

7 Scroll through the images until you find one you like, click that image, and then click **OK** to insert it.

If you want your screen to look like the one shown in the following graphics, click the stylized drawing of a cornucopia (a shell with food cascading out of it, symbolizing a plentiful harvest).

8 Drag the clip art image to the lower-right corner of the slide.

9 Click outside of the image to deselect it, and then click anywhere in the bulleted list.

10 Drag the right-middle handle to the right to enlarge the text object so that all the bullet points fit on one line, and then click a blank area of the slide.

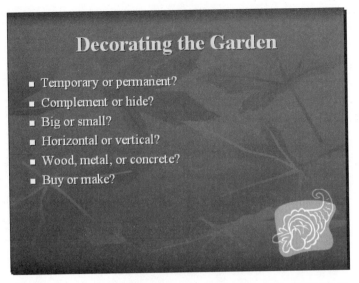

11 Display the Drawing toolbar, and click the **Insert Clip Art** button.

The Clip Art task pane appears.

12 At the bottom of the **Clip Art** task pane, click **Organize clips**.

13 If a message asks whether you want to catalog all the media files on your hard disk, click **Later**.

The Microsoft Clip Organizer window opens.

14 In the **Collections List**, under **My Collections**, click **Favorites**.

15 On the window's **File** menu, point to **Add Clips to Organizer,** and then click **On My Own**.

The Add Clips to Organizer dialog box appears.

16 On the Places bar, click **My Documents**. Then navigate to the *Microsoft Press \PowerPoint 2003 SBS\AddingPicture\InsertingClip* folder, and click the *Logo* file, and then click **Add**.

Tip To place images in a different collection, click Add To in the Add to Clips Organizer dialog box, and select the collection. You can click New to create a new collection.

The Garden Company's logo has been added to the Favorites collection.

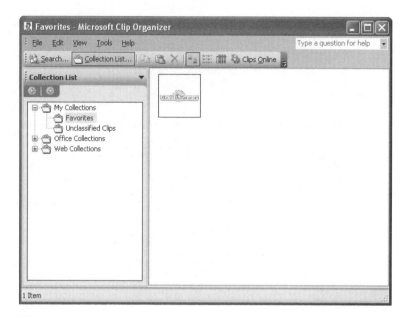

Tip   You can change the view of the list of clip art files by clicking buttons on the Clip Organizer window's toolbar.

17   Point to the thumbnail of the *Logo* file, click the down arrow that appears, and click **Edit Keywords**.

The Keywords dialog box appears.

18   In the **Keyword** box, type logo, and click **Add**.

The keyword *logo* is added to the "Keywords for current clip" list.

19   Click **OK** to close the **Edit Keywords** dialog box, and then close the Microsoft Clip Organizer window.

20   Double-click the entry in the **Search for** box at the top of the **Clip Art** task pane, type logo, and click **Go**.

The Garden Company logo appears in the clip art list.

21   Close the **Clip Art** task pane.

Save

22   On the Standard toolbar, click the **Save** button to save the presentation. If you have finished working with pictures, turn off the Drawing toolbar.

CLOSE the *InsertArt* presentation.

Modifying a Clip Art Image

Microsoft Office Specialist

Double-clicking a clip art image or selecting it and clicking Picture on the Format menu displays the Format Picture dialog box, where you can make the following modifications to an image:

- On the Colors and Lines tab, you can change the color of the image's background and its border.

- On the Size tab, you can enter specific dimensions for the height and width of the image, or you can *scale* the image as a percentage of its current size or of its original size. You can specify that the height and width must be scaled proportionally by selecting the "Lock aspect ratio" check box. You can also specify that the size of the image be optimized for a slide show screen by selecting the "Best scale for slide show" check box.

- On the Position tab, you can fine-tune the position of the image by entering exact dimensions in relation to either the upper-left corner or the center of the slide.

- On the Picture tab, you can crop away parts of an image. You can also specify whether the image should be colored (Automatic), gray, or black and white, and you can control its brightness and contrast.

You can change the colors used in a clip art image to create a different look or to match the current color scheme. Clicking the Recolor Picture button on the Picture toolbar displays a dialog box where you can change any of the image's existing colors.

In this exercise, you will scale a clip art image and then change its colors.

USE the *ChangeClip* presentation in the practice file folder for this topic. This practice file is located in the *My Documents\Microsoft Press\PowerPoint 2003 SBS\AddingPicture\ModifyingClip* folder and can also be accessed by clicking *Start/All Programs/Microsoft Press/PowerPoint 2003 Step by Step*.
OPEN the *ChangeClip* presentation.

1 Move to Slide 2, and double-click the clip art image.

  The Format Picture dialog box appears.

2 Drag the dialog box to the left by its title bar so that you can see the image in the right half of the slide, and then click the **Size** tab.

3 In the **Scale** area, select the number in the **Height** box, and type **150**.

4 Click **Preview** to view the image without closing the dialog box.

  Because the "Lock aspect ratio" check box is selected, the setting in the Width box has also changed to 150%.

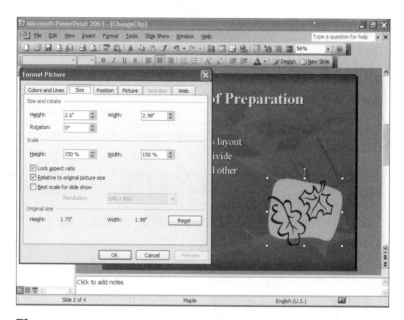

Tip If you change the size of an image and then want to restore the original size, you can set the scale back to 100% or click Reset in the Format Picture dialog box.

5 Click **OK** to close the **Format Picture** dialog box.

Recolor Picture

6 With the image still selected, click the **Recolor Picture** button on the **Picture** toolbar.

The Recolor Picture dialog box appears with the Colors option selected in the Change area.

7 Select the **Fills** option to display the fill colors of the image.

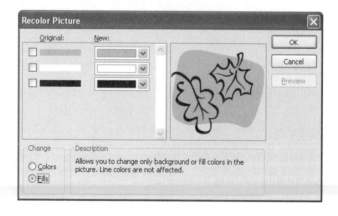

8   In the **New** area, click the down arrow to the right of the top box, and click the first color box in the color scheme.

The color swatch changes to dark orange, and the preview box on the right shows that all parts of the image that had been beige are now dark orange.

9   In the **New** area, click the down arrow to the right of the bottom box, and click the fourth color box in the color scheme.

10   Click **OK** to close the **Recolor Picture** dialog box, and click a blank area of the slide to deselect the image.

The clip art image now coordinates with the rest of the slide.

Save

11   On the Standard toolbar, click the **Save** button to save the presentation.

CLOSE the *ChangeClip* presentation.

Inserting a Picture

Microsoft Office Specialist

You can add graphics created in other programs, scanned photographs, or digital pictures to a slide by using the Picture command on the Insert menu. When you use this command, you specify the source of the picture, as follows:

- To insert a picture from a file on your hard disk, removable disk, or network, you use the From File command on the Picture submenu. You can also click the Insert Picture button in a content placeholder.

- To insert a picture from the clip art collection that comes with PowerPoint, you click the Clip Art command, which opens the Clip Art task pane.

See Also   For more information about clip art, see "Inserting a Clip Art Image," earlier in this chapter.

- If you have a scanner connected to the computer you are using, you can scan and insert a picture by using the From Scanner or Camera command. You can also use this command to download pictures from a digital camera.

When you insert pictures from files or from a scanner or digital camera, you can select multiple pictures, view thumbnails of them, and insert them all at once, which is faster than inserting them one at a time. After you insert any picture into your presentation, you can modify it by using the buttons on the Picture toolbar.

If you have a collection of pictures on your hard disk, you can use PowerPoint to create a *photo album*. You can customize the album by using layout options such as oval frames, and you can add captions to each picture.

In this exercise, you will add pictures to a slide, open a new photo album, and insert multiple pictures into the photo album.

USE the *InsertPic* presentation and the graphic files named *Picture01* through *Picture12* in the practice file folder for this topic. These practice files are located in the *My Documents\Microsoft Press \PowerPoint 2003 SBS\AddingPicture\InsertingPic* folder and can also be accessed by clicking *Start/All Programs/Microsoft Press/PowerPoint 2003 Step by Step*.
OPEN the *InsertPic* presentation.

Insert Picture

1 Move to Slide 4, and in the upper-left content placeholder, click the **Insert Picture** button.

The Insert Picture dialog box appears.

2 On the Places bar, click the **My Documents** icon. Then navigate to the *Microsoft Press \PowerPoint 2003 SBS\AddingPictures\InsertingPic* folder.

Views

Troubleshooting If you do not see thumbnails of the pictures in this folder, click the down arrow to the right of the Views button on the Insert Picture dialog box's toolbar, and click Thumbnails.

3 In the list box, click *Picture01*, and then click **Insert**.

The picture and the Picture toolbar appear.

4   Click a blank area of the upper-right content placeholder, and on the **Insert** menu, point to **Picture**, and then click **From File**.

5   In the **Insert Picture** dialog box, click *Picture02*, and click **Insert**.

6   Using either the **Insert Picture** button or the **Picture** command, insert *Picture03* in the lower-left content placeholder and *Picture04* in the lower-right placeholder.

7   Click a blank area of the slide to see the results.

Tip   You can save a PowerPoint slide as a picture that you can then use in other programs. Display the slide you want to save, and click Save As on the File menu. Click the down arrow to the right of the "Save as type" box, click Windows Metafile, and then click Save.

8   On the **Insert** menu, point to **Picture**, and then click **New Photo Album**.

The Photo Album dialog box appears.

9   Click **File/Disk**, and when the **Insert New Pictures** dialog box appears, make sure that the contents of the *My Documents\Microsoft Press\PowerPoint 2003 SBS \AddingPicture\InsertingPic* folder are displayed.

10   In the list box, click *Picture05*, scroll down to the bottom of the list box, hold down the [Shift] key, and then click *Picture12*.

Eight pictures—including Picture05 and Picture06, which are out of sight—are selected.

11 Click **Insert**.

The Photo Album dialog box appears with the eight pictures listed in the "Pictures in album" list.

12 In the **Album Layout** area, click the down arrow to the right of the **Picture layout** box, and then click **4 pictures with title** at the bottom of the drop-down list.

13 Click the down arrow to the right of the **Frame shape** box, and then click **Oval**.

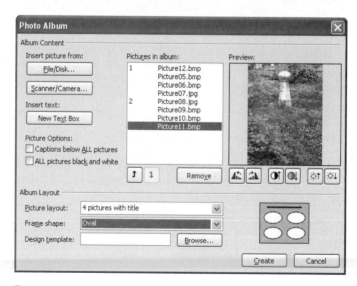

Because the Picture12 file was created before the other seven files, it appears at the top of the list.

Move Down

14 In the **Pictures in album** box, click **Picture12**, and then click the **Move Down** button until the selected picture is at the bottom of the list.

15 Click **Create**.

The Photo Album dialog box closes, and a new PowerPoint presentation called Photo Album opens with a title slide and two slides containing four pictures each.

16 On the **File** menu, click **Save As**, check that the presentation will be saved in the *My Documents\Microsoft Press\PowerPoint 2003 SBS\AddingPicture\InsertingPic* folder, and click **Save**.

PowerPoint saves the Photo Album presentation in the specified folder.

17 On the Formatting toolbar, click the **Design** button, and in the **Apply a design template** list in the **Slide Design** task pane, click the **Maple** template used in the InsertPic Presentation. Then close the task pane.

18 Move to Slide 2, click the title placeholder, and type **Artwork in the Herb Garden**. Then assign the title **More Garden Artwork** to Slide 3.

Close Window

19 Save the Photo Album presentation, and then at the right end of the menu bar, click the **Close Window** button (not the Close button at the right end of the title bar) to return to the InsertPic presentation.

Save

20 On the Standard toolbar, click the **Save** button to save the InsertPic presentation.

CLOSE the *InsertPic* presentation.

Modifying a Picture

Microsoft Office Specialist

After you have inserted a picture into a slide, you can work with it in several ways to create the effect you want. For example:

■ You can enhance the image's color, brightness, and contrast. After you make changes, you can click the Reset Picture button on the Picture toolbar to revert to the original settings.

■ If you need only part of a picture, you can use the Crop Picture command to *crop* the parts you don't want so that they do not show on the slide. The picture is not altered—parts of it are simply covered up.

■ You can rotate a picture to any angle by selecting it and dragging the green rotating handle.

■ You can *compress* pictures to minimize the file size of the image. In doing so, however, you might lose some visual quality, depending on the compression setting. You can pick the resolution you want for the pictures in a presentation based on where or how they'll be viewed (for example, on the Web or printed), and you can set other options, such as delete cropped areas of picture, to get the best balance between picture quality and file size.

In this exercise, you will modify a couple of pictures by changing their size, cropping, and moving them. You will then experiment with color and brightness, and finally, you will compress the pictures.

USE the *ModifyPic* presentation in the practice file folder for this topic. This practice file is located in the *My Documents\Microsoft Press\PowerPoint 2003 SBS\AddingPicture\ModifyingPic* folder and can also be accessed by clicking *Start/All Programs/Microsoft Press/PowerPoint 2003 Step by Step*.
OPEN the *ModifyPic* presentation.

1 Move to Slide 5, select the top picture, and drag the lower-right corner handle down until the picture covers about a third of the picture below it.

Crop

2 On the **Picture** toolbar, click the **Crop** button.

The handles around the selected picture change to cropping handles, and when you move the pointer over the slide, it changes to the cropping tool.

3 Position the center of the cropping tool over the lower-middle handle, and then drag up to crop the bottom of the picture to align with the word *expensive* in the adjacent text.

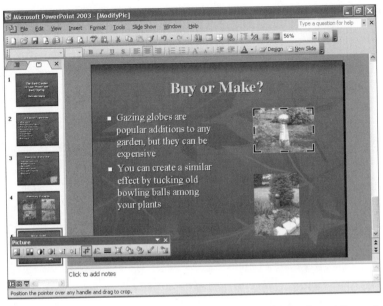

4 Click a blank area of the slide to turn off the cropping tool, and then click the bottom picture.

5 Drag the lower-right corner handle down and to the right until the picture is the same width as the one above it.

Troubleshooting If you have trouble resizing the picture, you can press the [Shift] key while dragging the sizing handles to turn off the "Snap objects to grid" feature, which aligns objects to an equally spaced grid on the slide.

6 On the **Picture** toolbar, click the **Crop** button, and crop the bottom picture from both the top and bottom.

You want the picture to be about the same size as the one above it, with the bowling ball and the gazing globe in about the same position in each picture.

7 Point to the bottom picture (not a handle), and when the pointer changes to a four-headed arrow, move the picture upward, aligning its bottom edge with the last line of the second bullet point.

8 Click a blank area of the slide to turn off the cropping tool, and click again to deselect the picture.

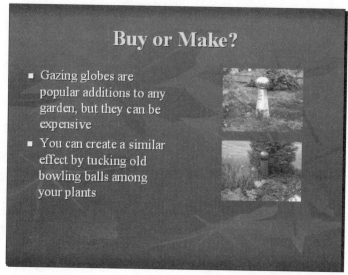

9   Click one picture, hold down the [Shift] key, and click the other picture so that both are selected.

Color

10   On the **Picture** toolbar, click the **Color** button, and then click **Grayscale**.

Both pictures are displayed in shades of gray.

More Brightness

11   On the **Picture** toolbar, click the **More Brightness** button twice.

The pictures are now brighter.

Less Contrast

12   On the **Picture** toolbar, click the **Less Contrast** button twice.

The picture contrast decreases to enhance the look of the pictures even more.

13   On the **Picture** toolbar, click the **Color** button, and then click **Automatic**.

The pictures are displayed in color but with the brightness and contrast settings you applied to the grayscale pictures.

Compress Pictures

14   On the **Picture** toolbar, click the **Compress Pictures** button.

The Compress Pictures dialog box appears.

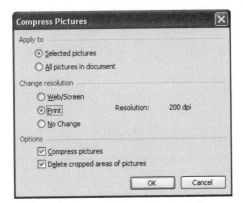

15 The current settings fit your needs, so click **OK**.

A warning box appears, letting you know that compressing pictures might reduce the quality of your images.

16 Click **Apply** to optimize the image.

17 On the Standard toolbar, click the **Save** button to save the presentation.

Save

CLOSE the *ModifyPic* presentation.

Inserting and Modifying Stylized Text

Microsoft Office Specialist

You can insert stylized text into a presentation by using *WordArt*. With WordArt, you can add visual enhancements to your text that go beyond changing a font or font size—in effect, you turn words into a picture. WordArt can be used to emphasize short phrases, such as *Our Customers Come First*, or a single word, such as *Welcome*.

You don't have to be an artist to create stylized text—WordArt includes a gallery of choices that enable you to stretch your text horizontally, vertically, or diagonally. You can also change the character spacing and reshape the text. You insert stylized text by first clicking the Insert WordArt button on the Drawing toolbar and then selecting a style.

In this exercise, you will insert WordArt into a slide and then format it.

USE the *InsertWordArt* presentation in the practice file folder for this topic. This practice file is located in the *My Documents\Microsoft Press\PowerPoint 2003 SBS\AddingPicture\InsertingArt* folder and can also be accessed by clicking *Start/All Programs/Microsoft Press/PowerPoint 2003 Step by Step*.
OPEN the *InsertWordArt* presentation.

1 On the **View** menu, point to **Toolbars**, and then click **Drawing** to turn on the Drawing toolbar.

Insert WordArt

2 With Slide 1 displayed, click the **Insert WordArt** button on the Drawing toolbar.

The WordArt Gallery dialog box appears, displaying a list of styles.

3 Click the style in the third column of the fourth row.

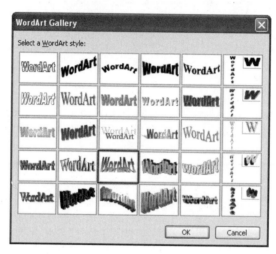

4 Click **OK**.

WordArt Gallery

> **Tip** If you want to change the shape of a WordArt object after you've created it, you can click the WordArt Gallery button on the WordArt toolbar. For even greater variety, you can select the object and then manually stretch and rotate it.

The Edit WordArt Text dialog box appears.

5 In the **Text** box, type **In the Herb Garden**.

The text appears in the Arial Black font at 36 points.

6 Change the **Size** setting to **60**, and click **OK**.

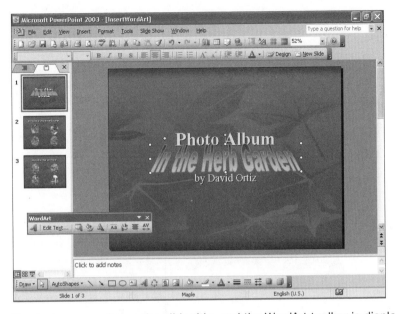

The text appears below the slide title, and the WordArt toolbar is displayed.

WordArt Shape

7 On the WordArt toolbar, click the **WordArt Shape** button, and then click the **Triangle Up** symbol in the first row.

The WordArt text appears as a triangle.

WordArt
Character
Spacing

8 On the WordArt toolbar, click the **WordArt Character Spacing** button, and then click **Very Loose** on the drop-down menu.

The width of the WordArt object increases to accommodate the additional space between the characters.

9 On the WordArt toolbar, click the **Format WordArt** button.

Format WordArt

The Format WordArt dialog box appears.

10 Click the **Size** tab, and in the **Size and rotate** area, click the up arrow to the right of the **Height** box until its setting is approximately **2"**.

11 Click the **Position** tab, and change the setting in the **Vertical** box to **0.5"** and click **OK**.

The WordArt object moves above the slide title.

Shadow Style

12 On the Drawing toolbar, click the **Shadow Style** button, and then click **Shadow Style 18** in the second column of the last row.

13 Click the **Shadow Style** button again, and then click **Shadow Settings** in the drop-down menu.

The Shadow Settings toolbar appears.

14 On the Shadow Settings toolbar, click the **Nudge Shadow Left** button five times.

Nudge Shadow
Left

The WordArt shadow increases in depth.

15 Turn off the Shadow Settings toolbar and the Drawing toolbar, and click a blank area of the slide.

The WordArt toolbar closes when you deselect the WordArt object, and you can see the results of your work.

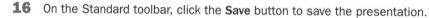

16 On the Standard toolbar, click the **Save** button to save the presentation.

Save

CLOSE the *InsertWordArt* presentation, and if you are not continuing on to the next chapter, quit PowerPoint.

Key Points

- You can insert any of the hundreds of clip art images included with The Microsoft Office System 2003 into a PowerPoint presentation. You can also search for additional images in Clips Online. You can then scale the image by a set percentage, size the image exactly by setting its dimensions, or size it manually by dragging its handles.

- You can change the color of clip art images to create a different look or to match the current color scheme.

- You can insert pictures created with another program or photographs from a scanner or digital camera into a slide. You can then size, crop, and move the pictures, and enhance their brightness and contrast.

- To reduce the size of presentations containing multiple pictures, you can compress the pictures.

- You can use WordArt to insert and format stylized text objects to create fancy titles.

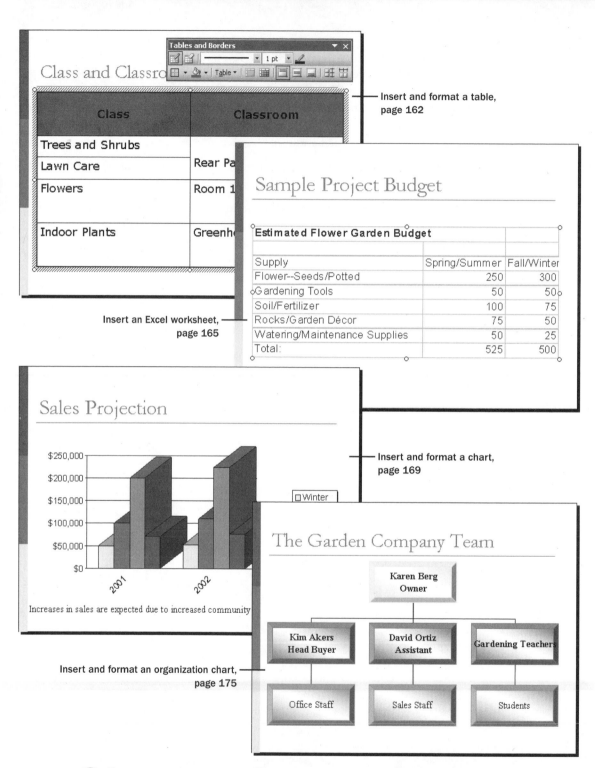

Insert and format a table, page 162

Insert an Excel worksheet, page 165

Insert and format a chart, page 169

Insert and format an organization chart, page 175

Chapter 9 at a Glance

9 Adding Tables, Charts, and Diagrams

In this chapter you will learn to:

✔   Insert and format a table.

✔   Insert an Excel worksheet.

✔   Insert and format a chart.

✔   Insert and format an organization chart.

Often you will want to bolster the argument you are making in a Microsoft Office PowerPoint 2003 presentation with facts and figures that are best presented in a table, chart, or diagram. These objects are all easily placed on PowerPoint slides that have been assigned a layout that includes a content placeholder. You use them as follows:

- You use tables to condense information into highly structured row and column grid formats that make it easy to identify categories or individual items and make comparisons. If the tabular information already exists—for example, as a Microsoft Office Excel worksheet—you can import it into a PowerPoint table or embed it as an object in a PowerPoint slide.

- You use charts to present numerical information in visual ways when it is more important for your audience to understand trends than identify precise values. If you have already created a chart in another program, you can embed it as an object.

- You use diagrams to depict hierarchies or processes. PowerPoint's diagramming tool enables you to easily create organization charts and cycle, radial, pyramid, Venn, and target diagrams.

In this chapter, you will insert and modify a table, a chart, and an organization chart. You will also import an Excel worksheet as an embedded object, and will modify the object from within PowerPoint.

See Also   Do you need only a quick refresher on the topics in this chapter? See the Quick Reference entries on pages xl–xli.

Important Before you can use the practice files in this chapter, you need to install them from the book's companion CD to their default location. See "Using the Book's CD-ROM" on page xiii for more information.

Inserting and Formatting a Table

Microsoft Office Specialist

When you want to present a lot of data in an organized and easy-to-read format, a table is often your best choice. PowerPoint makes it easy by including an Insert Table button in its content placeholders. You choose a layout that includes a content placeholder (among your choices is a layout designed specifically for tables), click the Insert Table button, specify the number of columns and rows, and then enter data in the resulting table structure.

A table's structure is a simple two-dimensional organization of rows and columns. The intersection of a row and a column is called a *cell*. The first row is commonly used for column headings; the leftmost column is ideal for row labels. After you create the table's structure, you type text in the cells just as you would in a paragraph, using the ⟨Tab⟩ key to move the insertion point from cell to cell.

You can customize and format individual cells as well as the entire table. For example, you can merge—combine—cells to create one cell that spans two or more columns or rows, and you can split a single cell into two or more cells. Using the buttons on the Formatting toolbar or the specialized Tables and Borders toolbar, you can add color and borders and change text alignment in a table.

In this exercise, you insert and format a table.

BE SURE TO start PowerPoint before beginning this exercise.
USE the *InsertTable* file in the practice file folder for this topic. This practice file is located in the *My Documents\Microsoft Press\PowerPoint 2003 SBS\AddingTable\InsertingTable* folder and can also be accessed by clicking *Start/All Programs/Microsoft Press/PowerPoint 2003 Step by Step.*
OPEN the *InsertTable* presentation.

1 Move to Slide 9, and double-click the table placeholder.

Slide 9 has already been formatted with the Table AutoLayout. Double-clicking the placeholder displays the Insert Table dialog box.

2 Click the up arrow to the right of the **Number of rows** box until the number reaches **4**.

3 Click **OK**.

A blank table with two columns and four rows appears, and the Tables and Borders toolbar is displayed.

Troubleshooting   If the Tables and Borders toolbar doesn't appear, point to Toolbars on the View menu, and click Tables and Borders.

4   Check that the insertion point is blinking in the upper-left cell of the table. Then type **Class**, press [Tab], type **Classroom**, and press [Tab] again.

The insertion point moves to the first cell of the second row.

Troubleshooting   If the Tables and Borders toolbar is floating and in the way, drag it by its title bar to a blank area of the slide.

5   Type **Trees and Shrubs**, press [Enter], type **Lawn Care**, and press [Tab]. Then type **Rear Patio**, and press [Tab] again.

6   Enter **Flowers** and **Room 1** in the third row, and **Indoor Plants** and **Greenhouse** in the fourth row.

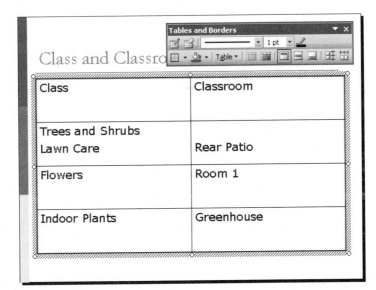

Bold

7   Drag through *Class* and *Classroom* to select their cells, and then on the Formatting toolbar, click the **Bold** button.

The column titles appear bold.

Center Vertically

8   On the Formatting toolbar, click the **Center** button to center the text in the cell, and then on the **Tables and Borders** toolbar, click the **Center Vertically** button.

The column titles are centered horizontally and vertically in their cells.

Fill Color

9   On the Tables and Borders toolbar, click the down arrow to the right of the **Fill Color** button, and click the **Red** box at the right end of the color scheme.

The cells with the column titles are filled with red.

Draw Table

10 On the Tables and Borders toolbar, click the **Draw Table** button, and draw a horizontal line between *Trees and Shrubs* and *Lawn Care*.

A dotted line appears as you draw the line. When you release the mouse button, the cell is split into two cells.

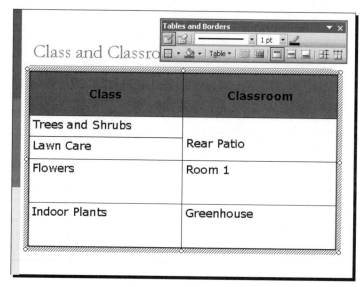

11 Draw a vertical line in the middle of the cell that contains the text *Room 1*.

The cell is split into two cells.

Eraser

12 On the Tables and Borders toolbar, click the **Eraser** button, and then click the vertical line you just drew.

The two cells merge back into one cell.

Tip　To add a column or row to a table, click in a cell adjacent to where you want to insert the column or row, click Table on the Tables and Borders toolbar, and then click Insert Columns to the Right, Insert Columns to the Left, Insert Rows Above, or Insert Rows Below. To delete a column or row, click anywhere in a column or row, click Table on the Tables and Borders toolbar, and then click Delete Rows or Delete Columns.

13 On the Tables and Borders toolbar, click the **Eraser** button to turn off the tool.

14 Click a blank area of the slide (not in the table) to deselect the table.

Save

15 On the Standard toolbar, click the **Save** button to save the presentation.

CLOSE the *InsertTable* presentation.

Inserting a Word Table

Microsoft Office Specialist

If you have already created a table in Word, you can insert that table into a PowerPoint slide as an embedded object instead of retyping it. For best results, the Word document containing the table should contain no other text.

See Also   For more information about embedded objects, see "Inserting an Excel Worksheet," below.

To insert an existing Word table:

1   On PowerPoint's **Insert** menu, click **Object**.

2   In the **Insert Object** dialog box, click **Create from file**.

3   Click the **Browse** button, navigate to the storage location of the Word document containing the table, double-click the file name, and click **OK**.

The table is embedded in the slide as an object.

4   Double-click the table object.

Word's menus and toolbars replace PowerPoint's. You can now use Word to format and otherwise manipulate the table.

5   Drag the object's handles to size its frame to fit snugly around the table, and then click outside the object to return to PowerPoint.

You can then move and size the object in PowerPoint to make sure it is readable and attractive.

Inserting an Excel Worksheet

Microsoft Office Specialist

PowerPoint's table capabilities are perfectly adequate for the display of simple information that is unlikely to change during the useful life of the presentation. However, if your data involves calculations or is likely to require updating, you will probably want to maintain the information in an Excel worksheet. You can then embed the worksheet in a slide as an object, or you can link the slide to the worksheet so that you won't have to worry about keeping the data up to date in more than one place.

Embedded objects and linked objects differ in the following ways:

■ An *embedded object* is an object that maintains a direct connection to its original program, known as the *source program*. After you insert an embedded object, you can easily edit it by double-clicking it, which opens the program in which it was originally created. Be aware that embedding an object in a presentation increases the presentation's file size because PowerPoint has to store not only the data itself but also information about how to display the data.

■ A *linked object* is a representation on a slide of information that is still stored in the original document, known as the *source document*. If you edit the source document in the source program after adding a linked object to a slide, PowerPoint updates the representation of the object. Because PowerPoint stores only the data needed to display the information, linking creates smaller file sizes than embedding.

For example, David Ortiz of The Garden Company might store past sales information and future sales projections in Excel worksheets. In a presentation he plans to deliver at a strategy meeting, he might embed the past sales information, which won't change, as an object on a slide. He might also link the future sales projections, which he is still in the process of fine-tuning, on another slide. Then as he updates the projections worksheet, the linked table in the PowerPoint presentation will automatically be updated as well.

Important   When working with a linked object, remember to make modifications in the source document, not in PowerPoint. Although you can make changes to the linked object on the slide, the next time you open the presentation, the object will be updated to reflect the version in the source document.

In this exercise, you will insert and format an Excel worksheet as an embedded object.

USE the *InsertWorksheet* presentation and *Budget* workbook in the practice file folder for this topic. These practice files are located in the *My Documents\Microsoft Press\PowerPoint 2003 SBS\AddingTable \InsertingWork* folder and can also be accessed by clicking *Start/All Programs/Microsoft Press/PowerPoint 2003 Step by Step*.
OPEN the *InsertWorksheet* presentation.

1   Move to Slide 8, and on the **Insert** menu, click **Object**.

The Insert Object dialog box appears.

2   Select the **Create from file** option, and then click **Browse**.

The Browse dialog box appears. It is similar to the Open dialog box.

3   If the contents of the *My Documents* folder are not displayed, click the **My Documents** icon on the Places bar, and then navigate to the *Microsoft Press \PowerPoint 2003 SBS\AddingTable\InsertingWork* folder.

4   Click *Budget* in the list box, and click **OK** to close the **Browse** dialog box.

The location of the file appears in the File text box.

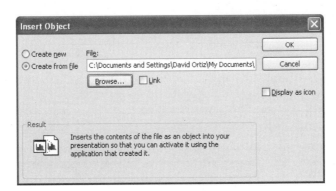

Tip   To link an object, you select the Link check box in the Insert Object dialog box.

5   Click **OK** to close the **Insert Object** dialog box.

The worksheet is embedded in the presentation slide.

6   Right-click the worksheet, point to **Worksheet Object** on the shortcut menu, and then click **Edit**.

Troubleshooting   If you move the mouse as you right click the table, the table will also move, and a different shortcut menu will appear—one without the Worksheet Object command. If this happens, click a blank area of the slide to close the shortcut menu, and then right-click again without moving the mouse.

The Excel workbook opens in PowerPoint with Sheet1 displayed. Excel's menus and Standard and Formatting toolbars replace PowerPoint's.

7   On the Standard toolbar, click the **Toolbar Options** button, and then click **Show Buttons on Two Rows**.

The two toolbars appear on two rows, making it easier to work with them because all their buttons are visible at a glance.

Troubleshooting   If you see three toolbars instead of two, the third toolbar is probably the Reviewing toolbar. On the View menu, point to Toolbars and then click Reviewing to turn it off.

Toolbar Options

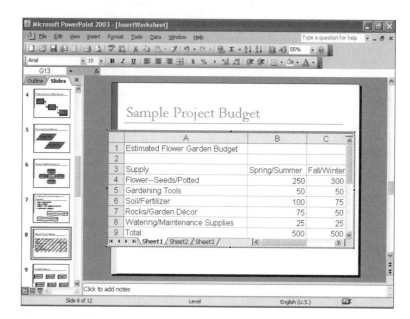

Important   The columns are labeled with letters (A, B, C, and so on), and the rows are labeled with numbers (1, 2, 3, and so on). Each cell can be referenced by its column letter followed by its row number (A1, A2, A3, and so on). A block of cells can be referenced by the cell in its upper-left corner and the cell in its lower-right corner, separated by a colon (A1:C3).

B
Bold

8   Click cell **A1**, and click the **Bold** button on the Formatting toolbar.

The title of the worksheet is now bold.

9   Click cell **B8**, type **50**, and press ⎡Enter⎤.

The new amount replaces 25 in the cell. The total in cell B9 is calculated by the formula shown in the formula bar below the Formatting toolbar, so the recalculated amount in B9 changes from 500 to 525.

10   Click a blank area of the slide.

Excel closes, PowerPoint's menus and toolbars are restored, and the embedded object is updated on the slide.

Sample Project Budget

Estimated Flower Garden Budget		
Supply	Spring/Summer	Fall/Winter
Flower--Seeds/Potted	250	300
Gardening Tools	50	50
Soil/Fertilizer	100	75
Rocks/Garden Décor	75	50
Watering/Maintenance Supplies	50	25
Total:	525	500

Save

11 On the Standard toolbar, click the **Save** button to save the presentation.

CLOSE the *InsertWorksheet* file.

Inserting and Formatting a Chart

Microsoft Office Specialist

For those occasions when you want to display numeric data visually, you can use Microsoft Graph, a program that works with PowerPoint to insert a chart into a presentation slide. After you create a chart, it becomes an embedded object on the slide.

You can start Graph in the following ways:

- By double-clicking a chart placeholder on a slide

- By clicking the Insert Chart button on the Standard toolbar

- By clicking Chart on the Insert menu

In Graph, data is displayed in a datasheet and represented in the chart, as follows:

- The *datasheet* is composed of rows and columns of *cells* that contain values, or *data points*, that make up a *data series*. Down the left side and across the top of the datasheet are gray *control boxes* that enable you to work with rows or columns of data. The first row and column of the datasheet hold the names of the data series.

■ The *chart* is made up of different elements that help display the data from the datasheet. A *data marker* is a graphical representation in the chart of each data point in a data series. The data is plotted against an *x-axis*—also called the category axis—and a *y-axis*—also called the value axis. (Three-dimensional charts also have a z-axis.) Along each axis are labels, called *tick-mark labels*, that identify the data. A *legend* provides a key for identifying the data series.

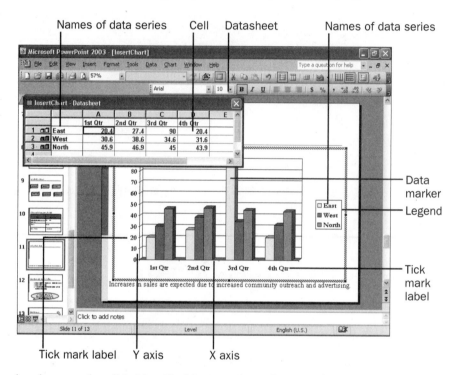

In a datasheet, each cell is identified by its column letter and row number, as in A1. To perform most tasks on the datasheet, you must first select a cell or a block of cells, called a *range*. When a cell is selected, it becomes the *active cell* and is distinguished by a heavy border. When a range is selected, the active cell is white with a heavy border, and all the other cells in the range are highlighted in black.

Tip   To select a single cell, simply click it. To select a range, click the first cell, hold down the [Shift] key, and then click the last cell. To select a row or column, click its control box. To select the entire datasheet, click the control box in the upper-left corner.

To enter data into the datasheet, you can do one or more of the following:

■ Type the data into the datasheet

■ Import information from another program, such as Excel

■ Copy and paste a specified range of data or a complete worksheet into the datasheet

After the data is entered into the datasheet, you can easily modify and format the associated chart. Graph comes with 14 types of charts, each with two-dimensional and three-dimensional variations. Having selected a chart type, you can format the chart to get the results that you want.

In this exercise, you will create a Graph chart by importing and entering data, and then you'll format the chart.

USE the *InsertChart* presentation and *Sales* worksheet in the practice file folder for this topic. These practice files are located in the *My Documents\Microsoft Press\PowerPoint 2003 SBS\AddingTable \InsertingChart* folder and can also be accessed by clicking *Start/All Programs/Microsoft Press /PowerPoint 2003 Step by Step.*
OPEN the *InsertChart* presentation.

1 Move to Slide 11, and double-click the chart placeholder.

Slide 11 has already been formatted with the Chart AutoLayout. When you double-click the chart placeholder, PowerPoint starts Microsoft Graph. The Graph menus and Standard and Formatting toolbars replace PowerPoint's, and the datasheet and chart appear with default data that you can replace with your own data.

View
Datasheet

Tip If the datasheet obstructs the chart, you can move the datasheet window out of the way by dragging its title bar or by clicking its Close button. If the data-sheet is closed, you can click the View Datasheet button on Graph's Standard toolbar to open it.

Toolbar Options

2 If the toolbars appear on one row, on the Standard toolbar, click the **Toolbar Options** button, and then click **Show Buttons on Two Rows**.

3 In the datasheet, click the blank cell above *East* and to the left of *1st Quarter*.

This is the cell Graph will use as the starting point for importing data into the datasheet.

Import File

4 On Graph's Standard toolbar, click the **Import File** button.

The Import File dialog box appears. This dialog box functions just like the Open dialog box.

5 If the contents of the *My Documents* folder are not displayed, click the **My Documents** icon on the Places bar, and then navigate to the *Microsoft Press \PowerPoint 2003 SBS\AddingTable\InsertingChart* folder.

6 In the list box, click *Sales*, and then click **Open**.

The Import Data Options dialog box appears. Sheet1 from the Excel workbook is selected as the one to be imported into the Graph chart.

7 Click **OK** to overwrite the current data in the datasheet.

Tip To change the size of the datasheet so that you can see all its data, drag the lower-right corner of the datasheet window.

8 Click cell **A4**, type $70,000, and press ⊞.

Graph accepts the new entry, and B4 becomes the active cell.

9 In cell **B4**, type $76,000, and press ⊞.

Graph accepts the new entry and moves the selection down to cell B5.

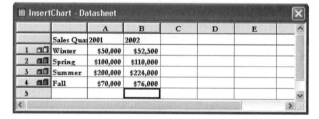

 By Column

Tip By default, Graph plots the series based on the rows in the datasheet. These series are identified in the legend. If you want to base the series on the columns instead, click the By Column button on Graph's Standard toolbar.

Chart Type

10 Close the datasheet window, and then on Graph's Standard toolbar, click the down arrow to the right of the **Chart Type** button, and then in the second column of the second row of the drop-down palette, click the **3-D Bar Chart**.

The chart changes to a three-dimensional bar chart.

Tip You can give your chart a dynamic look by changing the 3-D view. With Graph, you can control the elevation, rotation, position, and perspective for a 3-D chart by using the 3-D View command on the Chart menu.

11 On the **Chart** menu, click **Chart Type**.

The Chart Type dialog box appears with standard and custom chart types and formats.

12 Click the **Custom Types** tab, and in the **Chart type** list, click **Columns with Depth**. Then click **OK**.

The chart changes to the Columns with Depth chart type.

Chart Objects

13 On Graph's Standard toolbar, make sure the **Chart Area** appears in the **Chart Objects** box, so that the entire chart is selected.

Font Size

14 On Graph's Formatting toolbar, click the down arrow to the right of the **Font Size** button, and click **18**.

The font size used for the x-axis and y-axis data labels and the legend changes to 18 points.

15 On the **Chart** menu, click **Chart Options**, and then click the **Gridlines** tab.

The Chart Options dialog box appears with the Gridlines settings.

16 In the **Value (Z) axis** area, select the **Major gridlines** check box, and then click **OK**.

Gridlines appear on the chart.

17 In the chart, click the horizontal x-axis—the category axis—where the year values are plotted.

Black handles appear at the ends of the axis.

Tip You can double-click almost any chart object to edit its attributes. For example, you can double-click the y-axis to display the Format Axis dialog box, where you can apply patterns and change the font, style, number format, and alignment.

Angle
Counter-
clockwise

18 On Graph's Formatting toolbar, click the **Angle Counterclockwise** button.

The x-axis text angle changes to a 45-degree angle.

19   Click a blank area of the slide to deselect the chart object and quit Graph.

PowerPoint's menus and toolbars are restored, and the chart is embedded in the slide.

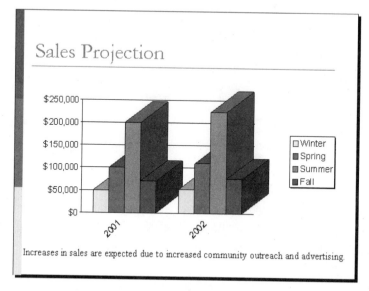

20   On the Standard toolbar, click the **Save** button to save the presentation.

Save

CLOSE the *InsertChart* presentation.

Inserting an Excel Chart

Microsoft Office Specialist

If you have already created a chart in Excel, you can import it into a slide instead of having to recreate it in PowerPoint.

To insert an Excel chart object into a slide:

1   On the **Insert** menu, click **Object**.

The Insert Object dialog box appears.

2   Select the **Create from file** option, and then click **Browse**.

3   Navigate to the folder where the Excel workbook containing the chart is stored, click **OK** to close the **Browse** dialog box, and then click **OK** to close the **Insert Object** dialog box.

PowerPoint embeds the chart in the slide.

Inserting and Formatting an Organization Chart

Microsoft
Office
Specialist

You can use PowerPoint's diagramming tool to create a variety of diagrams, including organization charts, or org charts. An *org chart* shows the relationships among the elements of an organization—for example, the relationship between a manager and her subordinates or between a parent company and its subsidiaries.

You create an org chart by double-clicking an org chart placeholder or by clicking the Insert Diagram or Organization Chart button on the Drawing toolbar. A sample org chart appears with boxes in which you can enter names. To add a new box to the chart, you select the adjacent box, click the down arrow to the right of the Insert Shape button on the Organization Chart toolbar, and do the following:

- Click Coworker to place the box next to the selected box and connect it to the boxes on the same level.

- Click Subordinate to place the new box below the selected box and connect it to other boxes below the selected box.

- Click Assistant to place the new box below the selected box and connect it only to the selected box.

After creating the org chart, you can double-click it to edit it at any time. If you add a chart box in the wrong place, you can select it and then press the ⌦ key to remove it. You can also rearrange boxes by dragging them.

By default, the org chart appears in a traditional hierarchy, with one manager at the top and subordinates below. You can use the AutoFormat button on the Organization Chart toolbar to change the chart style. You can also format the chart boxes and their connecting lines individually. You can change the chart box color, shadow, border style, border color, or border line style by clicking buttons on the Drawing toolbar.

Tip You can take advantage of the enhanced functionality of PowerPoint 2003's diagramming tool by converting org charts created with previous versions. After opening the presentation in PowerPoint 2003, double-click the org chart to convert it.

In this exercise, you will add an org chart to a slide, enter text, add a chart box, and then change the chart style.

USE the *InsertOrg* presentation in the practice file folder for this topic. This practice file is located in the *My Documents\Microsoft Press\PowerPoint 2003 SBS\AddingTable\InsertingOrg* folder and can also be accessed by clicking *Start/All Programs/Microsoft Press/PowerPoint 2003 Step by Step*. OPEN the *InsertOrg* presentation.

1 Move to Slide 12, and double-click the org chart placeholder.

 The Diagram Gallery dialog box appears with the Organization Chart option selected.

2 Click **OK**.

A default org chart object is inserted into the slide, with the top chart box selected. The Organization Chart toolbar is also displayed.

3 Click the top box, type Karen Berg, press ⌜Enter⌝, and type Owner.

4 Click the lower-left chart box, type Kim Akers, press ⌜Enter⌝, and type Head Buyer.

5 Click the lower-middle chart box, type David Ortiz, press ⌜Enter⌝, and type Assistant.

6 Click the lower-right chart box, type Gardening Teachers, and then click away from the chart boxes but within the org chart object.

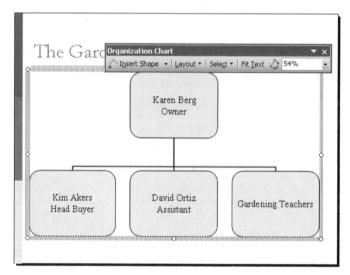

7 Click the lower-left chart box (don't click the text). Then on the Organization Chart toolbar, click the down arrow to the right of the **Insert Shape** button, and click **Subordinate** on the drop-down menu.

A subordinate chart box is placed below the selected chart box.

8   Click the subordinate chart box, and type **Office Staff**.

9   Click the lower-middle chart box. Then on the Organization Chart toolbar, click the down arrow to the right of the **Insert Shape** button, and click **Subordinate**.

10   Click the subordinate chart box, and type **Sales Staff**.

11   Add a subordinate box to the lower-right chart box, click it, and type **Students**.

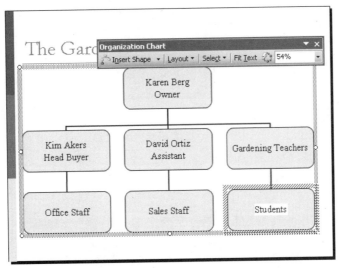

Autoformat

12   On the Organization Chart toolbar, click the **Autoformat** button.

The Organization Chart Style Gallery dialog box appears.

13   In the **Select a Diagram Style** list, click **Beveled Gradient**.

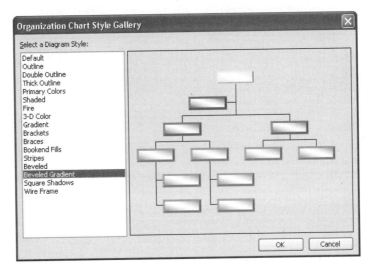

14   Click **OK**.

The style of the organization chart changes.

Select ▾

15   Click the *Kim Akers* chart box. Then on the Organization Chart toolbar, click the down arrow to the right of the **Select** button, and click **Level** on the drop-down menu.

All chart boxes at Kim Akers' level are selected.

B

Bold

16   Hold down Shift, click the *Karen Berg* chart box, and then click the **Bold** button on the Formatting toolbar.

The first two chart levels are now bold.

17   Click outside the org chart object to deselect it.

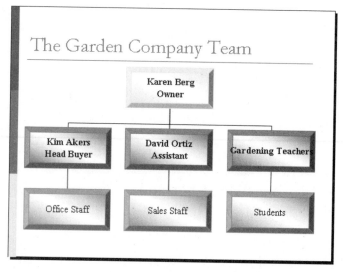

Save

18   On the Standard toolbar, click the **Save** button to save the presentation.

CLOSE the *InsertOrg* presentation, and if you are not continuing on to the next chapter, quit PowerPoint.

Inserting Other Types of Diagrams

In addition to org charts, you can create a variety of built-in diagrams, including cycle, radial, pyramid, Venn, and target diagrams. You can create and format these other types of diagrams by using techniques similar to those you use with org charts.

To insert and format a diagram:

Insert
Diagram or
Organization
Chart

1 Double-click a diagram placeholder, or on the Drawing toolbar, click the **Insert Diagram or Organization Chart** button.

The Diagram Gallery dialog box appears.

2 Click the diagram option you want, and click **OK**.

A sample diagram appears on the active slide with text shapes and labels appropriate to the type you chose.

3 Type information in the boxes and replace labels with your own text, as necessary.

Autoformat

4 If you want, use the **AutoFormat** button on the Diagram toolbar to change the format of the diagram.

Key Points

■ You can insert a table into a slide to organize information neatly in rows and columns. You can customize and format individual cells as well as the entire table.

■ You can embed an Excel worksheet in a slide. Double-clicking the worksheet object opens it in Excel so that you can edit it using Excel's formatting and calculating capabilities.

■ You can create a chart with Microsoft Graph to present numeric data in an easy-to-grasp visual format.

■ You can create a variety of diagrams, including organization charts. You can edit and format the diagram and change its layout to suit your needs.

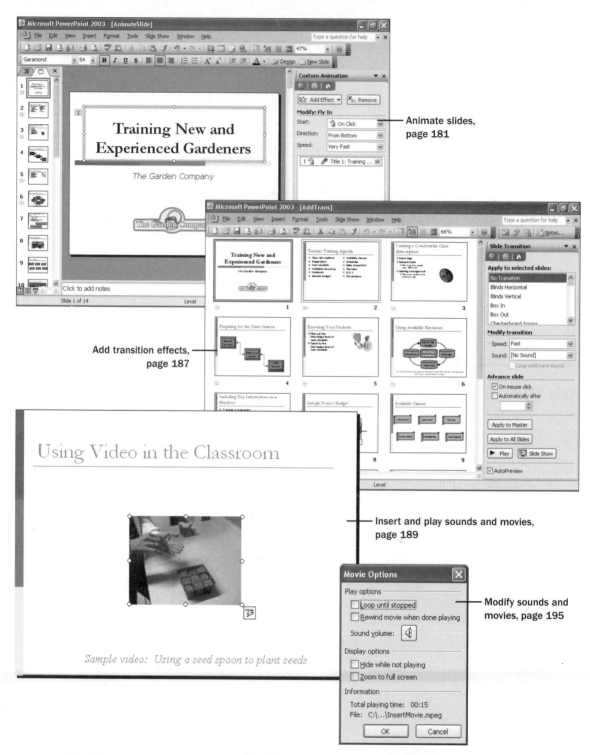

Animate slides,
page 181

Add transition effects,
page 187

Insert and play sounds and movies,
page 189

Modify sounds and
movies, page 195

Sample video: Using a seed spoon to plant seeds

Chapter 10 at a Glance

10 Creating a Multimedia Presentation

In this chapter you will learn to:

✔ Animate slides.

✔ Add transition effects.

✔ Insert and play sounds and movies.

✔ Modify sounds and movies.

With Microsoft Office PowerPoint 2003, you can transform a slide show into a multi-media presentation by animating text and objects, adding transitions between slides, and adding sounds and movie clips. You can set PowerPoint to play associated sounds and movies automatically when the slide containing them is displayed, or you can play them manually.

In this chapter, you will animate text and objects, and add slide transitions. You'll also insert sounds and movies into a presentation, and play the sounds and movies.

See Also Do you need only a quick refresher on the topics in this chapter? See the Quick Reference entries on pages xlii–xliv.

Important Before you can use the practice files in this chapter, you need to install them from the book's companion CD to their default location. See "Using the Book's CD-ROM" on page xiii for more information.

Animating Slides

Microsoft Office Specialist

You can make a slide show more engaging by animating the text and graphics on your slides. Common types of animation include the following:

■ You can apply *text animations* so that the text appears on the screen one para-graph, word, or letter at a time.

■ If a slide has more than one level of bullet points, you can animate different levels separately.

■ You can animate objects, such as shapes.

■ If an object has text, you can animate the object and the text together (the default type of animation) or separately, or you can animate one but not the other.

■ You can change the order of appearance of text or shapes.

■ You can animate charts created with Microsoft Graph or imported from Microsoft Excel—for example, you can animate each data series in a chart to appear at a different time.

The easiest way to apply animation effects to a slide show is to use Animation Schemes in the Slide Design task pane, which provides one-click access to professionally designed animations divided into three categories: Subtle, Moderate, and Exciting. Most of these animations have associated sound effects. To preview each animation scheme, you can cycle through the various options until you find the animation you want.

Tip   You can apply animation effects in Slide Sorter view or in Normal view. If you are in Slide Sorter view, PowerPoint applies the effect to every object on the slide except the title and background objects. If you are in Normal view, you must select the object you want to animate on the current slide and then apply the effect.

If you would rather create your own animation scheme, you can use the Custom Animation command on the Slide Show menu. You must be in Normal view. Custom animations include moving multiple objects simultaneously, moving objects along a path, and sequencing all the effects on the slide. You can add your animation scheme to each slide individually or, with one click, you can apply it to all the slides in a presentation.

In this exercise, you will apply an animation scheme to a slide from the Slide Design task pane, animate multiple slides, animate the text in a slide, change the text animation settings and levels for a slide, animate the text in a slide object, and change the order in which objects are animated.

BE SURE TO start PowerPoint before beginning this exercise.
USE the *AnimateSlide* presentation in the practice file folder for this topic. This practice file is located in the *My Documents\Microsoft Press\PowerPoint 2003 SBS\CreatingMultimedia\Animating* folder and can also be accessed by clicking *Start/All Programs/Microsoft Press/PowerPoint 2003 Step by Step*. OPEN the *AnimateSlide* presentation.

1   In the lower-left corner of the window, click the **Slide Sorter View** button, and then click Slide 3 in Slide Sorter view.

Slide Sorter View

2   On the **Slide Show** menu, click **Animation Schemes**.

The Slide Design task pane opens, displaying a selection of animation schemes.

3   In the **Apply to selected slides** area of the **Slide Design** task pane, click **Fade in all**.

PowerPoint applies the animation effect to the slide. An animation symbol appears below the lower-left corner of Slide 3.

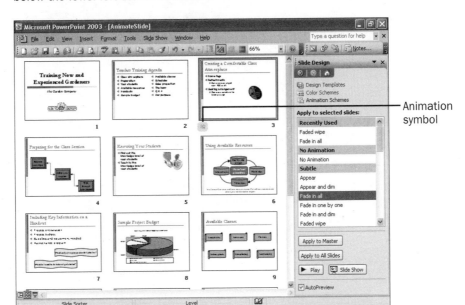

Animation symbol

4   Click Slide 2, hold down the Ctrl key, and then click Slides 5 and 6.

5   In the **Apply to selected slides** area of the **Slide Design** task pane, click **Faded wipe**.

PowerPoint applies the animation effect to all three slides. Because the AutoPreview check box is selected at the bottom of the Slide Design task pane, PowerPoint shows you how the animation will look when you deliver the slide show.

6   Double-click Slide 1 to switch to Normal view with Slide 1 displayed.

7   On the **Slide Show** menu, click **Custom Animation**.

The Custom Animation task pane opens.

8   Click the *Training New and Experienced Gardeners* title. Then in the **Custom Animation** task pane, click **Add Effect**, point to **Entrance**, and click **5. Fly In**.

The animation effect is demonstrated on Slide 1. In the Custom Animation task pane, the title text (item number 1) and a truncated description of the effect appear in the Animation Order list. (You can *hover* over the item number to see the full description.)

9   In the slide, click *The Garden Company*. Then in the **Custom Animation** task pane, click **Add Effect**, point to **Emphasis**, and click **5. Spin**.

PowerPoint demonstrates the animation effect. In the Custom Animation task pane, the subtitle text (item number 2) and a description of the effect appear in the Animation Order list.

10   At the bottom of the **Custom Animation** task pane, click the **Slide Show** button.

Slide 1 appears without the title.

11   Without moving the mouse, click to display the title with the Fly In effect, and then click a second time to spin the company name.

12   Press the [Esc] key to end the slide show.

Slide 1 reappears in Normal view.

13   In the **Custom Animation** task pane, click the first item in the **Animation Order** list, click the down arrow that appears to the item's right, and click **Effect Options**.

The Fly In dialog box appears, with the Effect tab active.

14   In the **Settings** area, click the down arrow to the right of the **Direction** box, and click **From Top**. Then select both the **Smooth start** and **Smooth end** check boxes.

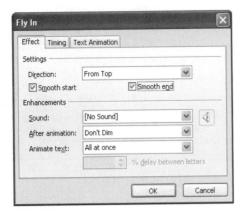

15 In the **Enhancements** area, click the down arrow to the right of the **Animate text** box, and click **By letter**. Then change the **% delay between letters** setting to **5**, and click **OK**.

PowerPoint demonstrates the animation effect.

Tip You can enhance an animation by dimming text after displaying it. In the Custom Animation task pane, click the down arrow to the right of the selected item in the Animation Order list, click Effect Options, click the Effect tab, click the down arrow to the right of the "After animation" box, and then click a color box or animation effect, such as Hide After Animation.

16 In the **Modify: Fly In** area of the **Custom Animation** task pane, click the down arrow to the right of the **Start** box, and click **With Previous**.

The animation effect is set to play without you having to click the mouse button to activate it.

17 Move to Slide 3. Then in the **Custom Animation** task pane, click the second animated item in the **Animation Order** list, click the down arrow, and click **Effect Options**.

The Fade dialog box appears.

18 Click the **Text Animation** tab, click the down arrow to the right of the **Group text** box, click **By 1st level paragraphs**, and then click **OK**.

The Fade dialog box closes, and PowerPoint demonstrates the effect.

Tip To print a presentation that contains animated slides, select the "Include animations" check box in the Print dialog box to print each stage of animation in the slide on a separate page.

19 Move to Slide 4, and drag a selection box around the three shapes and their connectors to select them all.

20 In the **Custom Animation** task pane, click **Add Effect**, point to **Entrance**, and click **4. Diamond**.

The number 1 appears next to each of the three shapes and two connector lines to show that they will all display their animation at the same time.

21 In the **Animation Order** list, click the first **Elbow connector**, and click the **Re-Order** up arrow at the bottom of the list two times.

This item is now second in the animation order.

22 Click the down arrow to the right of the **Start** box, and click **After Previous**.

23 In the **Animation Order** list, click the second **Elbow connector**, click the **Re-Order** up arrow once, click the down arrow to the right of the **Start** box, and click **After Previous**.

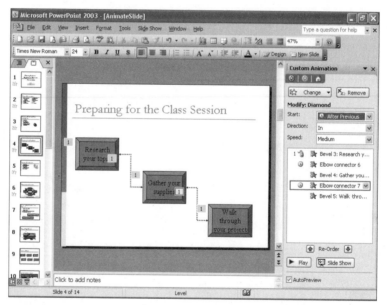

24 At the bottom of the **Custom Animation** task pane, click the **Slide Show** button, and then click the mouse button to display the shapes and their connectors in sequence.

The objects and connector lines appear one after another from top to bottom.

25 Press [Esc] to end the slide show, and then close the **Custom Animation** task pane.

Save

26 On the Standard toolbar, click the **Save** button to save the presentation.

CLOSE the *AnimateSlide* presentation.

Adding Transition Effects

Microsoft Office Specialist

Transition effects help a presentation make more of an impact by varying the way one slide replaces another. A *slide transition* is the visual effect of a slide as it moves on and off the screen during a slide show. Transitions include such effects as sliding into view from one of several directions, dissolving in from the outer edges or the center, and opening like a vertical blind.

Tip If you apply both a transition effect and an animation effect to a slide, the transition effect occurs first, followed by the animation effect.

Each slide can have only one transition. You can set transitions for slides one at a time, or apply the same transition to a group of slides by first selecting the slide or slides in Slide Sorter view or on the Slides tab of the Outline/Slides pane in Normal view. You can then use the Slide Transition task pane to apply the transition. You can also specify the following:

- The transition's speed
- The sound of the transition
- The direction of the transition
- When the transition takes place

In this exercise, you will apply a transition to a single slide, apply the same transition to multiple slides, and then set the transition speed.

USE the *AddTrans* presentation in the practice file folder for this topic. This practice file is located in the *My Documents\Microsoft Press\PowerPoint 2003 SBS\CreatingMultimedia\AddingTransition* folder and can also be accessed by clicking *Start/All Programs/Microsoft Press/PowerPoint 2003 Step by Step*. OPEN the *AddTrans* file.

Slide Sorter View

1 In the lower-left corner of the window, click the **Slide Sorter View** button.

2 On the **Slide Show** menu, click **Slide Transition**.

The Slide Transition task pane appears, displaying the slide transition option currently applied to the selected slide (Slide1).

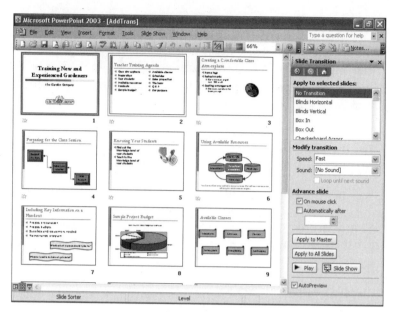

3 In the **Apply to selected slides** area of the **Slide Transition** task pane, scroll down the list, and click **Dissolve**.

PowerPoint demonstrates the transition effect on Slide 1.

4 Click the animation symbol below Slide 1.

PowerPoint demonstrates the Dissolve transition effect on Slide 1, followed by the animation effects that have already been applied to this slide.

5 At the bottom of the **Slide Transition** task pane, click the **Slide Show** button.

PowerPoint switches to Slide Show view and displays Slide 1 with the Dissolve transition effect, followed by the animation effect.

6 Click the mouse button to animate the subtitle, and press Esc to end the slide show.

7 On the **Edit** menu, click **Select All**.

All the slides are selected.

Tip You can also press Ctrl+A to select all the slides in a presentation.

8 Hold down the Ctrl key, and then click Slide 1 to deselect only that slide.

Slide 1 already has a slide transition, and you don't want to replace it.

9 In the **Apply to selected slides** area of the **Slide Transition** task pane, scroll down the list, and click **Random Bars Horizontal**.

The slide thumbnails demonstrate the transition effect. All the slides now have an animation symbol.

10 In the **Modify transition** area, click the down arrow to the right of the **Speed** box, and click **Medium**.

11 At the bottom of the **Slide Transition** task pane, click **Slide Show**.

PowerPoint switches to Slide Show view and displays Slide 2 with the Random Bars Horizontal effect.

12 Click the mouse button several times to advance through the slides, watching the transition and animation effects. Then press [Esc] to end the slide show.

PowerPoint returns to Slide Sorter view.

13 Close the **Slide Transition** task pane.

14 On the Standard toolbar, click the **Save** button to save the presentation.

Save

CLOSE the *AddTrans* presentation.

Inserting and Playing Sounds and Movies

*Microsoft
Office
Specialist*

A PowerPoint presentation is usually created to convey a lot of information in a short time to its audience. That information can be in the form of text, graphics, charts, and tables, but it might also consist of sounds and movie clips. In addition to simply conveying information, including a variety of media can make a presentation more interesting and help to hold the attention of an audience.

If a slide's layout includes a content placeholder, you can insert sounds and movies by clicking the Insert Media Clip button in the placeholder. You can also click Movies and Sounds on the Insert menu and choose whether to insert a sound or movie from the Microsoft Clip Organizer or from a file. PowerPoint inserts sounds and movies as objects, which you can then change and edit.

Sounds can be one of PowerPoint's sound effects (which include applause, a cash register, and a drum roll), music or another audio file, or a narration that you record yourself. To hear the sounds, you need sound hardware (such as a sound card and speakers) installed on your computer and on the computer from which you will deliver the slide show. To play the sound associated with a particular slide, you double-click the Play Animations icon on the Slides tab in the Outline/Slides pane in Normal view. During the slide show, sounds can either play automatically or play only when you activate them with your mouse.

Movies can be digital videos produced with digitized video equipment, or they can be *animated pictures*, also known as animated GIFs, such as cartoons. (GIF stands for Graphics Interchange Format.) To play a movie, you double-click the movie object. After the movie starts, you can click the movie object to pause and restart it.

In this exercise, you will add sound to a slide transition, insert a sound into a slide, and insert and play one movie clip from the Clip Organizer and another from a file.

BE SURE TO have a sound card and speakers installed on your computer for this exercise. (If you do not have this hardware, you can still follow the steps but you won't be able to hear the sound.)
USE the *InsertMedia* presentation and the *InsertMovie* movie file in the practice file folder for this topic. These practice files are located in the *My Documents\Microsoft Press\PowerPoint 2003 SBS \CreatingMultimedia\InsertingSound* folder and can also be accessed by clicking *Start/All Programs/ Microsoft Press/PowerPoint 2003 Step by Step*.
OPEN the *InsertMedia* presentation.

1   On the **Slide Show** menu, click **Slide Transition**.

The Slide Transition task pane appears.

2   In the **Modify transition** area of the **Slide Transition** task pane, click the down arrow to the right of the **Speed** box, and click **Slow**. Then click the down arrow to the right of the **Sound** box, and click **Chime**.

Troubleshooting   If a message tells you that this feature is not yet installed on your computer, click Yes to install it.

PowerPoint applies the sound to the first slide and plays the sound.

Tip   For additional sound selections, click Other Sound at the bottom of the Sound list. Then in the Add Sound dialog box, find and select the sound file you want to add, and click OK.

3   At the bottom of the **Slide Transition** task pane, click the **Slide Show** button.

The sound plays during the animation of the first slide.

4   Press the [Esc] key to stop the slide show and return to Normal view.

5   Move to Slide 3, and on the **Insert** menu, point to **Movies and Sounds**, and then click **Sound from Clip Organizer**.

The Clip Art task pane appears with a selection of sounds.

6   In the **Clip Art** task pane, click **Claps Cheers**.

Tip   If you are connected to the Internet, you can click the "Clip art on Office Online" button at the bottom of the Clip Art task pane to open your browser and go to the Microsoft Office Online Clip Art and Media Web site, where you have access to hundreds of clip art images, photos, sounds, and movies.

A message asks whether you want the sound to play automatically or only when clicked.

7   Click **Automatically**.

A small sound icon appears in the middle of the slide.

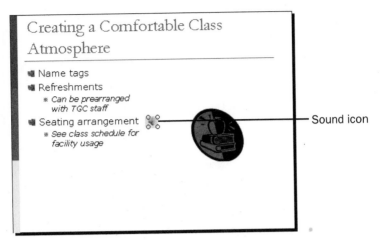

Sound icon

Tip   To make the sound icon easier to see when delivering a slide show, you can enlarge it by dragging its sizing handles.

8   Click the sound icon (not one of its handles), and drag it to the lower-right corner of the slide. Then double-click the sound icon to hear the sound.

The sound plays.

9   Close the **Clip Art** task pane.

Insert
Media Clip

10   Move to Slide 6, and in the content placeholder, click the **Insert Media Clip** button.

The Media Clip dialog box appears, displaying a selection of movie clips.

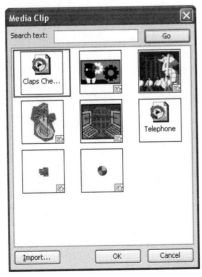

If you are connected to the Internet, you will have more movie clips to choose from.

11 Click the **communication, computers** movie clip (the two computers with the globe behind them), and click **OK**.

Tip If you can't locate the specified clip, type "communication, computers" in the "Search text" box, and then click Go.

12 The movie clip is inserted as an object in the middle of the content placeholder, and the Picture toolbar appears.

Tip Most of the movies in the Clip Organizer are actually animated GIF files. Like movies, animated GIFs add interest to your presentation. However, you can edit them by using the same techniques you use to edit pictures.

13 Adjust the size and position of the movie clip until it is about the same height as the two adjacent bullet points and closer to the right margin of the slide, giving the whole slide a balanced look.

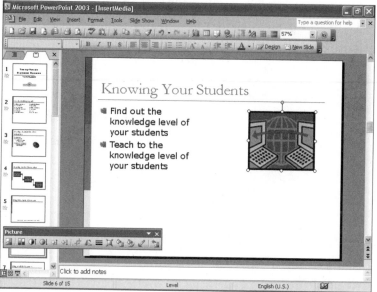

14 In the lower-left corner of the window, click the **Slide Show** button.

Slide 6 appears, and the movie clip plays.

Slide Show

15 Press [Esc] to stop the slide show and return to Normal view.

16 Move to Slide 5, and on the **Insert** menu, point to **Movies and Sounds**, and then click **Movie from File**.

The Insert Movie dialog box appears.

17 Navigate to the *My Documents\Microsoft Press\PowerPoint 2003 SBS \CreatingMultimedia\InsertingSound* folder, and then double-click the *InsertMovie* file.

18 When a message asks how you want the movie to start, click **When Clicked**.

The movie clip is inserted as an object in the middle of Slide 5.

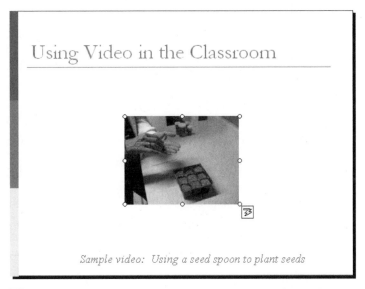

Using Video in the Classroom

Sample video: Using a seed spoon to plant seeds

Automatic
Layout Options

Tip When you insert an object such as a movie, PowerPoint adjusts the layout of the slide to accommodate the type of object. You can control these automatic adjustments by clicking the Automatic Layout Options button that appears below the lower-right corner of the movie object.

19 In the lower-left corner of the window, click the **Slide Show** button, click to display the slide title, click to display the caption, and then double-click the movie object.

The movie object starts to play.

20 Click the movie object to pause the movie.

21 Click the movie object again to play the rest of the movie.

22 Press Esc to end the slide show.

23 On the Standard toolbar, click the **Save** button to save the presentation.

Save

Close the *InsertMedia* presentation.

Recording a Narration

If you are creating a presentation that people will view on their own machines rather than at a speaker-led meeting, or if you are archiving a presentation and want to include the speaker's comments, you can add voice narration to a presentation. To record a narration, your computer must be equipped with a sound card and microphone. (If you don't have the necessary hardware installed on your computer, the Record Narration command on the Slide Show menu might be dimmed.) As you record, you can pause or stop at any time. If you are not satisfied with a narration, you can delete it just like any other PowerPoint object.

To record a presentation narration:

1 On the **Slide Show** menu, click **Record Narration**.

The Record Narration dialog box appears, showing the amount of free disk space and the number of minutes that you can record.

Important You can insert narration into slides in one of two ways. Embedding the narration adds the sound objects to the presentation (and increases the size of the file), while linking the narration stores the sound objects in separate files. To insert the narration into slides as an embedded object, click OK to begin recording. To insert the narration as a linked object, select the "Link narrations in" check box, and click OK.

2 Click **OK**.

3 Discuss the points associated with the first slide, just as if you were giving the presentation to a live audience, and click the mouse button to advance to the next slide.

4 Repeat step 3 for all the slides.

5 If you need to pause for a while, right-click the mouse button, and click **Pause Narration** on the shortcut menu.

6 To resume recording, right-click, and click **Resume Narration** on the shortcut menu.

7 When you have finished the narration, right-click, and click **End Show**, and then click Save to save your narration.

A sound icon appears in the lower-right corner of each slide that has narration.

8 Test the narration by running the presentation in Slide Show view.

The narration plays with the slide show.

Modifying Sounds and Movies

Microsoft Office Specialist

New in Office 2003

Improved media playback

After you insert a sound or movie object, you can change the way it plays. You can modify the animation or action settings, and you can adjust the play settings so that PowerPoint plays the movie with the playback options that you set in the Play Options dialog box. You can also change the action settings to play a movie or sound by moving the mouse over the object instead of clicking the object. Additionally, you can change the animation order so that the movie plays either before PowerPoint animates the text or at the same time as PowerPoint animates the text. To find out the total playing time of the movie or to set play options, you right-click the movie object, and then click Edit Movie Object.

In this exercise, you will modify the sound and animation settings of a sound object and a movie object.

USE the *ModMedia* presentation in the practice file folder for this topic. This practice file is located in the *My Documents\Microsoft Press\PowerPoint 2003 SBS\CreatingMultimedia\ModifyingSound* folder and can also be accessed by clicking *Start/All Programs/Microsoft Press/PowerPoint 2003 Step by Step*. OPEN the *ModMedia* presentation.

1 Move to Slide 5, right-click the movie object, and then click **Edit Movie Object** on the shortcut menu.

The Movie Options dialog box appears, displaying the total playing time and file name of the movie.

2 In the **Play options** area, select the **Loop until stopped** check box.

Now when the movie object plays, the media clip will play repeatedly until you stop it.

3   Click **OK** to close the **Movie Options** dialog box.

4   Double-click the movie object, play the movie until it starts a second time, and then click the movie object to stop the movie.

5   Right-click the movie object, and click **Custom Animation** on the shortcut menu.

The Custom Animation task pane appears, displaying the movie object in the Animation Order list.

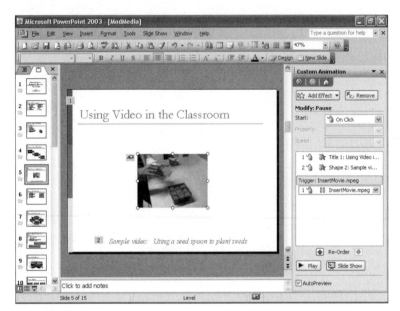

6   With the *InsertMovie.mpg* item selected in the **Animation Order** list in the **Custom Animation** task pane, click the down arrow to the right of the **Start** box, and click **With Previous**.

The mouse icon is removed from the item. The movie clip will now begin playing when the item above it in the Animation Order list is displayed.

Tip   To customize other animation settings for a specific media object, click the object's item in the Animation Order list, click the down arrow, click Effect Options or Show Advanced Timeline, and make any necessary changes. To remove a custom animation, click the down arrow, and click Remove.

7   Click the **Re-Order** up arrow near the bottom of the **Custom Animation** task pane.

During the slide show, the movie will now play before the appearance of the text at the bottom of the slide.

8   In the **Animation Order** list, click the down arrow to the right of the **InsertMovie** item, and click **Show Advanced Timeline**.

A timeline appears at the bottom of the Animation Order list.

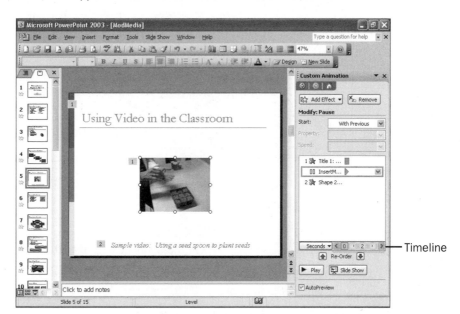

Timeline

9   At the bottom of the **Custom Animation** task pane, click the **Play** button.

The slide appears in Normal view in the same way as in a slide show, displaying the timeline indicator.

10 Move to Slide 3, and click the sound icon in the lower-right corner to select the object.

11 On the **Slide Show** menu, click **Action Settings**.

The Action Settings dialog box appears.

12 Click the **Mouse Over** tab, and then select the **Object action** option.

The Play option appears in the box below.

Slide Show

13 Click **OK**, and then click the **Slide Show** button.

14 Move the mouse pointer over the sound icon to play the sound.

15 Move the pointer away from the icon, click the mouse button to display the next set of bullet points, and point to the icon again.

16 Repeat step 15 for the last set of bullet points, and then press Esc to stop the slide show.

Save

17 On the Standard toolbar, click the **Save** button to save the presentation.

CLOSE the *ModMedia* presentation, and if you are not continuing on to the next chapter, quit PowerPoint.

Key Points

- You can add animation to the text and graphics on your slides, and you can customize how and when the animation occurs.

- You can apply transition effects to smoothly replace one slide with another. You can also set the transition time, the direction of the transition, and when the transition takes place.

- You can add sounds and movie clips to convey information or add interest. You can use sounds and movies that come with PowerPoint or supply your own sound and movie files.

- After you insert a sound or movie object, you can change the way it plays by modifying the animation or action settings.

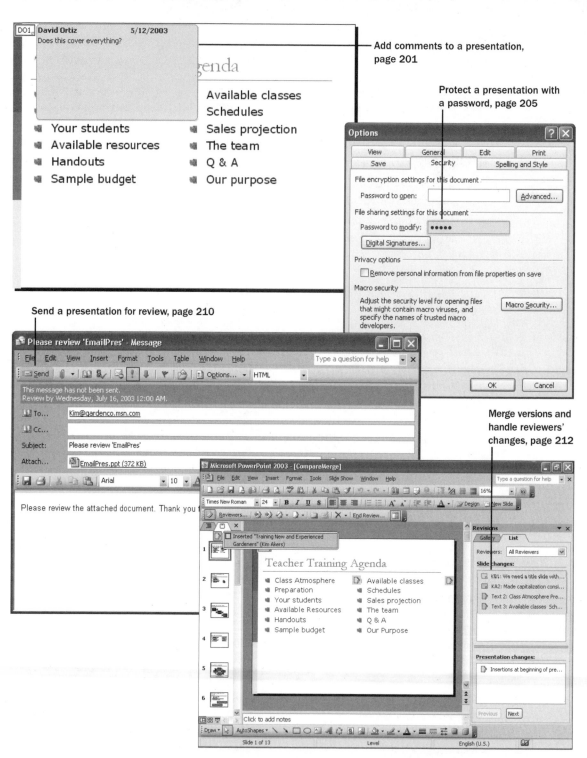

Add comments to a presentation, page 201

Protect a presentation with a password, page 205

Send a presentation for review, page 210

Merge versions and handle reviewers' changes, page 212

11 Reviewing and Sharing a Presentation

In this chapter you will learn to:

✔ Add comments to a presentation.

✔ Protect a presentation with a password.

✔ Send a presentation for review.

✔ Merge versions and handle reviewers' changes.

After you create a draft of a presentation, you might want to distribute it to your co-workers for feedback. Collaborating with others can help you produce accurate and thorough presentations.

Before you send a Microsoft Office PowerPoint 2003 presentation out for review, you might want to protect it with a password that will allow only specified people to open the document. You can send a presentation to reviewers electronically so that they can read, revise, and comment on the presentation without having to print it. When reviewers return the edited presentation to you, you can merge the different versions into the original, evaluate all the revisions and comments, and accept or reject the edits.

In this chapter, you'll insert comments into a presentation, assign a password to protect the presentation, send a presentation for review through e-mail, and then merge presentations received back from reviewers. You'll also accept and reject changes as appropriate.

See Also Do you need only a quick refresher on the topics in this chapter? See the Quick Reference entries on pages xliv–xlv.

Important Before you can use the practice files in this chapter, you need to install them from the book's companion CD to their default location. See "Using the Book's CD-ROM" on page xiii for more information.

Adding Comments to a Presentation

Microsoft Office Specialist

Before declaring a presentation final, you will probably want to ask other people to review and comment on it. You or your reviewers can insert *comments* without disrupting the text and layout of the slides by using the Comment command on the Insert menu.

After comments are added to a presentation, you can edit or delete them, and you can choose to show or hide them. To edit or delete a comment, you right-click the commented text and then click Edit Comment or Delete Comment on the shortcut menu. To hide or show a comment, you need to open the Reviewing toolbar and click the Markup button, which toggles the display of comments on and off. You can then use the buttons on the Reviewing toolbar to insert, delete, or edit comments. You can also right-click any toolbar and then click Revisions on the shortcut menu to open the Revisions task pane, where you can view the comments on the current slide.

In this exercise, you will add and modify comments, display the Reviewing toolbar and the Revisions task pane, hide and show the comments, and delete comments that you no longer need.

BE SURE TO start PowerPoint before beginning this exercise.
USE the *AddComments* presentation in the practice file folder for this topic. This practice file is located in the *My Documents\Microsoft Press\PowerPoint 2003 SBS\ReviewingShare\AddingComment* folder and can also be accessed by clicking *Start/All Programs/Microsoft Press/PowerPoint 2003 Step by Step*.
OPEN the *AddComments* presentation.

1 On the **Insert** menu, click **Comment**.

A comment box opens with your name, today's date, and a blinking insertion point where you can begin typing your comment.

2 In the comment box, type Does this cover everything?

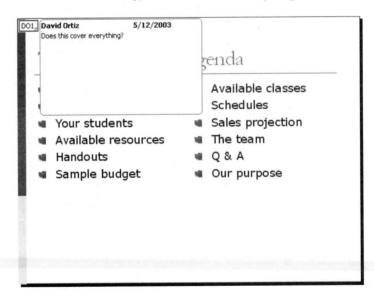

Tip   To change the name of the person making the comments, click Options on the Tools menu, and in the "User information" area of the General tab, change the entries in the Name and Initials boxes, and click OK. All new comments will then have the new user information attached to them.

3   Click anywhere outside the comment box.

The comment box closes, and a small box with your initials and the number 1 appears in the upper-left corner.

4   Point to the small box to display the comment.

5   Move to Slide 3, select the first square object, and on the **Insert** menu, click **Comment**.

6   In the comment box, type Any ideas for improving this slide?, and click anywhere outside the comment box.

7   Double-click the small box.

The comment box opens so that you can edit the comment.

8   Click between the word *slide* and the question mark, press [Space], type visually, and click outside the comment box to close it.

9   On the **View** menu, point to **Toolbars**, and then click **Reviewing**.

PowerPoint displays the Reviewing toolbar.

Markup

10   On the Reviewing toolbar, click the **Markup** button.

The small box on Slide 3 disappears.

11   On the Reviewing toolbar, click the **Markup** button again.

The small box reappears.

Insert
Comment

12   Move to Slide 9, and then on the Reviewing toolbar, click the **Insert Comment** button.

13   In the comment box, type Ask Kim to prepare a report on potential class sizes and class costs.

14   Click anywhere outside the comment box.

The comment box closes, and a small box with your initials and the number 3 appears in the upper-left corner.

15   Right-click any toolbar, and then click **Revisions**.

The Revisions task pane opens, showing the third comment in the "Slide changes" box.

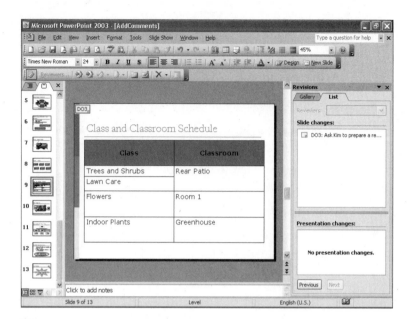

Tip If you want to change the width of the Revisions task pane, point to the pane's left border, and when the pointer changes to a double-headed arrow, drag to the left to make the pane wider or to the right to make it narrower.

16 Right-click the small box on the slide, and click **Delete Comment** on the shortcut menu.

The comment is deleted from the slide and also from the Revisions task pane.

17 At the bottom of the **Revisions** task pane, click **Previous**.

Slide 3 appears, and comment number 2 is displayed in the Revisions task pane.

18 In the **Revisions** task pane, click **Previous**.

Slide 1 appears, and comment number 1 is displayed in the Revisions task pane.

X ▾
Delete
Comment

19 Double-click the slide's small box to display its comment, and then on the Reviewing toolbar, click the **Delete Comment** button.

The comment is removed.

🖫
Save

20 On the Standard toolbar, click the **Save** button to save the presentation. Then turn off the Reviewing toolbar, and close the **Revisions** task pane.

CLOSE the *AddComments* presentation.

Entering Handwritten Changes

While giving a presentation, you can use the Ink Annotations feature to take notes, circle or underline important points, or draw arrows and diagrams. In addition, PowerPoint 2003 supports the insertion of handwritten notes directly onto slides on a Tablet PC. While reviewing a presentation in Normal view, you can mark up slides with changes in your own handwriting. You can turn the markup on and off by clicking the "Show/Hide Comments and Changes" button on the Ink Annotations toolbar, which is effective if you need to view a slide both with and without its markup.

To add ink annotations while running PowerPoint on a Tablet PC:

1   Open the presentation in Normal view, and display the slide that you want to mark.

2   On the **Insert** menu, tap **Ink Annotations** to display the Ink Annotations toolbar.

3   Add your notes or drawing to the slide.

4   After you finish, tap **Stop Inking** on the Ink Annotations toolbar.

PowerPoint offers several different pen styles and colors for marking slides, and ink annotations can also be printed.

If your presentation is opened on a desktop or laptop computer, your handwritten notes can still be seen. The annotations will appear as objects in the presentation, where they can be moved, resized, or deleted when no longer necessary.

Protecting a Presentation with a Password

If you don't want reviewers to edit your work, you can protect a presentation with a *password* so that others can only read it. For greater protection, you can assign a password that must be entered to open the presentation. You can use the password and other security options in PowerPoint to protect the integrity of your presentation as it moves from person to person. At times, you will want the information to be used but not changed; at other times, you will want only specified people to be able to view the presentation.

To protect a presentation, you click Options on the Tools menu and then use the options on the Security tab of the Options dialog box.

- Assign a password that must be entered in order to open the presentation. The presentation is then *encrypted* according to the settings you make by clicking the adjacent Advanced button so that only people with the password are able to open the presentation.

- Assign a password that must be entered in order to modify the presentation. People who don't have the password can open a *read-only* version of the presentation and can save a copy with a different name, but they cannot make changes to the original.

Tip   Setting presentations such as company-wide bulletins as read-only is useful when you want them to be distributed and read, but not changed.

- Assign a *digital signature* that certifies the original of the presentation and guarantees that it has not been changed since the signature was attached.

- Remove information about the creator of the presentation so that this information is not publicly available.

- Assign a *security level* that determines whether presentations that contain macros can be opened on your computer.

The next time you open a presentation after setting a password, a Password dialog box appears. You can either enter the password exactly as it was set—including spaces, symbols, and uppercase and lowercase characters—or click Read Only to open a version of the presentation that you can view but not modify.

Important   In the following exercise we use a common word that is easy to type as a password. To protect your presentations from being opened by unauthorized people, passwords should include combinations of uppercase and lowercase letters, digits, and punctuation symbols. The same password should never be used for multiple presentations. When you set a password, take a moment to write it down, and keep it in a safe place. PowerPoint doesn't maintain a list of passwords, so if you lose or forget the password for a protected presentation, you will not be able to open it.

In this exercise, you will assign a password to a presentation. You will then open a presentation that has been protected with a password, change the password protection, and remove the protection so that reviewers can use it easily.

Attaching a Digital Signature

New in
Office 2003
Digital
signatures

When you create a presentation that will be circulated to other people via e-mail or the Web, you might want to consider attaching a *digital signature*, which is an electronic stamp of authentication. Certified digital signatures can be obtained from companies such as VeriSign. The digital signature confirms the origin of the presentation and that no one has tampered with it since it was signed.

To add a digital signature to a PowerPoint presentation:

1   With the presentation open, click **Options** on the **Tools** menu, and click the **Security** tab.

2   Click **Digital Signatures**, and in the **Digital Signature** dialog box, click **Add**.

3   In the **Select Certificate** dialog box, click a certificate in the list, and click **OK**.

4   Click **OK** twice to close the **Digital Signature** and **Options** dialog boxes.

The word *(Signed)* now appears in PowerPoint's title bar.

5   On the Standard toolbar, click the **Save** button to save the presentation.

Save

To view the digital signature attached to a signed presentation:

1   Click **Options** on the **Tools** menu, and click the **Security** tab.

2   Click **Digital Signatures** to open the **Digital Signature** dialog box, where you can view a list of signers and see who issued their digital IDs.

3   Click **OK** twice to close the **Digital Signature** and **Options** dialog boxes.

USE the *AddPassword* presentation in the practice file folder for this topic. This practice file is located in the *My Documents\Microsoft Press\PowerPoint 2003 SBS\ReviewingShare\ProtectingPresent* folder and can also be accessed by clicking *Start/All Programs/Microsoft Press/PowerPoint 2003 Step by Step*. OPEN the *AddPassword* presentation.

1   On the **Tools** menu, click **Options**, and then click the **Security** tab.

2   In the **Password to modify** box, type tulip.

As you type the password, asterisks appear in place of characters to keep your password confidential.

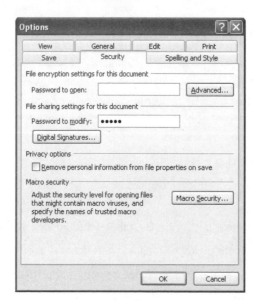

3 Click **OK** to close the **Options** dialog box.

The Confirm Password dialog box appears.

4 In the **Reenter password to modify** box, type **tulip**, and click **OK**.

The password is set. To test the password protection, you need to close the presentation and open it again.

Save

5 On the Standard toolbar, click the **Save** button.

The presentation is saved.

Close Window

6 At the right end of the menu bar, click the **Close Window** button to close the presentation window.

Open

7 On the Standard toolbar, click the **Open** button.

The Open dialog box appears.

8 Navigate to the *My Documents\Microsoft Press\PowerPoint 2003 SBS\ReviewingShare \ProtectingPresent* folder, and double-click the *AddPassword* file.

The Password dialog box appears.

9 In the **Password** box, type **roses**, and click **OK**.

A message tells you that the password you have typed is incorrect.

10 Click **OK**, and then in the **Password** dialog box, click **Read Only**.

A read-only version of the *AddPassword* presentation opens, displaying Slide 1 in Normal view.

11 Close the presentation, click the **Open** button on the Standard toolbar, navigate to the *My Documents\Microsoft Press\PowerPoint 2003 SBS\ReviewingShare \ProtectingPresent* folder, and double-click the *AddPassword* file.

The Password dialog box appears.

12 In the **Password** box, type tulip, and click **OK**.

The *AddPassword* presentation opens, displaying Slide 1 in Normal view.

13 On the **Tools** menu, click **Options**, and then click the **Security** tab, if necessary.

14 Select the contents in the **Password to modify** box, and press the [Del] key to remove the password protection.

15 Click **OK** to close the **Options** dialog box.

16 On the Standard toolbar, click the **Save** button to save the presentation.

CLOSE the *AddPassword* presentation.

Information Rights Management

New in Office 2003
Information Rights Management

If you work for a company that frequently handles sensitive or proprietary information, the ability to protect that information from unauthorized access—whether from nosy employees or from computer criminals—can be critical. The Information Rights Management feature available with The Microsoft Office System 2003 provides the basis for a secure information system.

If your company or organization has implemented the Information Rights Management feature, you can restrict who can change, print, or copy a presentation, and you can limit these *permissions* for a specified period of time. If Microsoft Windows Rights Management Services is running on your company's Microsoft Windows Server 2003 system, your system administrator can establish policies that further restrict how presentations can be manipulated and circulated and can create templates for use with confidential or otherwise sensitive documents.

Important You might have to download the Windows Rights Management client software to assign permissions to files. Check PowerPoint's Help system for more information.

To set the permissions for the open presentation:

Permission

1 Click the **Permission** button on the Standard toolbar.

The Permission dialog box opens.

2 Select the **Restrict permission to this presentation** check box to activate the other features in the dialog box.

3 To grant users permission to only read the presentation, enter their e-mail addresses in the **Read** box. To grant users permission to read, edit, and save changes to the presentation (but not print it), enter their e-mail addresses in the **Change** box. You can also click the **Read** or **Change** buttons to select names from your **Outlook Address Book**.

4 If you want to grant additional permissions, such as permission to print or copy presentation contents, or if you want to set an expiration date for permissions, click the **More Options** button, set the permissions, and then click **OK**.

If you send a presentation with restricted permissions to someone who uses a version of Microsoft Office that's older than Microsoft Office 2003, that person can still use the presentation by opening it in a version of Microsoft Internet Explorer that has been updated with rights management software.

Sending a Presentation for Review

After you finish making changes to a presentation, you can quickly send it via e-mail to another person for review. You can send the presentation from within PowerPoint, so you don't even have to open your e-mail program.

To send a presentation to other people, you use the Send To command on the File menu. The Send To submenu includes the Mail Recipient (for Review) and Mail Recipient (as Attachment) commands. Clicking either of these commands opens a message window in which the presentation is already listed as an attachment.

E-mail (as
Attachment)

Tip To send a copy of the current presentation as an attachment to an e-mail message, you can also click the E-mail (as Attachment) button on the Standard toolbar.

If you use the Mail Recipient (for Review) command, the Subject box contains the file name of the presentation you are sending and the message area includes the text *Please review the attached document*. If you use the Mail Recipient (as Attachment) command, the message box is blank. To send the presentation, you simply enter the recipient's e-mail address in the To box, and the e-mail address for anyone who should receive a copy of the message and its attachments in the Cc or Bcc box.

In this exercise, you will send a presentation for review by attaching it to an e-mail message.

BE SURE TO have an e-mail program installed on your computer and an e-mail account set up before starting this exercise.

USE the *EmailPres* presentation in the practice file folder for this topic. This practice file is located in the *My Documents\Microsoft Press\PowerPoint 2003 SBS\ReviewingShare\SendingPresent* folder and can also be accessed by clicking *Start/All Programs/Microsoft Press/PowerPoint 2003 Step by Step*.

OPEN the *EmailPres* presentation.

1 On the **File** menu, point to **Send To**, and then click **Mail Recipient (for Review)**.

A message window opens, ready for you to type in the recipient's address.

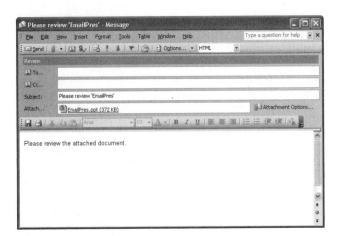

2 In the **To** box, type **Kim@gardenco.msn.com**.

Troubleshooting This e-mail address is fictitious and will result in an undeliverable message being posted in your Inbox. If you prefer, send the message to a cooperative colleague or to yourself.

Tip To select a name from your address book or contacts list, click the To button, click a name in the Name list, click To, and then click OK.

Importance: High

3 On the E-mail toolbar, click the **Importance: High** button.

The message is set for delivery with high priority and will appear in the recipient's Inbox with an exclamation mark.

Message Flag

4 On the E-mail toolbar, click the **Message Flag** button.

The Flag for Follow Up dialog box appears.

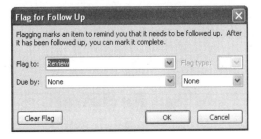

5 Click the down arrow to the right of the **Due by** box.

A calendar appears.

6 Click a date two days from the current date, and then click **OK**.

The review by date appears in the bar above the To: box.

7 Click immediately to the right of the period following *Please review the attached document*, press [Space], and type **Thank you for the quick turn around. DO**.

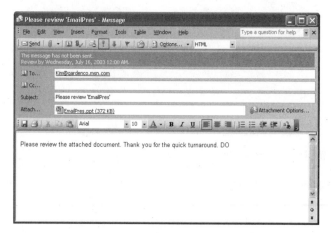

8 On the E-mail toolbar, click the **Send** button.

The e-mail with the attached presentation is sent out for review, and you return to the PowerPoint presentation.

New in Office 2003
Document Workspaces

Tip If your team is running Microsoft Windows SharePoint Services, you can send a shared attachment to create a Document Workspace, a team Web site where your group can collaborate on a project. Before you send your message, click Attachment Options in the message header to open the Attachment Options task pane, then click the "Shared attachments" option and specify the URL for the Document Workspace server (you must have appropriate permissions to access this server). After creating the Document Workspace, use the Shared Workspace task pane to monitor progress.

CLOSE the *EmailPres* presentation.

Merging Versions and Handling Reviewers' Changes

Microsoft Office Specialist

After you send a presentation for review, reviewers make changes and add comments, and then send the presentation back to you. You can then merge their versions of the presentation into the original so that you can see all the changes in one place.

When you merge presentations, PowerPoint shows the differences between the original and the reviewed versions with *change markers*. When more than one person has reviewed the same presentation, PowerPoint uses a different color marker for each reviewer so that you can quickly identify who made what change. These markers show the details of the changes without obscuring the presentation or affecting its layout. You can accept or reject one marker at a time, all markers on a slide, or all markers in a presentation. When you accept a change, PowerPoint incorporates it into the appropriate slide. When you reject a change, PowerPoint restores the original slide.

When you open a presentation that contains comments or changes, PowerPoint displays the Reviewing toolbar so that you can easily work with the markers. The following table lists the Reviewing toolbar buttons and a brief description of each one.

Button name	Icon	Description
Markup		Turns the tracking of changes on and off.
Reviewers	Reviewers...	Displays changes made by specific reviewers or by all reviewers.
Previous Item		Moves to the previous comment or tracked change.
Next Item		Moves to the next comment or tracked change.
Apply		Accepts a single change, all changes to a slide, or all changes to the presentation.
Unapply		Rejects a single change in a presentation, all changes to a slide, or all changes to the presentation.
Insert Comment		Inserts a comment on the displayed slide.
Edit Comment		Edits the selected comment.
Delete Comment/Marker		Deletes a single comment or change, or all comments or changes in the presentation. (The name is either Delete Comment or Delete Marker depending on what type of revision is selected.)
Revisions Pane		Shows or hides the Revisions task pane.

You can also use the Revisions task pane to see the details of the changes. On the list tab, you can see a list of the changes made to the current slide by all reviewers or by a selected reviewer, or on the Gallery tab, you can see a graphical representation of the changes.

In this exercise, you will open one presentation and merge two other versions of the presentation into it. You will then review comments and changes, accept and reject changes, and save the revised presentation.

USE the *CompareMerge, CompareMerge_KA,* and *CompareMerge_KB* presentations in the practice file folder for this topic. These practice files are located in the *My Documents\Microsoft Press\PowerPoint 2003 SBS \ReviewingShare\MergingVersion* folder and can also be accessed by clicking *Start/All Programs/Microsoft Press/PowerPoint 2003 Step by Step.*
OPEN the *CompareMerge* presentation.

1   On the **Tools** menu, click **Compare and Merge Presentations**.

The Choose Files to Merge with Current Presentation dialog box appears.

2   Navigate to the *My Documents\Microsoft Press\PowerPoint 2003 SBS\ReviewingShare \MergingVersion* folder, click the *CompareMerge_KA* file, hold down the ⎡Shift⎤ key, and click the *CompareMerge_KB* file.

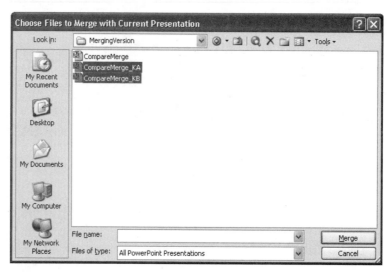

3   Click **Merge**.

A message warns that the presentations you have selected were not sent to reviewers via the Send To command on the File menu and that changes you have made to the presentation might consequently show up as reviewer changes.

Troubleshooting   This message appears only because you are working with the practice files provided for this exercise. When working with real files that you sent to and received from reviewers, you will not see this message.

4   Click **Continue**.

The Revisions task pane opens, showing the comments and changes made to the first slide in the presentation. The comments and changes from each reviewer appear in a different color with their initials.

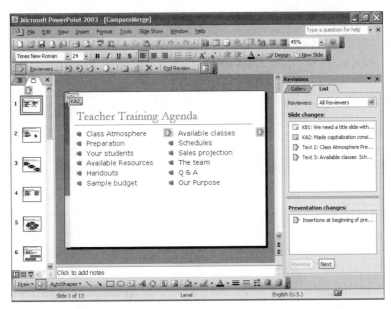

5   On the Reviewing toolbar, click the **Reviewers** button, clear the **Kim Akers** check box in the drop-down list, and then click anywhere on the screen.

The comments and revisions made by Kim Akers are hidden, leaving only those made by Karen Berg, the owner of The Garden Company.

6   On the Reviewing toolbar, click the **Reviewers** button, select the **All Reviewers** check box, and then click anywhere on the screen.

Troubleshooting   If clicking the All Reviewers check box clears it, click it again to make sure it is selected.

The comments and revisions made by both reviewers are now shown.

7   Click the change marker at the top of the **Slides** tab in the **Outline/Slides** pane.

The ScreenTip indicates that Kim Akers has added a slide titled *Training New and Experienced Gardeners* to the beginning of the presentation.

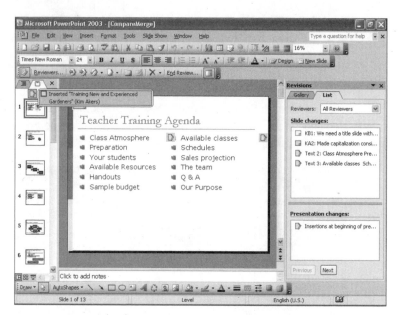

Apply

8 On the Reviewing toolbar, click the **Apply** button.

The title slide inserted by Kim in her version of the presentation appears as Slide 1 of the presentation.

Delete
Comment

9 Click the comment icon on the title slide, read it, and then on the Reviewing toolbar, click the down arrow to the right of the **Delete Comment** button, and click **Delete All Markup on the Current Slide**.

10 Move to Slide 2, and in the **Slide changes** area on the **List** tab of the **Revisions** task pane, click the **KB1** comment.

Karen Berg's first comment, *We need a title slide with our logo*, is displayed.

Tip When you display a comment or change, the name that appears in the ScreenTip is that of the user identified on the General tab of the Options dialog box in the reviewer's installation of PowerPoint. If no user information is entered, "end user" appears in the ScreenTip.

11 In turn, click the **KA2** comment and the two change markers.

You agree with Kim's changes and want to accept them.

12 On the Reviewing toolbar, click the down arrow to the right of the **Apply** button, and click **Apply All Changes to the Current Slide**.

13 On the Reviewing toolbar, click the down arrow to the right of the **Delete Comment** button, and click **Delete All Markup on the Current Slide**.

Tip   To delete a single comment or change marker, you can right-click it, and then click Delete Comment or Delete Marker on the shortcut menu.

The Revisions task pane indicates that the next change is on Slide 3.

14   At the bottom of the **Revisions** task pane, click **Next**.

15   Review the comment and the changes, accept them, and delete the markers.

16   On the Reviewing toolbar, click the **Next Item** button.

Next Item

PowerPoint displays Slide 4.

Unapply

17   Apply all the changes to the slide. Then on the Reviewing toolbar, click the down arrow to the right of the **Unapply** button, and click **Unapply All Changes to the Current Slide**. Then apply the changes again.

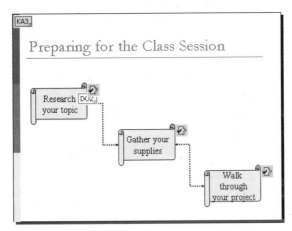

Undo   Redo

Tip   After accepting a change, you can also use the Undo and Redo buttons on the Standard toolbar to flip back and forth to see which version of a slide you prefer.

18   Delete all the markers from Slide 4.

19   In the **Revisions** task pane, click the down arrow to the right of the **Reviewers** box, clear the **Kim Akers** check box, and click away from the drop-down list to close it.

The message in the "Slide changes" area tells you that Karen Berg's next change is on Slide 11.

20   At the bottom of the **Revisions** task pane, click **Next** to move to Slide 11.

21   Read Karen's comment, and then on the **Edit** menu, click **Delete Slide** to comply with her request.

22   In the **Revisions** task pane, click **Next**, apply the changes, and delete the markers.

The message in the "Slide changes" area indicates that Karen has made no more comments or changes, and the setting in the Reviewers box changes to All Reviewers.

23 Press ⌃Ctrl+Home to move to Slide 1, and then on the Reviewing toolbar, click the **Next Item** button.

You move to Slide 7, the next slide to which Kim Akers has made changes.

24 In the **Revisions** task pane, click the **Gallery** tab.

This tab shows you what Slide 7 will look like if you accept Kim's changes.

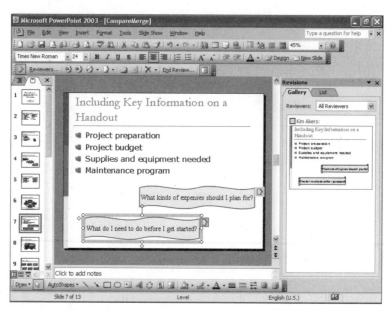

25 Review all the remaining changes to the presentation, and then on the Reviewing toolbar, click the down arrow to the right of the **Apply** button, and click **Apply All Changes to the Presentation**.

26 On the Reviewing toolbar, click the down arrow to the right of the **Delete Comment** button, and then click **Delete All Markup in this Presentation**.

27 In the message box that appears, click **Yes** to confirm that you want to delete all comments and markers.

Save

28 On the Standard toolbar, click the **Save** button to save the presentation.

CLOSE the *CompareMerge* presentation, and if you are not continuing on to the next chapter, quit PowerPoint.

Key Points

- You can insert comments in a presentation and then view them in the Revisions task pane.

- You can set a password that must be entered before someone can modify a presentation. If you want others to be able to read or copy the presentation but not make changes to it, you can also set a password that must be entered before someone can open the presentation.

- You can quickly send a presentation to another person for review by using e-mail.

- You can merge different versions of a presentation into the original and then review revisions and comments all in one place. You can use the buttons on the Reviewing toolbar to view, accept, and reject revisions.

- PowerPoint uses a different color to identify the comments and changes made by different reviewers, so you can review all comments and changes at once or work with those of each reviewer separately.

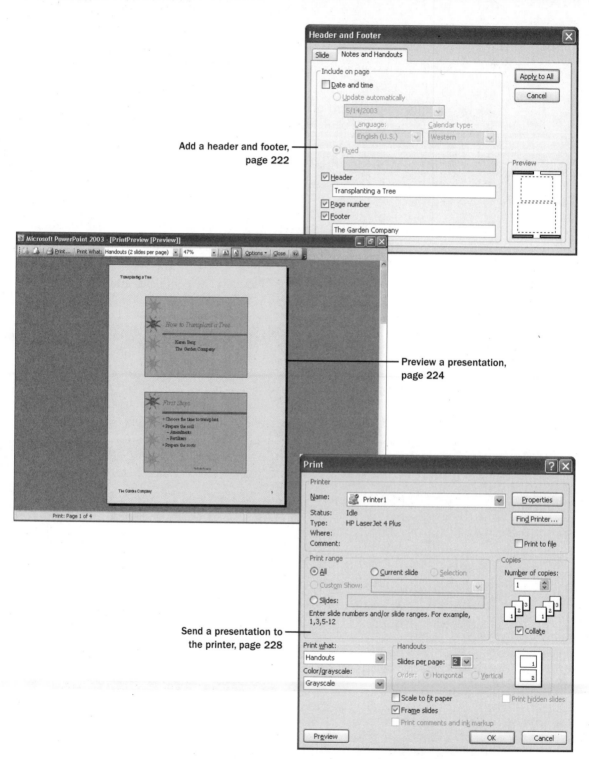

Add a header and footer, page 222

Preview a presentation, page 224

Send a presentation to the printer, page 228

12 Printing Presentations

In this chapter you will learn to:

✔   Add a header and footer.

✔   Preview a presentation.

✔   Send a presentation to the printer.

Although the current trend is toward delivering presentations as electronic slide shows, you might sometimes need to print your slides as transparencies for delivery using an overhead projector. Even if you plan to deliver an electronic slide show, you might need to print out an outline, audience handouts, or speaker notes. So knowing how to print presentations is a necessary presenter's skill.

Tip   Even if you plan to deliver a slide show electronically, it is wise to print a set of transparencies and audience handouts and to have them with you in case something should go wrong with your equipment.

With Microsoft Office PowerPoint 2003, you have flexibility when you are preparing to print slides, outlines, handouts, and speaker notes. Before you print your presentation, you can add a header and footer to display the date and time, page number, or other important information. You can easily customize your printouts by selecting the paper size, page orientation, print range, and printer type that meet your needs. When you are ready to print, you can preview your presentation on the screen to make sure it appears the way you want. If you are working on a color presentation, you can preview your presentation in black and white to see how color slides will look after they are printed on a grayscale printer.

In this chapter, you'll open an existing presentation, add a header and footer, and preview the slides. Then you will choose the right printer settings, and print slides, audience handouts, and accompanying speaker notes.

See Also   Do you need only a quick refresher on the topics in this chapter? See the Quick Reference entries on pages xlvi–xlvii.

Important   Before you can use the practice files in this chapter, you need to install them from the book's companion CD to their default location. See "Using the Book's CD-ROM" on page xiii for more information.

Adding a Header and Footer

Microsoft Office Specialist

Before you print your presentation, you can add a header and footer that will appear on every slide, handout, or notes page. Headers and footers contain useful information about the presentation, such as the author or company name, the date and time, and the slide number. Because you can add more than one header and footer to a presentation, you can have different headers and footers for slides and for notes and handouts.

Header and footer information is stored on the presentation's master slides. You can quickly add a header and footer to slides, audience handouts, outlines, and speaker notes with the Header and Footer command on the View menu.

In this exercise, you will add a header and footer to a presentation.

BE SURE TO start PowerPoint before beginning this exercise.
USE the *HeaderFooter* presentation in the practice file folder for this topic. This practice file is located in the *My Documents\Microsoft Press\PowerPoint 2003 SBS\PrintingPresent\AddingHeader* folder and can also be accessed by clicking *Start/All Programs/Microsoft Press/PowerPoint 2003 Step by Step*.
OPEN the *HeaderFooter* presentation.

1 On the **View** menu, click **Header and Footer**.

The Header and Footer dialog box appears, displaying the Slide tab.

2 Clear the **Date and time** check box to eliminate the date and time from the slides.

3 Select the **Footer** check box, and in the box below it, type **The Garden Company**.

In the Preview box, a black rectangle highlights the placement of the footer on the slides.

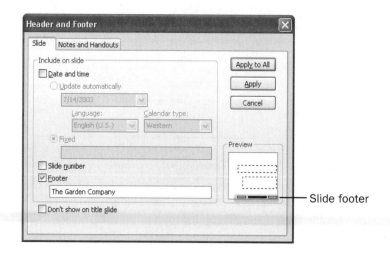

Slide footer

4 Select the **Don't show on title slide** check box so that the footer won't appear on the title slide.

5 Click the **Notes and Handouts** tab.

The header and footer settings for the notes and handout pages appear. All four check boxes are selected.

Tip The settings for notes and handouts will also be applied if you print an outline of your presentation.

6 Clear the **Date and time** check box so that the date and time won't appear on each printout.

7 Click the **Header** text box, and type Transplanting a Tree.

8 Click the **Footer** text box, and type The Garden Company.

PowerPoint will include the header, footer, and page number on each notes or handout page that you print.

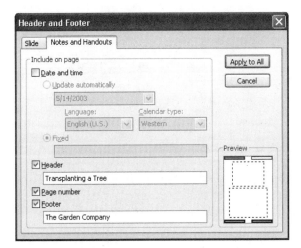

9 Click **Apply to All**.

PowerPoint applies the header and footer information to the slides, notes pages, and handouts pages.

10 Move to Slide 2 to see the footer in place on the slide, and then on the **View** menu, click **Notes Page** to see the header and footer in place on the notes page.

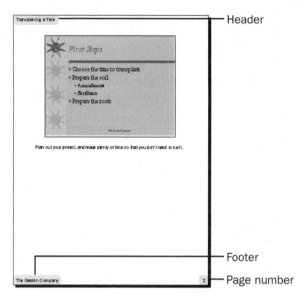

Header

Footer

Page number

Normal View

11 In the lower-left corner of the screen, click the **Normal View** button.

You return to Normal view.

12 On the Standard toolbar, click the **Save** button to save the presentation.

Save

CLOSE the *HeaderFooter* file.

Previewing a Presentation

Microsoft Office Specialist

You can use print preview to see how your presentation will look before you print it. While in print preview, you have the option of switching between various views, such as notes, slides, outlines, and handouts, or even between *landscape* and *portrait* orientation.

If you are using a black and white printer to print a color presentation, you need to verify that the printed presentation will be legible. For example, red text against a shaded background shows up well in color, but when seen in black and white or shades of gray, the text tends to be indistinguishable from the background. To prevent this problem, you can preview your color slides in pure black and white or grayscale to see how they will look when you print them. Pure black and white displays colors in black and white, whereas grayscale displays colors in shades of gray.

You can see how your slides will look when printed on a non-color printer while working in Normal view. On the View menu, point to Color/Grayscale, and then click Grayscale or Pure Black and White.

In this exercise, you will preview presentation handouts. Then you'll switch to Pure Black and White view and change the way a slide looks in black and white.

USE the *PrintPreview* presentation in the practice file folder for this topic. This practice file is located in the *My Documents\Microsoft Press\PowerPoint 2003 SBS\PrintingPresent\PreviewingPresent* folder and can also be accessed by clicking *Start/All Programs/Microsoft Press/PowerPoint 2003 Step by Step.* OPEN the *PrintPreview* presentation.

Print Preview

1 On the Standard toolbar, click the **Print Preview** button.

The screen switches to print preview and displays the first slide as it will print with the current settings.

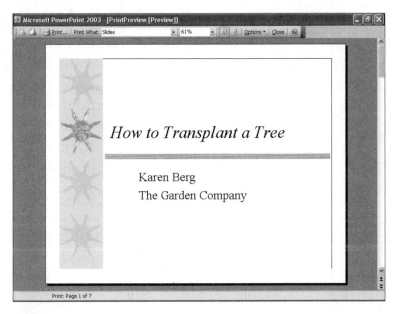

Important If you are printing on a non-color printer, the slide is shown in grayscale.

2 On the Print Preview toolbar, click the down arrow to the right of the **Print What** box, and click **Handouts (2 slides per page)**.

The preview screen displays your presentation in handout format with two slides per page.

3 On the Print Preview toolbar, click the **Options** button, point to **Color/Grayscale**, and then click **Color (On Black and White Printer)**.

Troubleshooting If you are printing to a color printer, click Color instead.

The preview screen displays your presentation with a shaded background.

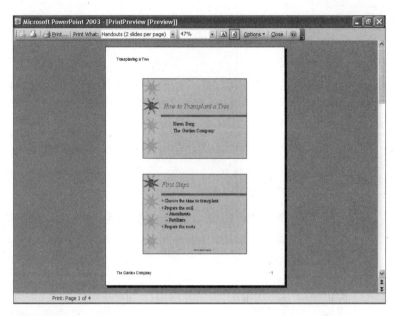

Troubleshooting   Don't worry if your slides are more or less shaded than the ones shown here. Different printers can produce slightly different preview results.

Next Page

4   On the Print Preview toolbar, click the **Next Page** button.

The preview screen displays the next handout page.

5   Position the pointer (which changes to a magnifying glass with a plus sign) in the preview area, and then click the center of the top slide.

The zoom percentage increases to display a magnified view of the slide.

6   Click the center of the slide again.

The zoom percentage decreases to display the original view of the slide.

Previous Page

7   On the Print Preview toolbar, click the **Previous Page** button.

The preview screen displays the previous handout page.

Close Preview

8   On the Print Preview toolbar, click the **Close Preview** button.

The preview screen closes, and your slide appears in Normal view with the Slides tab of the Outline/Slides pane active.

Troubleshooting   If your screen is not in Normal view, click Normal on the View menu, and then click the Slides tab.

Color/
Grayscale

9 On the Standard toolbar, click the **Color/Grayscale** button, and then click **Grayscale**.

The slide switches from color to grayscale and the Grayscale View toolbar opens. You can still see the slide thumbnails in color on the Slides tab, making it easier to compare the active slide in color and black and white.

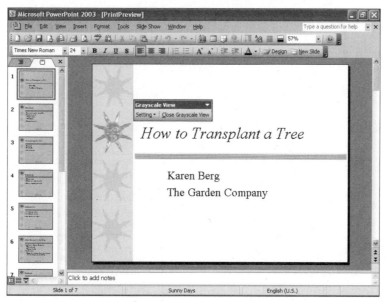

Next Slide

10 At the bottom of the scroll bar to the right of the **Slide** pane, click the **Next Slide** button.

The next slide appears in black and white with its slide thumbnail in color.

Slide Sorter
View

11 In the lower-left corner of the window, click the **Slide Sorter View** button.

All of the slides appear in the Slide Sorter view in black and white.

12 Double-click Slide 1 to display it in Normal view.

13 On the Grayscale View toolbar, click the **Setting** button, and then click **Black with Grayscale Fill**.

The slide background changes from white to gray.

14 On the Grayscale View toolbar, click the **Setting** button, and then click **White**.

The slide background is white again.

Close Grayscale View

15 On the Grayscale View toolbar, click the **Close Grayscale View** button.

The slide switches back to color.

Save

16 On the Standard toolbar, click the **Save** button to save the presentation.

CLOSE the *PrintPreview* presentation.

Sending a Presentation to the Printer

Microsoft Office Specialist

Before you print a presentation, you should review the settings in the Page Setup dialog box and the Print dialog box.

You can use the Page Setup dialog box to set the proportions and orientation of your slides, notes pages, handouts, and outlines on the printed page. For a new presentation, PowerPoint opens with default slide page settings: on-screen slide show, landscape orientation (10 x 7.5 inches), and slides starting at number one. Notes, handouts, and outlines are printed in portrait orientation (7.5 x 10 inches). In the Page Setup dialog box, you can choose from the eleven slide sizes listed in the following table.

Size	Description
On-screen Show	For an on-screen slide show. The slide size for the screen is smaller than the Letter Paper size.
Letter Paper (8.5x11 in)	For a presentation printed on U.S. letter-size paper.
Ledger Paper (11x17 in)	For a presentation printed on legal-size paper.
A3 Paper (297x420 mm), A4 Paper (210x297 mm), B4 (ISO) Paper (250x353 mm), B5 (ISO) Paper (176x250 mm)	For a presentation printed on international paper sizes.
35mm Slides	For 35mm slides. The slide size is slightly reduced to produce the slides.
Overhead	For transparencies for an overhead projector (8.5x11 in).
Banner	For a banner (8x1 in) for a Web page.
Custom	For slides that are a non-standard size.

2   Click the down arrow to the right of the **Slides sized for** box, and then click **Letter Paper (8.5x11 in)**.

3   Click **OK**.

The slide size changes to fit letter-sized paper.

4   On the **File** menu, click **Print**.

The Print dialog box appears.

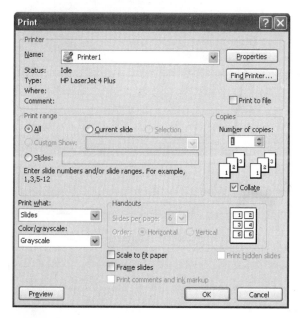

5   In the **Printer** area, click the down arrow to the right of the **Name** box.

A drop-down list displays the names of all the printers installed on your computer.

6   Click one of the printers in the list.

After choosing a printer, you can customize its settings for this particular print operation.

7   Click **Properties**.

The Properties dialog box appears, showing the current printer settings.

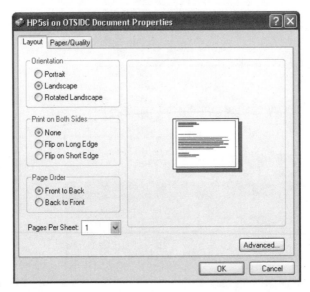

The settings in this dialog box vary depending on the printer you selected. The settings shown here are for a printer that can print on both sides of a sheet of paper (duplex).

8   In the **Properties** dialog box, click **OK** to accept the current settings.

The Properties dialog box closes, and the print setup is complete.

9   In the **Print range** area of the **Print** dialog box, select the **Current slide** option.

10   Click the down arrow to the right of the **Print what** box, and then click **Slides**.

11   Click the down arrow to the right of the **Color/grayscale** box, and then click **Grayscale**.

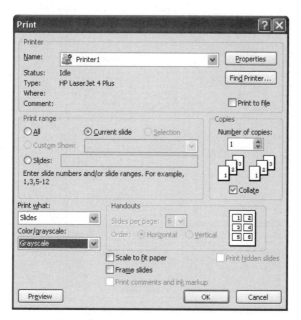

12 Click **OK**.

PowerPoint prints the current slide.

Tip   Every printer prints text and graphics slightly differently. PowerPoint sizes presentation slides to fit the requirements of the printer you choose. By using *scalable fonts*, such as TrueType fonts, you can print a presentation on different printers with the same results, because PowerPoint reduces or enlarges the size of the text in the slides as necessary.

13 On the **File** menu, click **Print**.

14 In the **Print range** area of the **Print** dialog box, select the **All** option.

15 Click the down arrow to the right of the **Print what** box, and then click **Handouts**.

PowerPoint activates the Handouts area and selects the "Frame slides" check box when you specify that you want to print handouts.

16 Click the down arrow to the right of the **Slides per page** box, and click **2**.

Tip   You can print audience handouts in six formats: one, two, three, four, six, or nine slides per page.

17 Click **OK**.

PowerPoint prints the presentation's slides as handout pages.

18 On the **File** menu, click **Print**.

19 In the **Print range** area of the **Print** dialog box, click the **Slides** option, and in the adjacent box, type **1-2,4**.

> **Tip** You can print slides or notes pages in any order by entering slide numbers and ranges separated by commas (no spaces). For example, if you enter 1,3,5-12 in the Slides box in the Print dialog box, PowerPoint prints slides 1, 3, and 5 through 12.

20 Click the down arrow to the right of the **Print what** box, and then click **Notes Pages**.

21 Click **OK**.

PowerPoint prints notes pages 1, 2, and 4.

Save

22 On the Standard toolbar, click the **Save** button to save the presentation.

CLOSE the *PrintFile* presentation, and if you are not continuing on to the next chapter, quit PowerPoint.

Key Points

■ You can add useful information about a presentation, such as the author or company name, the date and time, and the page number, in a header and footer that will appear on every slide, handout, or notes page.

■ You can use print preview to see how your presentation will look before you print it. While in print preview, you can switch the view from slides to notes, outlines, or handouts, and you can switch between landscape and portrait orientation.

■ You can use the Page Setup dialog box to set the proportions and orientation of your slides, notes pages, handouts, and outlines on the printed page.

■ You can print your PowerPoint presentation in several ways: as slides, speaker notes, audience handouts, or an outline. PowerPoint prints slides and supplement materials based on settings in the Print dialog box.

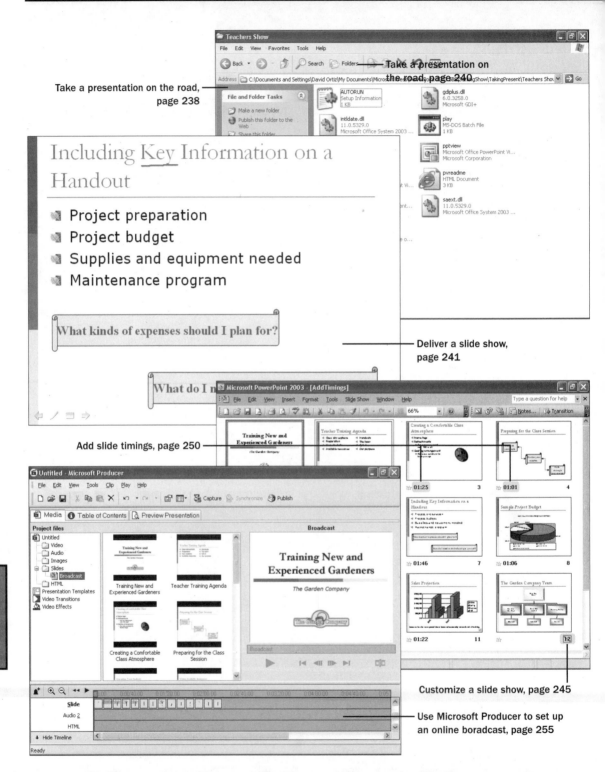

Take a presentation on the road, page 238

Take a presentation on the road page 240

Deliver a slide show, page 241

Add slide timings, page 250

Customize a slide show, page 245

Use Microsoft Producer to set up an online boradcast, page 255

Chapter 13 at a Glance

13 Setting Up and Delivering Slide Shows

In this chapter you will learn to:

✔ Take a presentation on the road.

✔ Deliver a slide show.

✔ Customizing a slide show.

✔ Add slide timings.

✔ Use Microsoft Producer to set up an online broadcast.

The goal of all the effort involved in creating a presentation is to be able to effectively deliver it to a specific audience. In Microsoft Office PowerPoint 2003, you can deliver a presentation as an electronic slide show in Slide Show view. In this view, instead of the slide appearing in a presentation window within the PowerPoint program window, the slide occupies the entire screen.

When you deliver an electronic slide show you navigate through the slides by clicking the mouse button. You can move forward and backward one slide at a time, and you can jump to specific slides as the needs of your audience dictate. You can hide individual slides, or if you know that you will be giving variations of the same presentation to several different audiences, you can hide sets of slides as separate presentations that you show only if appropriate. You can rehearse a presentation and add timings to slides so that you can pace your presentation. You can also use slide timings to set up a slide show to run unattended, either just once or continuously.

If your computer is on a network or if you have access to the Internet, you can give a slide show on any other computer on the network by using PowerPoint 2003's online broadcasting feature. You can also set up and deliver an online presentation via Microsoft NetMeeting. PowerPoint also includes features to help you deliver a presentation on the road.

In this chapter, you'll first use the Package for CD feature to package a presentation so that everything is available when you move it to another computer. Then you'll explore various navigation tools as you deliver a presentation. You'll see how to take notes, create custom and self-running presentations, and broadcast a presentation over a network.

See Also Do you need only a quick refresher on the topics in this chapter? See the Quick Reference entries on pages xlvii–l.

Important Before you can use the practice files in this chapter, you need to install them from the book's companion CD to their default location. See "Using the Book's CD-ROM" on page xiii for more information.

Taking a Presentation on the Road

Microsoft Office Specialist

When you develop a presentation on the computer from which you will be delivering it, you will have all the fonts, linked objects, and other components of the presentation available when the lights go down and you launch your first slide. However, if you need to transport your presentation to a different computer in order to deliver it, you need to be sure you have everything you need.

New in Office 2003
Package for CD

Microsoft Office PowerPoint 2003 provides a feature called *Package for CD* for when you have to transport your presentation. It helps to gather all the presentation components and then compress and save them to a CD, floppy disk, or other type of removable media, or to a hard disk. Linked files are included in the presentation package by default. TrueType fonts are stored with the presentation if you select the Embed TrueType Fonts option.

Tip You can embed fonts when you package a presentation, or you can do it when you save a new presentation. In the Save As dialog box, click Tools, click Save Options, and on the Save tab select the "Embed TrueType fonts" check box. Then select the "Embed characters in use only (best for reducing file size)" option to embed only those characters used in the presentation, or select the "Embed all characters (best for editing by others)" option to embed all the characters in the font set.

New in Office 2003
Updated PowerPoint Viewer program

PowerPoint comes with a special program called the *PowerPoint Viewer*, which you can use to deliver a presentation on a computer that does not have PowerPoint installed. You can easily install the PowerPoint Viewer program on any compatible system (one that uses the Microsoft Windows operating system). When you run Package for CD, you have the option of including the PowerPoint Viewer with the packed presentation.

When you complete the Package for CD process, PowerPoint creates two files:

■ *Pngsetup* is a setup file that takes apart the presentation package and sets up the presentation for delivery.

■ *Pres0.ppz* is a compressed version of your presentation.

The Pngsetup and Pres0.ppz files need to be stored in the same folder for the slide show delivery to be successful. To unpack and deliver your presentation, simply double-click the Pngsetup file, and follow the instructions that appear.

In this exercise, you will use Package for CD to create a presentation package in a folder on your hard drive. You will then deliver the presentation using the PowerPoint Viewer.

BE SURE TO start PowerPoint before beginning this exercise.
USE the *RoadPres* presentation in the practice file folder for this topic. This practice file is located in the *My Documents\Microsoft Press\PowerPoint 2003 SBS\SettingShow\TakingPresent* folder and can also be accessed by clicking *Start/All Programs/Microsoft Press/PowerPoint 2003 Step by Step.*
OPEN the *RoadPres* presentation.

1 On the **File** menu, click **Package for CD**.

The Package for CD dialog box appears.

2 In the **Name the CD** box, type Teachers Show.

PowerPoint will include the open presentation, all its linked files, and the PowerPoint Viewer in the presentation package, but you need to specifically tell it to include embedded fonts.

3 Click **Options**.

The Options dialog box appears.

4 Select the **Embedded TrueType fonts** check box, and click **OK**.

Important   It is especially important to select the "Embedded TrueType fonts" check box if you are using fonts that are not typically installed by Windows. Then when you open the presentation on a computer that doesn't have these TrueType fonts installed, the presentation looks the same as it did on your computer. Be aware that including embedded fonts in a presentation package can increase the file size dramatically.

5 Click **Copy to Folder**.

The Copy to Folder dialog box appears.

6 Click **Browse**, navigate to the *My Documents\Microsoft Press\PowerPoint 2003 SBS \SettingShow\TakingPresent* folder, and click **Select**.

7 When you return to the **Copy to Folder** dialog box, click **OK**.

PowerPoint displays a message box that reports its progress as it creates the presentation package.

8 Click **Close** to close the **Package for CD** dialog box.

Close

9 At the right end of the title bar, click the **Close** button to close the presentation and quit PowerPoint.

10 Display the taskbar, click the **Start** button, and then click **My Documents**.

The My Documents window opens.

11 Navigate to the *Microsoft Press\PowerPoint 2003 SBS\SettingShow\TakingPresent \Teachers Show* folder on your hard disk.

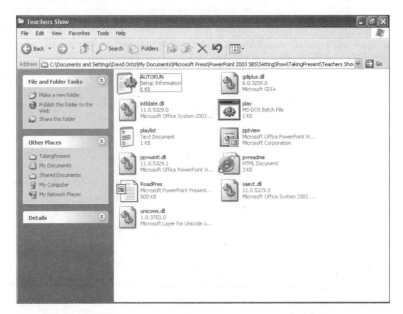

12 In the list of file and folder names, right-click the *RoadPres* file, and click **Open With** on the shortcut menu.

Troubleshooting If clicking Open With displays a submenu that lists the Microsoft Office PowerPoint Viewer, click that option and skip steps 13 through 15. If the submenu doesn't list the viewer, click Choose Program, and continue with step 13.

13 If the **Programs** list in the **Open With** dialog box includes **Microsoft Office PowerPoint Viewer**, click that option, click **OK**, and skip steps 14 and 15. Otherwise, click **Browse**:

14 Double-click **Microsoft Office**, double-click **OFFICE11**, and then double-click **PPTVIEW**.

15 With **Microsoft Office PowerPoint Viewer** selected in the **Programs** list, click **OK**.

The PowerPoint Viewer displays the presentation's title slide, and the title and subtitle automatically fly in from the right.

16 Click the mouse button to advance to the next slide.

17 Press the [Esc] key to end the presentation.

The PowerPoint Viewer closes.

18 Close the Teachers Show window.

Delivering a Slide Show

Microsoft Office Specialist

The simplest way to advance from one slide to the next in Slide Show view is to click the mouse button. However, PowerPoint 2003 provides a popup toolbar that appears when you move the mouse while in Slide Show view to enable you to move around in other ways.

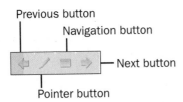

Previous button

Navigation button

Next button

Pointer button

New in Office 2003
New slide show navigation tools

You can use the following techniques to navigate through a slide show:

- To start a slide show with a particular slide, select the slide in Normal or Slide Sorter view, and then click the Slide Show button.

- To move to the next slide, press [Space] or the → key; click the Next button on the popup toolbar that appears when you move the mouse during a slide show; or right-click the screen, and click Next on the shortcut menu.

- To move to the previous slide, press the ← key; click the Previous button on the popup toolbar that appears when you move the mouse during a slide show; or right-click the screen, and click Previous on the shortcut menu.

- To jump to a slide out of sequence (even one that is hidden), click the Navigation button on the popup toolbar that appears when you move the mouse during a slide show, click Go to Slide, and then click the slide on the submenu; or right-click the screen, click Go to Slide, and then click the slide on the submenu.

See Also For information about hiding slides, see "Customizing a Slide Show" in this chapter.

- To display the slides in a custom slide show, click the Navigation button on the popup toolbar that appears when you move the mouse during a slide show, click Custom Show, and click the show on the submenu; or right-click the screen, click Custom Show, and click the show on the submenu.

See Also For information about custom slide shows, see "Customizing a Slide Show" in this chapter.

- To end a slide show at any time, click the Navigation button on the popup toolbar, and click End Show; right-click the screen, and click End Show on the shortcut menu; or press [Esc].

Tip If you are in the middle of a slide show and can't remember how to move to a particular slide, click the Navigation button on the popup toolbar, and then click Help. PowerPoint displays a long list of keyboard shortcuts for carrying out slide show tasks. For example, you can press N to go to the next slide, press H to show a hidden slide, press E to erase pen annotations, or press A to show the pointer arrow.

New in Office 2003
Improved ink annotations

During a slide show, you can annotate slides by drawing freehand lines and shapes to emphasize a point. To do this, you click the Pointer arrow on the popup toolbar, click a pen tool, and then begin drawing. You can change the ink color at any time during the presentation by clicking the Pointer arrow, clicking Ink Color, and clicking a color in the palette that appears.

In this exercise, you will use the popup toolbar to navigate through a presentation in Slide Show view and to end a slide show. You'll also use the pen tool to mark up a slide during a slide show, and you'll change the pen color.

USE the *DeliverShow* presentation in the practice file folder for this topic. This practice file is located in the *My Documents\Microsoft Press\PowerPoint 2003 SBS\SettingShow\DeliveringShow* folder and can also be accessed by clicking *Start/All Programs/Microsoft Press/PowerPoint 2003 Step by Step.*
OPEN the *DeliverShow* presentation.

Slide Show

1 With Slide 1 selected, click the **Slide Show** button.

PowerPoint displays the first slide in the presentation, and the title and subtitle fly in from the right.

2 Click anywhere on the screen, or press [Space].

The slide show advances to the next slide.

3 Press the ← key twice to display the previous slide, and then press the → key to display the next slide.

4 Move the mouse.

PowerPoint displays the pointer, and the popup toolbar appears in the lower-left corner of the screen.

Troubleshooting If the popup toolbar doesn't appear, press [Esc] to end the slide show, and then on the Tools menu, click Options. On the View tab, select the "Show popup toolbar" check box, and click OK.

Next

5 On the popup toolbar, click the **Next** button.

The first bullet point on Slide 2 appears.

6 Right-click anywhere on the screen, and then on the shortcut menu, click **Previous**.

The bullet point disappears.

7 Right-click anywhere on the screen, and point to **Go to Slide**.

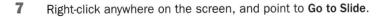

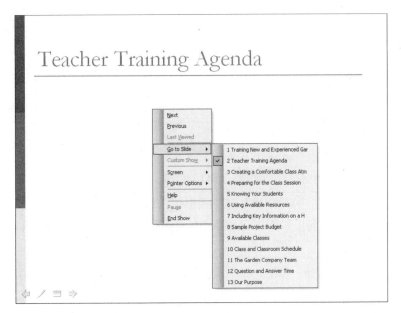

8 In the list of slide names, click **8 Sample Project Budget**.

9 Display the popup toolbar, click the **Navigation** button, and click **Next**.

Navigation

A budget chart appears on Slide 8.

10 Right-click anywhere on the screen, and click **End Show**.

Slide 8 appears in Normal view.

> **Tip** If you click all the way through to the end of the slide show, PowerPoint displays a black screen to indicate that the next click will return you to the previous view. If you do not want the black screen to appear at the end of a slide show, click Options on the Tools menu. Then on the View tab, clear the "End with black slide" check box, and click OK. Clicking while the last slide is displayed will then return you directly to the previous view.

11 Move to Slide 7, and click the **Slide Show** button.

PowerPoint displays the current slide in Slide Show view.

12 Right-click anywhere on the screen, point to **Pointer Options** on the shortcut menu, and then click **Felt Tip Pen**.

The pointer changes to resemble the tip of a felt tip pen.

Important When the pen tool is active in Slide Show view, clicking the mouse does not advance the slide show to the next slide. You need to switch back to the regular pointer to advance the slide using the mouse.

13 Draw a line under the word *Key* in the title.

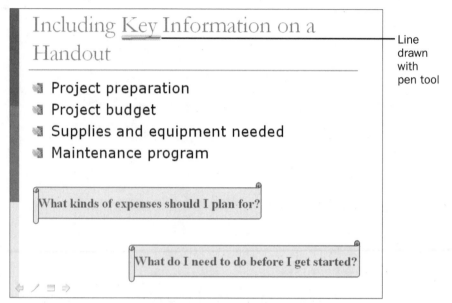

Line drawn with pen tool

14 Right-click anywhere on the screen, point to **Pointer Options**, and then click **Erase All Ink on Slide**.

The line is erased.

15 Press [Space] twice to display the Sample Project Budget slide and its chart.

16 On the popup toolbar, click the **Pointer** arrow, and then click **Ink Color**.

Pointer arrow

The Ink Color palette appears with a selection of colors.

17 On the **Ink Color** palette, click any color box.

18 Draw circles around *$500* and *Fall/Winter* in the chart's title.

19 Right-click anywhere on the screen, point to **Pointer Options**, and then click **Arrow**.

The pen tool changes back to the regular pointer, and you can now click the mouse button to advance to the next slide.

20 Press [Esc] to stop the slide show.

A message asks whether you want to keep your ink annotations.

21 Click **Discard**.

Slide 8 appears in Normal view.

CLOSE the *DeliverShow* presentation.

Using Presenter View with Multiple Monitors

If your computer is connected to two monitors, you can view a slide show on one monitor while you control it from the other. This is useful when you want to control a slide show and run other programs that the audience doesn't need to see.

You can set up your presentation to use multiple monitors by clicking Set Up Show on the Slide Show menu, and then in the "Multiple monitors" area of the Set Up Show dialog box, specifying which monitor the slide show should be displayed on and selecting the Show Presenter View check box. You can then control the slide show by using special presenter tools in Presenter view. You can see details about what bullet point or slide is coming next, see your speaker notes, and jump directly to any slide.

Important   Before you can use multiple monitors, you need to install the proper hardware and software. Install the secondary monitor or projecting device according to the manufacturer's instructions. Check with your computer manufacturer to find out whether integrated dual-monitor support is available so that you can utilize the Presenter view.

To deliver a slide show on one monitor and use Presenter view on another:

1 Open the PowerPoint presentation you want to set up.

2 On the **Slide Show** menu, click **Set Up Show**.

The Set Up Show dialog box appears.

3 In the **Multiple monitors** area, click the down arrow to the right of the **Display slide show on** box, and click the name of the monitor you want to use to project the slide show.

The slide show will run full-screen on the specified monitor, but will appear in Normal view on the other monitor.

4 In the **Multiple monitors** area, select the **Show Presenter View** check box, and click **OK**.

5 Click **Slide Show** button to start the slide show.

6 In Presenter view, use the navigation tools to deliver the presentation.

SlideShow ▾

Customizing a Slide Show

*Microsoft
Office
Specialist*

If you plan to present variations of the same slide show to different audiences, you don't have to create a separate presentation for each audience. Instead, you can select slides from the presentation that are appropriate for a particular audience and group them as a custom show. You can then run the custom show using just those slides. For example, a slide show to train The Garden Company employees in how to conduct classes for customers might include slides that are not appropriate for a training session for people hired on contract. Because the training materials are similar for the two groups, rather than creating two presentations, The Garden Company can develop the employee presentation first and then create a custom show for contractors using a subset of the slides in the employee presentation.

Sometimes you might want to be able to make an on-the-spot decision during a presentation about whether to display a particular slide. You can give yourself this flexibility by hiding the slide so that you can skip over it if its information doesn't seem useful to a particular audience. If you decide to include the slide's information in the presentation, you can display it by using the Go to Slide command and clicking that slide in a list, or you can insert an action button on a visible slide that you can click to jump to that slide.

In this exercise, you will create and edit a custom show. You will also hide a slide and use an action button to display it when necessary. Finally, you will run the slide show to see how custom shows, hidden slides, and action buttons work.

USE the *CustomShow* presentation in the practice file folder for this topic. This practice file is located in the *My Documents\Microsoft Press\PowerPoint 2003 SBS\SettingShow\CreatingCustom* folder and can also be accessed by clicking *Start/All Programs/Microsoft Press/PowerPoint 2003 Step by Step*.
OPEN the *CustomShow* presentation.

1   On the **Slide Show** menu, click **Custom Shows**.

    The Custom Shows dialog box appears.

2   Click **New**.

    The Define Custom Show dialog box appears. The default custom show name is selected in the "Slide show name" box.

3   In the **Slide show name** box, type Contractors.

4   In the **Slides in presentation** box, click slide 8, and then click **Add**.

    Slide 8 appears as Slide 1 in the "Slides in custom show" box on the right.

5 In turn, select Slides 2 through 7, and 12 through 14 in the **Slides in presentation** list, and add them to the custom slide show.

The slides appear in sequential order in the "Slides in custom show" box on the right.

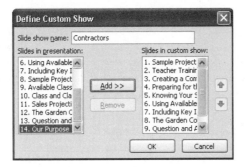

6 Click **OK**.

7 In the **Custom Shows** dialog box, click **Show** to start the custom slide show.

8 Click through all the slides, including the blank one at the end of the show.

9 In Normal view, click **Custom Shows** on the **Slide Show** menu.

10 In the **Custom shows** list, verify that **Contractors** is selected, and then click **Edit**.

The Define Custom Show dialog box appears.

11 In the **Slides in custom show** box, click Slide 8 to select the item.

12 Click **Remove**.

PowerPoint removes the slide from the custom show, but not from the main presentation.

Tip To change the order of the list, move a slide by selecting it and clicking the up arrow or the down arrow to the right of the "Slides in custom show" box.

13 Click **OK** to close the **Define Custom Show** dialog box, and click **Close** to close the **Custom Shows** dialog box.

14 Scroll to the bottom of the **Outline/Slides** pane. Then on the **Slides** tab, right-click Slide 12, and click **Hide Slide** on the shortcut menu.

PowerPoint puts a shadow box around and a diagonal line through the number 12 to indicate that the slide is hidden.

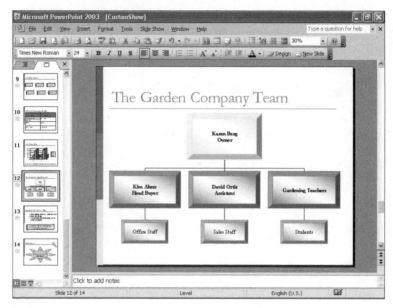

Hide Slide

Tip In Slide Sorter view, you can select a slide and then click the Hide Slide button on the Slide Sorter toolbar.

Slide Show

15 Click Slide 11, click the **Slide Show** button, and then press [Space] to move to the next slide.

Because Slide 12 is hidden, PowerPoint skips from Slide 11 to Slide 13.

16 Press the ← key to return to the previous slide, Slide 11.

17 Right-click anywhere on the screen, point to **Go To Slide**, and then click (**12**) **The Garden Company Team**.

The hidden slide appears in Slide Show view.

18 Press [Esc] to end the slide show.

Action Button:
Return

19 Move to Slide 11, and on the **Slide Show** menu, point to **Action Buttons**, and then click the **Action Button: Return** button in the lower-left corner of the menu.

20 Click the lower-right corner of the slide.

PowerPoint inserts a large action button where you clicked and displays the Action Settings dialog box.

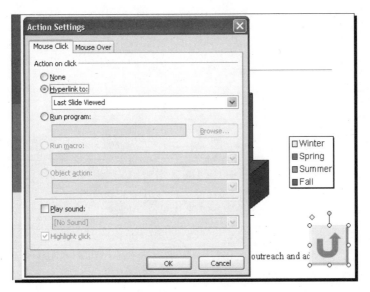

21 In the **Action on click** area, click the down arrow to the right of the box below **Hyperlink to**, and click **Slide** in the drop-down list.

The Hyperlink to Slide dialog box appears.

22 Scroll to the bottom of the **Slide title** list, and click **(12) The Garden Company Team**.

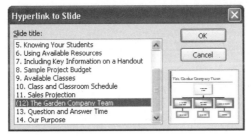

23 Click **OK** to close the **Hyperlink to Slide** dialog box, and click **OK** again to close the **Action Settings** dialog box.

24 Use the action button's sizing handles to make it smaller, and then position it in the lower-right corner of the slide.

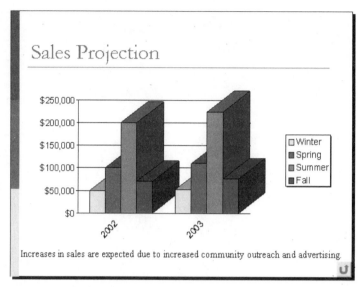

25 Click the **Slide Show** button, and then click the slide's action button.

PowerPoint displays the hidden slide.

26 Press Esc to end the slide show.

Save

27 On the Standard toolbar, click the **Save** button to save the presentation.

CLOSE the *CustomShow* presentation.

Adding Slide Timings

Microsoft Office Specialist

You can advance through a slide show in one of two ways:

- Manual advance, which you control by clicking the mouse button, pressing keys, or clicking commands.

- Automatic advance, which moves through the slide show automatically, keeping each slide on the screen for the length of time you specify.

The length of time a slide appears on the screen is controlled by its *slide timing*. You can apply a timing to a single slide, to a group of slides, or to an entire presentation by selecting the slides, clicking Slide Transition on the Slide Show menu, and in the "Advance slide" area of the Slide Transition task pane, entering the number of minutes and seconds in the "Automatically after" box.

If you are unsure how much time to allow for the slide timings of a presentation, you can rehearse the slide show while PowerPoint automatically tracks and sets the timing for you, reflecting the amount of time you spend on each slide during the rehearsal.

This technique allows you to spend more time talking about some slides than others. You set slide timings during the rehearsal by clicking Rehearse Timings on the Slide Show menu, or in Slide Sorter view, clicking the Rehearse Timings button on the Slide Sorter toolbar.

In this exercise, you will first set slide timings manually and then you will set them automatically during a slide show rehearsal.

USE the *AddTimings* presentation in the practice file folder for this topic. This practice file is located in the *My Documents\Microsoft Press\PowerPoint 2003 SBS\SettingShow\AddingTiming* folder and can also be accessed by clicking *Start/All Programs/Microsoft Press/PowerPoint 2003 Step by Step*.
OPEN the *AddTimings* presentation.

Slide Sorter
View

1   Click the **Slide Sorter View** button, and then click Slide 3.

2   On the Slide Sorter toolbar, click the **Slide Transition** button.

Slide Transition

Troubleshooting   In Slide Sorter view, the toolbars appear on a single row. If you don't see the Slide Transition button, click the Toolbar Options button, and then click the Slide Transition button on the drop-down menu.

The Slide Transition task pane appears.

3   In the **Advance slide** area, select the **Automatically after** check box, and then click the up arrow twice to show **00:02**.

Because both check boxes in the "Advance slide" area are selected, the slide will advance either after two seconds or when you click the mouse.

Tip   When both check boxes are selected, a mouse click in Slide Show view always advances to the next bullet point or slide, even if the slide's timing has not elapsed. If you want to prevent PowerPoint from advancing to the next bullet point or slide, right-click the current slide, and click Pause on the shortcut menu.

4   Click **Slide Show**.

Slide 3 appears, its bullet points are displayed one at a time, and then PowerPoint moves to Slide 4.

Tip   Slide timings are divided equally among the animations for each slide. So if a slide has a title and four bullet points that are all animated and you assign a timing of 1 minute to the slide, the elements will appear at 12-second intervals.

5   Press [Esc] to end the show, and then in Slide Sorter view, click Slide 3.

Adjacent to the animation icon below the lower-left corner of Slide 3 is the slide timing you just applied.

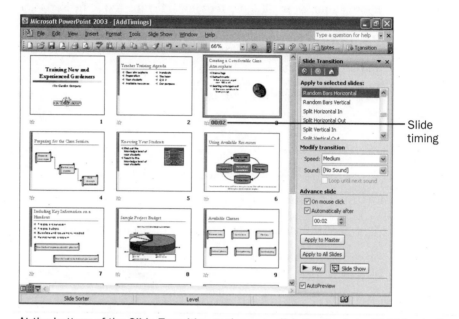

Slide timing

6 At the bottom of the **Slide Transition** task pane, click the **Apply to All Slides** button.

PowerPoint applies the current Slide Transition settings, including the slide timing, to all the slides.

Important When you click Apply to All Slides, all the transition effects applied to the active slide are transferred to the other slides. If you have applied different transitions to different slides, those individually specified transitions are overwritten. So it's a good idea to apply all the effects that you want the slides to have in common first. Then if you want, you can select each slide and customize its effects. (Bear in mind, though, that too many effects in one presentation can distract the audience from your message.)

7 Click **Slide Show**, watch as the slides advance, and click the mouse button when the black screen is displayed.

8 In the **Advance slide** area of the **Slide Transition** task pane, clear the **Automatically after** check box, and then click **Apply to All Slides**.

The slide timings disappear from below the slides.

Important Before you carry out the remaining steps in this exercise, read all the steps carefully so that you understand what you need to do after you begin rehearsing the presentation.

Rehearse
Timings

9 Click Slide 1, and then on the Slide Sorter toolbar, click the **Rehearse Timings** button.

PowerPoint switches to Slide Show view, starts the show, and displays the Rehearsal toolbar in the upper-left corner of the screen. A Slide Time counter is timing the length of time Slide 1 remains on the screen.

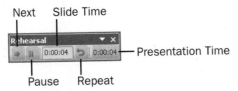

10 Wait about 10 seconds, and then click the **Next** button.

Next

11 Work your way slowly through the slide show, clicking **Next** to display each bullet point on each slide and then move to the next slide.

12 If you want to repeat the rehearsal for a particular slide, click the **Repeat** button on the Rehearsal toolbar to reset the Slide Time for that slide to 0.00.00.

Repeat

Close

Tip If you want to start the entire rehearsal over again, click the Rehearsal toolbar's Close button, and when a message asks whether you want to keep the existing timings, click No.

When you reach the end of the slide show, a message box displays the elapsed time for the presentation and asks whether you want to apply the recorded slide timings.

13 Click **Yes**.

You return to Slide Sorter view, where the recorded timings have been added below each slide. The timing for the active slide, Slide 1, appears in the "Automatically after" box in the "Advance slide" area of the Slide Transition task pane, and you can manually adjust the timing if you want.

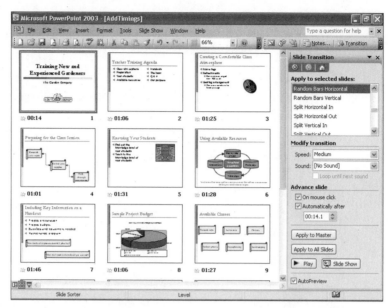

14 At the bottom of the **Slide Transition** task pane, click the **Slide Show** button.

PowerPoint runs the slide show, using the recorded timings.

15 Press [Esc] at any time to stop the slide show.

16 On the Standard toolbar, click the **Save** button to save the presentation, and then close the **Slide Transition** task pane.

Save

CLOSE the *AddTimings* presentation.

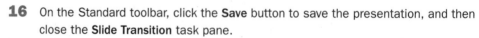

Creating a Self-Running Presentation

When slide timings have been applied to a PowerPoint presentation, the presentation can be set up to run automatically, either once or continuously. Self-running slide shows are a great way to communicate information without a presenter needing to be in attendance. You might want to set up a presentation to run unattended in a booth at a trade show or as a product demonstration in a store. A self-running show turns off all navigation tools except action buttons and other action settings available to the viewer.

To set up a self-running slide show.

1   Open the presentation, and then on the **Slide Show** menu, click **Set Up Show**.

The Set Up Show dialog box appears.

2   In the **Show type** area, select the **Browsed at a kiosk (full screen)** option.

When you select this option, PowerPoint selects the "Loop continuously until 'Esc'" check box in the "Show options" area and dims the option so that you cannot clear it. If you have attached a recorded narration to the presentation, it will play with the presentation unless you select the "Show without narration" check box.

See Also   For information about recording narrations, see the sidebar titled "Recording a Narration" in Chapter 10.

---

3   Click **OK**.

Slide Show

4   To test the show, move to Slide 1, and click the **Slide Show** button.

The presentation runs continuously, using its transitions, animations, and slide timings.

5   Press [Esc] to stop the slide show.

6   On the **File** menu, click **Save As**.

The Save As dialog box appears.

7   Navigate to the folder where you want to store the self-running presentation.

8   Click the down arrow to the right of the **Save as type** box, and click **PowerPoint Show** in the drop-down list.

9   In the **File name** box, assign a name to the self-running version of the show, and click **Save**.

PowerPoint saves the presentation as a slide show.

10   Close the presentation.

11   When you are ready to run the show, click the **Start** button on the taskbar, click **My Documents**, navigate to the folder where the slide show file is stored, and double-click it.

The slide show opens in Slide Show view and begins to play.

12   Press [Esc] to stop the slide show and exit the presentation.

Using Microsoft Producer to Set Up an Online Broadcast

Microsoft Office Specialist

These days, it is not unusual for an organization to have employees or members in different cities or even in different countries. When it is not possible or desirable to gather people together for a presentation, you can prepare the presentation for broadcast over a computer network or even the Internet by using Microsoft Producer. You can also save the presentation on a Web server so that people who are not able to attend the broadcast can view it later.

Important   To broadcast a presentation, you need Microsoft Producer installed on your computer. This program is not installed by default; to install and use it, you will need to download the necessary software from the Microsoft Office Online Web site. On the Help menu, click Microsoft Office Online, and click Downloads in the left pane of the Web site's home page. Then in the Search box, type *Producer*, and click the Go button. Click the link to the PowerPoint 2003 add-in called Microsoft Producer, and follow the download instructions.

In this exercise, you will use Producer to publish a presentation for online broadcast.

BE SURE TO download Microsoft Producer for PowerPoint 2003 from the Microsoft Office Online Web site before beginning this exercise.
USE the *Broadcast* presentation in the practice file folder for this topic. This practice file is located in the *My Documents\Microsoft Press\PowerPoint 2003 SBS\SettingShow\Broad-castingPresent* folder and can also be accessed by clicking *Start/All Programs/Microsoft Press/PowerPoint 2003 Step by Step*.

1   Click the **Start** menu, point to **All Programs**, point to **Microsoft Office**, and then click **Microsoft Producer for PowerPoint 2003**.

 If the Microsoft Producer dialog box appears asking how you want to create your presentation, click Cancel.

2   On the **File** menu, click **Import**.

 The Import File dialog box appears.

3   Navigate to the *My Documents\Microsoft Press\PowerPoint 2003 SBS\Setting-Show\BroadcastingPresent* folder, and double-click the *Broadcast* file.

 The Import dialog box appears, showing a progress bar while Producer imports your presentation. When the process is complete, your presentation appears on Producer's Media tab.

4   In the **Project Files** pane, click the **Broadcast** presentation icon, and drag it to the **Timeline** at the bottom of the screen.

Producer adds the slides in your presentation to the Slide Track of the Timeline, using the order and duration specified in PowerPoint for each slide.

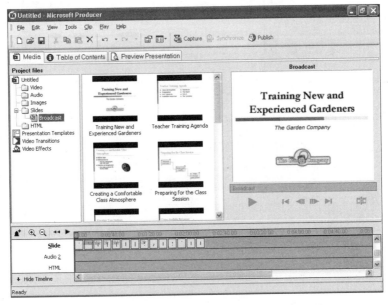

5   Click the **Table of Contents** tab. In the **Introduction** area, type Training New and Experienced Gardeners in the **Title** box, and in the **Presenter** box, type The Garden Company.

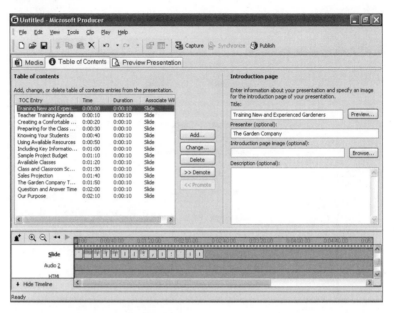

6 On the toolbar, click the **Publish** button.

The first page of the Publish Wizard appears.

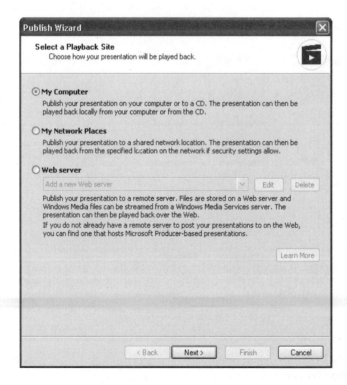

7   Click **Next** to accept My Computer as the location for publishing your presentation.

(You also have the option of publishing the presentation on a network or on a Web server.) The Publishing Destination page appears.

8   In the **File name** box, type Training1. Make sure that the **Publish files to** box specifies that the presentation will be saved in your My Documents folder, and click **Next**.

The Presentation Information page appears.

9   You already specified a title and a presenter on the Producer Table of Contents tab, so click **Next** to continue.

The Publish Setting page appears.

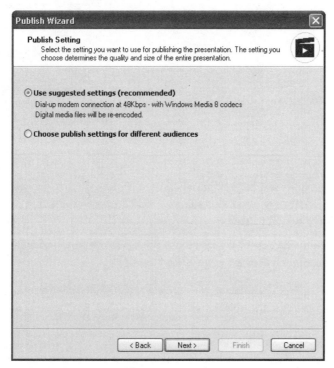

10   Click **Next** to use the suggested settings.

The Publish Your Presentation page appears.

11   Click **Next** to publish your presentation.

The Presentation Preview page appears. You could finish the publication process by clicking Finish, but this page also gives you the opportunity to preview your presentation in a Web browser.

12   In the **Preview presentation for playback in** area, click the **Internet Explorer 5.0 or later for Windows** link.

259

The presentation's Introduction page appears in a browser window, displaying the text you entered on the Producer Table of Contents tab.

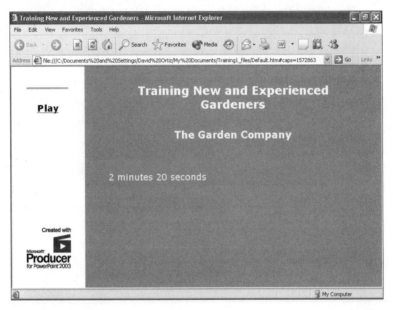

13 Click the **Play** link.

The slide show begins playing in the browser window, just as it would if you were viewing it as a remote broadcast. You can watch the entire slide show, or click the Pause button to stop it.

14 Click the browser window's **Close** button to return to Producer, and on the wizard's **Presentation Preview** page, click **Finish**.

CLOSE Producer, saving your project if you wish, and if you are not continuing on to the next chapter, quit PowerPoint.

Key Points

- You can use Package for CD to create a presentation package that you can copy to a CD or a folder on another computer. This package contains everything you need to run the presentation.

- You can include the PowerPoint Viewer in a presentation package so that you can run the presentation on a computer on which PowerPoint is not installed.

- You can use a variety of toolbar buttons, commands, and keyboard shortcuts to navigate through a presentation in Slide Show view. You can also add actions buttons to slides to assist in navigation.

- You can use different types of pen tools and different pen colors to mark up slides during a slide show, and you can save or discard these annotations.

- When the complete slide show is not desired or required for a particular audience, you can select slides from among all those available to create a custom show.

- You can hide slides and then decide to display them only if they are appropriate for a particular situation or audience.

- You can assign timings to slides manually, or you can practice the slide show and have PowerPoint record the slide timing that you use in rehearsal. You can then use these timings to automatically advance from one slide to the next.

- When you need to give a presentation to a remote audience, you can schedule and host an online broadcast. You can also participate in an online broadcast as an audience member.

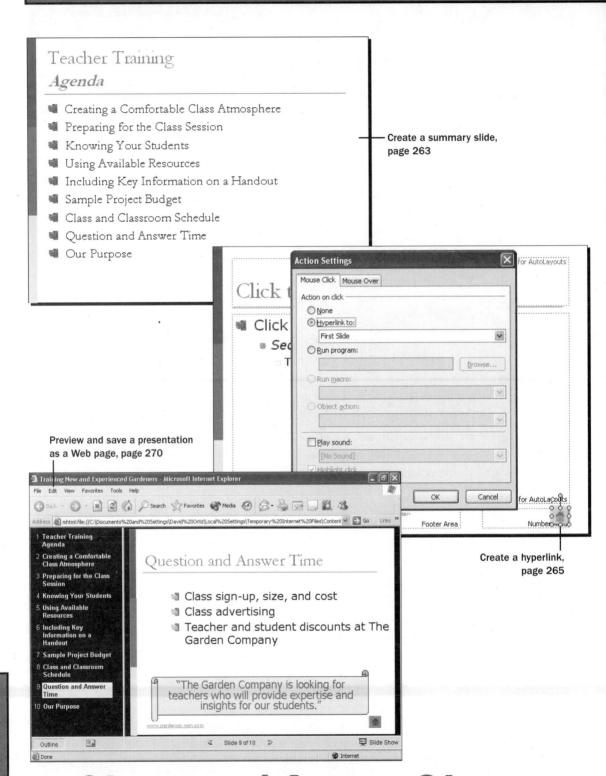

Create a summary slide, page 263

Preview and save a presentation as a Web page, page 270

Create a hyperlink, page 265

14 Creating Web Presentations

In this chapter you will learn to:

✔ Create a summary slide.

✔ Create a hyperlink.

✔ Preview and save a presentation as a Web page.

With Microsoft Office PowerPoint 2003, you can save a presentation as a Web page that can be viewed in a Web browser. PowerPoint provides all the tools you need to convert and display the presentation over an intranet or the Internet. The converted presentation is viewed as a single Web page with a navigation bar that provides easy access to each slide.

To maximize the usefulness of the presentation, you can create a summary slide to serve as a "home page" for your Web-based slide show. You can also create hyperlinks that enable viewers to move to specific slides, to other presentations, or to Web sites. Hyperlinks can also be used to display files created with other programs, such as Microsoft Office Excel worksheets, to clarify assumptions, or to support conclusions.

In this chapter, you'll create a summary slide that can be used as an agenda slide to introduce a presentation. You'll also create hyperlinks to another slide, an Excel · chart, and a Web site, and you'll create an action button that enables viewers of the presentation to jump back to the agenda slide at any time. Finally, you will see how to preview a presentation as a Web page and save a Web version of the presentation.

See Also Do you need only a quick refresher on the topics in this chapter? See the Quick Reference entries on pages l–li.

Important Before you can use the practice files in this chapter, you need to install them from the book's companion CD to their default location. See "Using the Book's CD-ROM" on page xiii for more information.

Creating a Summary Slide

A *summary slide* is a list of the titles, formatted as bullet points, from selected slides in your presentation. You can create a summary slide to use as an *agenda slide* or as the *home page* for an online presentation.

To create a summary slide, you select the slides you want to include from Slide Sorter view, and then you click the Summary Slide button on the Slide Sorter toolbar. In front of the first selected slide, PowerPoint creates a new slide with the titles of the selected slides as bullet points.

In this exercise, you will create a summary slide to be used as an agenda slide for a Web-based presentation.

BE SURE TO start PowerPoint before beginning this exercise.
USE the *CreateAgenda* presentation in the practice file folder for this topic. This practice file is located in the *My Documents\Microsoft Press\PowerPoint 2003 SBS\CreatingWeb\CreatingSummary* folder and can also be accessed by clicking *Start/All Programs/Microsoft Press/PowerPoint 2003 Step by Step.*
OPEN the *CreateAgenda* presentation.

Slide Sorter View

1 In the lower-left corner of the presentation window, click the **Slide Sorter View** button.

Slide Sorter view appears with Slide 1 selected.

2 On the **Edit** menu, click **Select All** to select all of the slides in the presentation.

Summary Slide

3 On the Slide Sorter toolbar, click the **Summary Slide** button.

PowerPoint creates a new Slide 1 with the titles of the selected slides as bullet points.

New summary slide

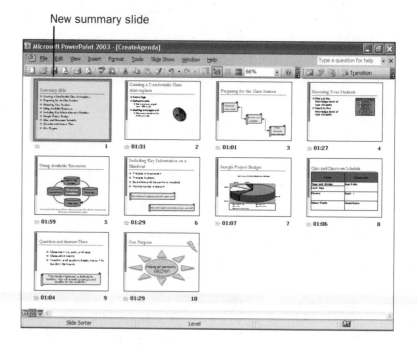

Normal View

4 In the lower-left corner of the presentation window, click the **Normal View** button to display Slide 1 in Normal view.

5 Select the *Summary Slide* title text.

6 Type **Teacher Training**, and press the ⌈Enter⌋ key.

The *Teacher Training* text moves up and becomes smaller to leave room for a second line of text within the title text object.

18 ▾
Font Size

7 On the Formatting toolbar, click the down arrow to the right of the **Font Size** box, and click **36**.

The text of the second line will be smaller than the first.

B **I**
Bold Italic

8 On the Formatting toolbar, click the **Bold** button, and then click the **Italic** button.

9 Type **Agenda**.

10 Click a blank area of the slide to deselect the object.

Teacher Training

Agenda

- Creating a Comfortable Class Atmosphere
- Preparing for the Class Session
- Knowing Your Students
- Using Available Resources
- Including Key Information on a Handout
- Sample Project Budget
- Class and Classroom Schedule
- Question and Answer Time
- Our Purpose

Save

11 On the Standard toolbar, click the **Save** button to save the presentation.

CLOSE the *CreateAgenda* presentation.

Creating a Hyperlink

Microsoft Office Specialist

The power of a Web presentation lies in its ability to include *hyperlinks* to different places: to another slide in the presentation, to another slide show, to a file on your computer or your company's intranet, or to a Web address. You use the Action Settings command on the Slide Show menu to create these hyperlinks.

You can add a hyperlink to any text or object—a shape, table, graph, or picture. Then you can jump directly to the linked location by clicking the text or object. If you have text within a shape, you can establish separate hyperlinks for the text and the shape. After creating a hyperlink, you can edit the object without losing the hyperlink (although deleting the object also deletes the hyperlink).

In addition to attaching hyperlinks to text or objects, you can also attach them to PowerPoint's predefined *action buttons*, which include the Home, Help, Information, Back, Next, Beginning, End, and Return buttons. You add an action button to a slide by clicking Action Buttons on the Slide Show menu, clicking a button type, dragging to create a button of that type on a slide or the Slide Master, and then specifying its link.

In this exercise, you will create a hyperlink from one slide to another. You will also create hyperlinks to an Excel chart and to a Web site. You will then create an action button that jumps to the presentation's agenda page, add a sound to the button, and then test it.

USE the *CreateLink* presentation and *GardenBudget* workbook in the practice file folder for this topic. These practice files are located in the *My Documents\Microsoft Press\PowerPoint 2003 SBS \CreatingWeb\CreatingHyperlink* folder and can also be accessed by clicking *Start/All Programs/Microsoft Press/PowerPoint 2003 Step by Step*.
OPEN the *CreateLink* presentation.

1. Move to Slide 3, select *Gather your supplies* in the middle text box, and on the **Slide Show** menu, click **Action Settings**.

   The Action Settings dialog box appears, displaying the Mouse Click tab.

2. Select the **Hyperlink to** option, click the down arrow to the right of the box below **Hyperlink to**, scroll down the list of destinations, and click **Slide**.

   The Hyperlink to Slide dialog box appears.

3. In the **Slide title** list, click **5. Using Available Resources**.

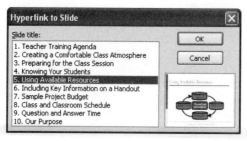

4. Click **OK**.

5. In the **Action Settings** dialog box, click **OK**, and then click a blank area of the slide.

   The text is underlined to indicate that it is a hyperlink, and it takes on the accent and hyperlink color in the slide color scheme, which is gold.

Slide Show

6 In the lower-left corner of the presentation window, click the **Slide Show** button.

PowerPoint displays Slide 3 in Slide Show view, and the slide title appears.

7 Click the mouse button to display the boxes and connectors.

8 Move the mouse to display the pointer, and then click the *Gather your supplies* hyperlink.

The slide show jumps to Slide 5.

9 Press the [Esc] key to end the slide show.

10 Move to Slide 7, click the chart object, and on the **Slide Show** menu, click **Action Settings**.

The Action Settings dialog box appears, displaying the Mouse Click tab.

11 Select the **Hyperlink to** option, click the down arrow to the right of the box below **Hyperlink to**, and then click **Other File** at the bottom of the list.

The Hyperlink to Other File dialog box appears.

12 Navigate to the *My Documents\Microsoft Press\PowerPoint 2003 SBS\CreatingWeb \Creating Hyperlink* folder, and double-click the *GardenBudget* file.

The path of the file you selected appears in the box below "Hyperlink to" in the Action Settings dialog box.

13 Click **OK**.

14 Click the **Slide Show** button, and when the chart appears on Slide 7, click it.

Tip The pointer changes to a pointing hand when you move it over the chart object. Any time the pointer has this shape, you can click to follow a hyperlink.

Excel opens and displays a pie chart showing the flower garden budget.

15 On the **File** menu, click **Exit**, and then click **No** when you are prompted to save changes to the Excel file.

Excel quits, and you return to the slide show.

16 Press [Esc] to end the slide show.

17 On the **View** menu, point to **Master**, and click **Slide Master**.

The Slide Master appears.

Insert
Hyperlink

18 In the lower-left corner of the slide, select *www.gardenco.msn.com*, and on the Standard toolbar, click the **Insert Hyperlink** button. Then if necessary, click the **Existing File or Web Page** option in the **Link to** bar.

The Insert Hyperlink dialog box appears. A blinking insertion point in the Address box indicates where you should type the Web site's *URL (Uniform Resource Locator)*.

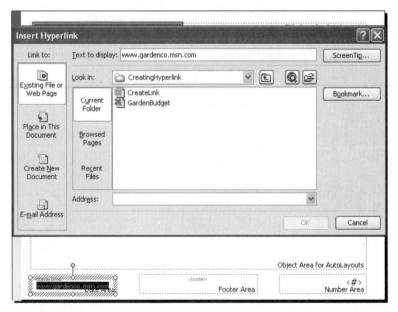

Important   A Web site's URL consists of three parts: the prefix, in this case *http://*, which indicates that the *Hypertext Transfer Protocol* is being used to access an address on the Internet; a network identification, such as *www* for *World Wide Web*; and a site or domain name, such as *gardenco.msn.com* (which is fictitious).

19 In the **Address** box, type **http://www.gardenco.msn.com**, and click **OK**. Then click a blank area of the slide

The Web site address in the lower-left corner of the slide is now gold and underlined and is recognizable as a hyperlink.

Action button:
Home

20 On the **Slide Show** menu, point to **Action Buttons**, and in the second column of the first row of the button palette, click the **Action Button: Home** button.

The pointer changes to a cross-hair pointer.

21 In the lower-right corner of the slide, drag to create a Home action button.

When you release the mouse button, the Action Settings dialog box appears with the "Hyperlink to" option selected and First Slide in the box below. At the bottom of the dialog box, the "Highlight click" check box is selected, but dimmed to indicate that you cannot change this setting.

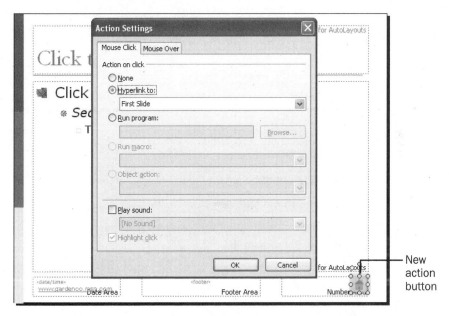

New action button

22 Select the **Play sound** check box, click the down arrow to the right of the box below **Play sound**, scroll down the list, click **Camera**, and then click **OK**.

The selected sound will play when the Home button is clicked.

23 Right-click the action button, and click **Format AutoShape** on the shortcut menu.

24 On the **Colors and Lines** tab, click the down arrow to the right of the **Color** box, click the **Gold** box in the color scheme area, and click **OK**.

The Home button is now the accent and hyperlink color.

25 On the Slide Master View toolbar, click the **Close Master View** button.

Slide 7 appears in Normal view with the hyperlinked Web address in the lower-left corner and the Home button in the lower-right corner.

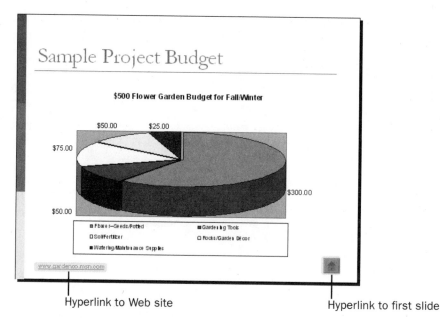

Hyperlink to Web site   Hyperlink to first slide

26 Click the **Slide Show** button.

The slide entitled *Sample Project Budget* appears.

27 Click the **Home** button.

The slide show jumps to the first slide in the presentation—the agenda slide—and the camera sound plays.

Save

28 Press [Esc] to end the slide show, and then on the Standard toolbar, click the **Save** button to save the presentation.

CLOSE the *CreateLink* presentation.

Previewing and Saving a Presentation as a Web Page

Microsoft Office Specialist

With PowerPoint, you can easily save a presentation as a Web page in *HTML (Hypertext Markup Language)* format with the extension *.html*. HTML consists of codes called *tags* that determine how text and graphics are displayed in a *Web browser* such as Microsoft Internet Explorer.

Before you save a presentation as a Web page, you should preview the presentation to see what it will look like when it's displayed in a Web browser. You can preview a presentation by using the Web Page Preview command on the File menu. You can then make adjustments to your presentation in PowerPoint before converting it to Web format. In addition, before saving a Web presentation you might want to save the presentation's graphics in PNG (Portable Networks Graphics) format. PNG graphic files are smaller than those of most other graphic formats, so they can be saved and downloaded faster.

Important Although PNG format is recommended for Microsoft Internet Explorer 5.0 or later, not all browsers support it. If you know that some viewers of your presentation use a different browser, you might not want to save your graphics in this format.

When you are ready to convert your presentation to HTML for display in a Web browser, you use the Save as Web Page command on the File menu. PowerPoint creates a folder with the same name as the Web presentation. In this folder is a set of files that PowerPoint uses to display the presentation as a Web page. If you move the Web presentation to another location, you must also move this folder; otherwise your Web browser won't be able to display the presentation.

Tip You can also create a Web page from a presentation by using the Save As command on the File menu. In the Save As dialog box, click the down arrow to the right of the "Save as type" box, and then click Web Page or Web Archive. The Web Page type produces the same results as the Save as Web Page command. The Web Archive type saves all the elements of the presentation, including text and graphics, in a single file with the extension *.mht*. In your browser, you can open a PowerPoint presentation that has been saved in either Web Page or Web Archive format.

When PowerPoint previews or saves a presentation as a Web page, it puts the title specified in the presentation's *properties* in the title bar and sets up a *navigation frame* down the left side of the page. This frame resembles the Outline tab of the Outline/ Slides pane in Normal view, except that it contains only the slides' titles. Clicking a title in the navigation frame displays that slide in the adjacent frame.

Tip To view the properties assigned to a presentation, click Properties on PowerPoint's File menu. The Summary tab lists a number of properties, including the title, subject, and author. If you created the presentation, you can change these properties to suit your needs. (Whether other people can change them depends on the security settings assigned to the presentation on the Security tab of the Options dialog box or via Information Rights Manager.)

After a Web presentation is converted to HTML, it is not cast in stone. You can open the presentation in PowerPoint and make changes just as you normally would. Clicking the Save button saves the changes to the HTML file. You can also save the changes in a regular PowerPoint presentation by clicking the Save As command on the File menu and changing the "Save as type" setting to Presentation.

In this exercise, you will preview a presentation as a Web page and save its graphics in PNG format. You will then convert the presentation to a Web page, view the presentation in your Web browser, edit it in PowerPoint, and save the changes.

USE the *CreateWeb* presentation in the practice file folder for this topic. This practice file is located in the *My Documents\Microsoft Press\PowerPoint 2003 SBS\CreatingWeb\PreviewingPage* folder and can also be accessed by clicking *Start/All Programs/Microsoft Press/PowerPoint 2003 Step by Step*.
OPEN the *CreateWeb* presentation.

Maximize

1 On the **File** menu, click **Web Page Preview**, and then click your Web browser's **Maximize** button, if necessary.

Troubleshooting If Internet Explorer is not your default Web browser, follow the necessary prompts to proceed in Netscape Navigator or a different browser.

The message *Preparing for Web Page Preview* appears in the status bar, along with a status indicator, and then your Web browser opens, displaying the presentation as a Web page. The title bar displays the name assigned to the presentation in the Properties dialog box, and a navigation frame on the left side of the window lists all the slide titles.

2 In the list of slide titles in the navigation frame, click *9 Question and Answer Time*.

Slide 9 appears in the frame on the right.

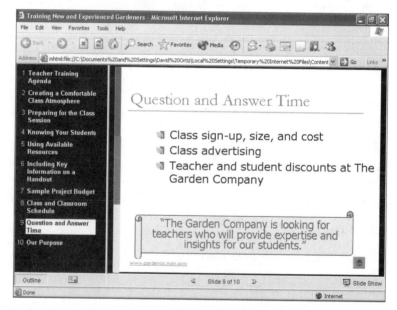

3 In the lower-right corner of the slide, click the **Home** button to jump back to Slide 1.

4   On the **File** menu, click **Close**.

Your browser closes, and you return to PowerPoint.

5   On the **Tools** menu, click **Options**.

The Options dialog box appears.

6   Click the **General** tab, and then click **Web Options**.

The Web Options dialog box appears.

7   Click the **Browsers** tab.

8   Select the **Allow PNG as a graphics format** check box.

9   Click the **General** tab.

10 Make sure that the **Add slide navigation controls** check box is selected, and then click the down arrow to the right of the **Colors** box, and click **Presentation colors (accent color)**.

11 Select the **Show slide animation while browsing** check box.

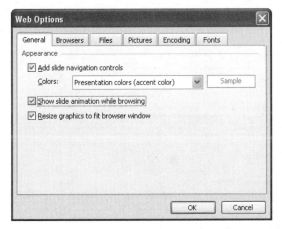

12 Click **OK** to close the **Web Options** dialog box, and then click **OK** to close the **Options** dialog box.

13 On the **File** menu, click **Save as Web Page**.

The Save As dialog box appears with Single File Web Page specified in the "Save as type" box at the bottom of the dialog box.

14 In the **File name** box, click to the right of the existing file name, and type Page.

The Web page will be saved with the name *CreateWebPage*.

15 Click the down arrow to the right of the **Save in** box, and make sure that the file will be saved in the *My Documents\Microsoft Press\PowerPoint 2003 SBS\CreatingWeb \PreviewingPage* folder.

Tip You can also save a presentation to an FTP site. *FTP (File Transfer Protocol)* is a communications method that you can use to quickly transfer files to a different location over the Internet. To save a presentation to an FTP site, click the down arrow to the right of the "Save in" box in the Save As dialog box, click FTP Locations in the list, and navigate to the location where you want to save the presentation. Then assign the presentation a name, and click Save.

16 Click **Publish**.

The Publish as Web Page dialog box appears.

17 In the **Browser support** area, select the **All browsers listed above (creates larger files)** option.

This option makes the Web presentation compatible with all browsers.

18 Make sure that the **Complete presentation** option is selected and that the **Open published Web page in browser** check box at the bottom of the dialog box is cleared.

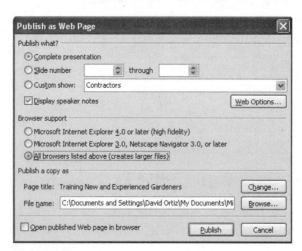

19 Click **Publish**.

PowerPoint saves the presentation as a Web page.

20 On the Standard toolbar, click the **Save** button.

Save

PowerPoint saves the CreateWeb presentation.

Close Window

Open

21 At the right end of the menu bar, click the **Close Window** button.

The CreateWeb presentation closes.

22 On the Standard toolbar, click the **Open** button.

The Open dialog box appears. The file list includes a new folder with the same name as the Web page file that you just saved.

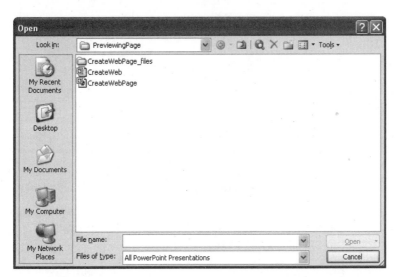

23 In the list of folders and files, click the *CreateWebPage* file (not the *CreateWebPage_files* folder).

24 Click the down arrow to the right of the **Open** button, click **Open in Browser**, and when a message warns you to click only those hyperlinks that are from trusted sources, click **Yes**.

Your Web browser opens and displays Slide 1.

25 Click a few slide titles to move around the presentation, and then on the browser's **File** menu, click **Close**.

Your browser closes, and you return to PowerPoint.

26 On the Standard toolbar, click the **Open** button, and in the **Open** dialog box, double-click *CreateWebPage*.

The Web presentation opens in PowerPoint, where it looks like a regular presentation.

27 Display the Drawing toolbar, click **AutoShapes**, click **Stars and Banners**, click the banner in the second column of the last row, and drag to create a banner in the upper-right corner of the agenda slide.

28 On the Standard toolbar, click the **Save** button to save the presentation, and then click the **Close Window** button to close it.

29 On the Standard toolbar, click the **Open** button, and in the **Open** dialog box, click *CreateWebPage*. Then click the down arrow to the right of the **Open** button, click **Open in Browser**, and click **Yes** in the trusted hyperlinks message box.

Your Web browser opens and displays Slide 1 with the banner AutoShape you just added.

30 On the browser's **File** menu, click **Close**.

Your browser closes, and you return to PowerPoint.

BE SURE TO turn off the Drawing toolbar if you want to save screen space, and if you are not continuing on to the next chapter, quit PowerPoint.

Creating a Web Presentation by Using the AutoContent Wizard

You can use the AutoContent Wizard to create a presentation designed for Web viewing. When you create this type of presentation, PowerPoint places action buttons on the screen for the user to click to navigate through the slide show.

To create a Web presentation with the AutoContent Wizard:

1 On the **View** menu, click **Task Pane**, and then if the New Presentation task pane is not displayed, click the task pane's down arrow and click **New Presentation** in the drop-down list.

2   In the **New** area, click **From AutoContent wizard**.

The AutoContent Wizard opens.

3   After reading the introduction, click **Next**.

4   Select a presentation type, and click **Next**.

5   Select the **Web presentation** option, and click **Next**.

6   Type the title for the presentation's first slide, add information to the footer, if desired, and then click **Next**.

7   Click **Finish** to create the Web presentation.

8   On the **File** menu, click **Save As**, change the **Save as type** setting to **Single File Web Page**, and click **Publish**.

9   Set up the Web options as you want them, click **Publish**, and close the presentation without saving it.

10   Click the **Open** button, click the Web presentation, click the down arrow to the right of the **Open** button, and click **Open in Browser**.

11   Read any security messages that appear, clicking **Yes** or **OK** if you want to proceed, and then test your Web presentation in your browser.

Key Points

- You can create a summary slide to use as an agenda slide or as the home page for a Web presentation.

- You can add a hyperlink to any text or object to directly link it to another slide, presentation, file, or Web address.

- You can create action buttons to which you can attach navigational hyperlinks.

- You can save a presentation as a Web page in HTML. When it is displayed in a Web browser, the page has a navigation frame with hyperlinks that enable the viewer to jump from slide to slide.

- After you save a Web presentation, you don't have to edit the HTML file to make changes. You can open the Web presentation in PowerPoint and make and save changes that will be reflected in the presentation the next time it is viewed in a Web browser.

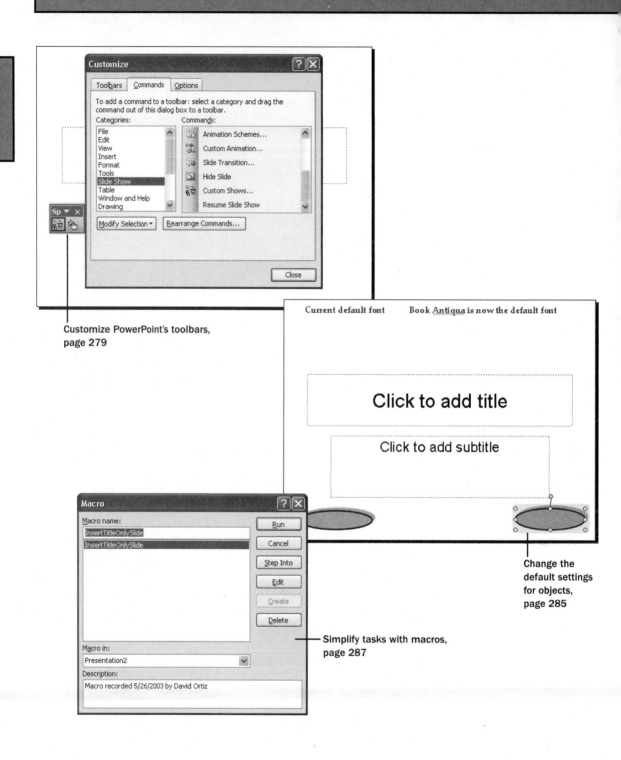

Customize PowerPoint's toolbars,
page 279

Change the
default settings
for objects,
page 285

Simplify tasks with macros,
page 287

Chapter 15 at a Glance

15 Customizing PowerPoint

In this chapter you will learn to:

✔   Customize PowerPoint's toolbars.

✔   Change the default settings for objects.

✔   Simplify tasks with macros.

Microsoft Office PowerPoint 2003 has many optional settings that can affect either the screen display or the operation of certain functions. You can customize these settings to optimize the way you work and perform tasks. For example, you can change toolbars so that the tools that you use most often are readily found. Or you can change the initial formatting of text that appears in text boxes and of other objects. If you frequently perform a repetitive task in PowerPoint, you can also record the sequence of steps as a macro to automate the task and save time.

In this chapter, you'll customize the PowerPoint screen display to meet your needs. You'll also change toolbars so that the tools that you use most often are easy to find. In addition, you will find out how to customize default drawing and font attributes. Finally, you'll create macros to help you automate a repetitive task.

See Also   Do you need only a quick refresher on the topics in this chapter? See the Quick Reference entries on pages lii–liii.

Important   You will create all the files that you need during the course of this chapter, so you will not need any practice files.

Customizing PowerPoint's Toolbars

PowerPoint has several preset toolbars with buttons that can save you time and effort. Different toolbars appear depending on which view is active and which object is selected. In Normal view, for example, you see the Standard and Formatting toolbars, and the Drawing toolbar might also appear unless you have turned it off to save screen space. If you select a picture on a slide, the Picture toolbar is also displayed.

In this book, the Standard and Formatting toolbars appear on two rows to make locating specific buttons easier. You can also arrange these toolbars on the same row below the menu bar by clicking the Toolbar Options button at the right end of a toolbar and then clicking Show Buttons on One Row. You can move a toolbar to a new location on the screen by dragging its *move handle*—the four dots at the left end of the toolbar. If you drag a toolbar to an edge of the screen, it is *docked* along that edge, and if you drag it anywhere else, it becomes a *floating toolbar*, with a title bar, a Toolbar Options down arrow, and a Close button. You move a floating toolbar by dragging its title bar, or you can double-click the title bar to dock the toolbar.

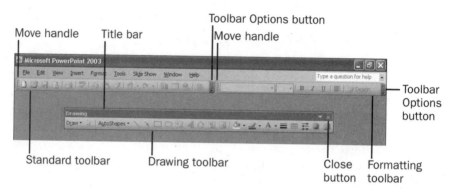

Move handle   Title bar   Toolbar Options button   Move handle

Standard toolbar   Drawing toolbar   Close button   Formatting toolbar   Toolbar Options button

If you display the Standard and Formatting toolbars on one row, not all their buttons can be visible at once, so PowerPoint hides the buttons you use less frequently, leaving visible the buttons you use the most or are most likely to use. You can display hidden buttons by clicking the Toolbar Options button and then clicking the button you want on a drop-down palette. (That button then replaces one you have not used lately on the toolbar.)

You can customize both the Standard and Formatting toolbars by adding or removing buttons, not just hiding or showing them. You can add buttons by clicking the Add or Remove Buttons command on the Toolbar Options drop-down palette, clicking the name of the toolbar, and then clicking the button you want to add or remove. You can also create new toolbars that contain only the buttons you need or use most frequently by clicking Customize on the Tools menu. You can use the Customize dialog box to rearrange buttons on a new or existing toolbar, to move buttons from one toolbar to another, or to delete the toolbars you have created. (You can't delete the built-in toolbars.)

In this exercise, you will move the Formatting toolbar, arrange the Standard and Formatting toolbars on the same row, reset the toolbars to show the default buttons, and add and remove a toolbar button. You will also create a new toolbar and add, arrange, and delete buttons.

BE SURE TO start PowerPoint before beginning this exercise. If your Standard and Formatting toolbars don't appear on two rows before you begin, click Customize on the Tools menu, click the Options tab, check the "Show Standard and Formatting toolbars on two rows" check box, and click OK. OPEN a new, blank presentation, and close the task pane.

1 Point to the move handle (the four dots) at the left end of the Formatting toolbar.

The pointer changes to a four-headed arrow.

2 Drag the toolbar down and to the right.

The toolbar becomes a floating toolbar with a title bar, a Toolbar Options down arrow, and a Close box.

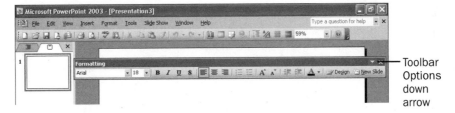

Toolbar Options down arrow

3 On the **Tools** menu, click **Customize**.

The Customize dialog box appears.

4 Click the **Options** tab, if necessary.

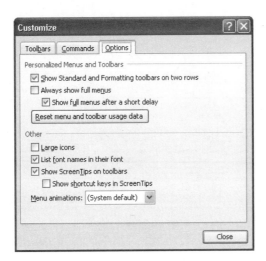

5 Clear the **Show Standard and Formatting toolbars on two rows** check box.

Behind the dialog box, the Formatting toolbar returns to its former position—docked below the Standard toolbar.

6 Click **Reset menu and toolbar usage data**, and when PowerPoint warns that the record of commands you have used will be deleted, click **Yes** to continue.

7 Click **Close**.

The Customize dialog box closes and the toolbars arrange themselves on one row.

8 On either toolbar, click the **Toolbar Options** button.

Toolbar Options

9 Point to **Add or Remove Buttons**, and then point to **Formatting**.

A submenu opens, displaying buttons that you can add to or delete from the Formatting toolbar. The buttons with a check mark next to them currently appear on the Formatting Toolbar or on the Toolbar Options button palette; those without a check mark can be added.

10 Click the **Layout** button in the submenu.

A check mark appears next to it, and the button appears on the Formatting toolbar just to the left of the Toolbar Options down arrow.

Click a button in this submenu to add it to the toolbar.

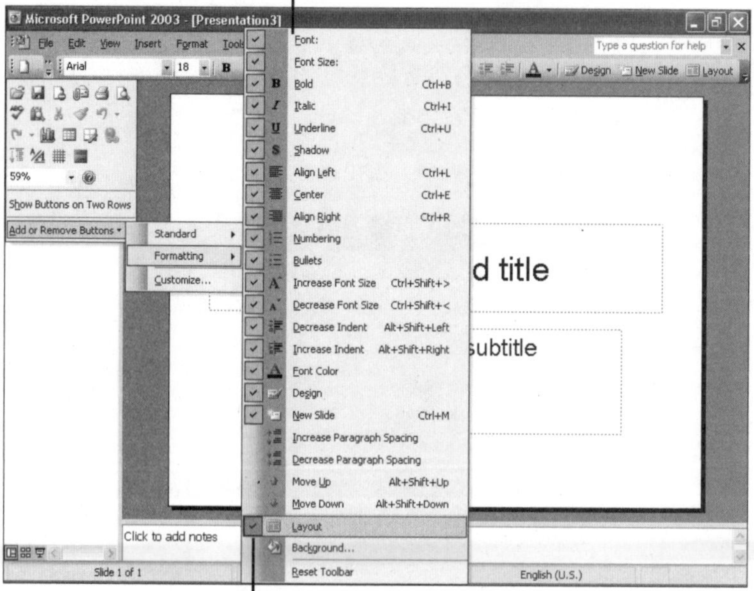

This button has been added.

11 Click the **Layout** button again.

The button is removed from the toolbar.

12 Click anywhere in the presentation window to close the list.

13 On the **Tools** menu, click **Customize**.

The Customize dialog box appears.

14 Click the **Toolbars** tab.

15 Click **New**.

The New Toolbar dialog box appears.

16 In the **Toolbar name** box, type Special, and click **OK**.

In the Toolbars list, *Special* appears at the bottom of the list with a check mark next to it. A small empty toolbar appears in the presentation window.

New toolbar

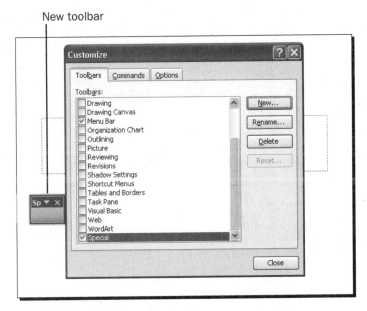

Troubleshooting   You might have to move the dialog box out of the way (by dragging its title bar) to see the new toolbar.

17 Click the **Commands** tab to display a list of available PowerPoint commands.

18 In the **Categories** list, click **Slide Show** to display a list of commands related to setting up and running a slide show.

19 In the **Commands** list, click **Action Settings**, and then drag it to the Special toolbar.

As you drag the button onto the Special toolbar, a black insertion bar appears to indicate the location of the button. When you release the mouse button, the Action Settings button appears on the Special toolbar.

20 Scroll to the bottom of the **Commands** list, and then drag the **Custom Shows** button to the right end of the Special toolbar.

The Custom Shows button appears on the Special toolbar.

21 Drag the **Custom Shows** button to the left of the **Action Settings** button.

The Custom Shows button appears in its new location on the toolbar.

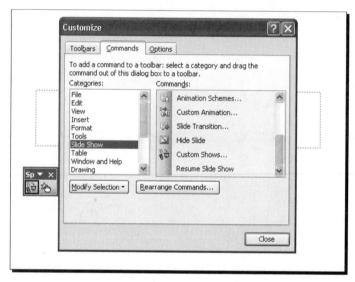

22 Drag the **Custom Shows** button off the toolbar.

The button is removed from the Special toolbar.

23 In the **Customize** dialog box, click the **Toolbars** tab to display a list of current toolbars.

24 With **Special** highlighted in the **Toolbars** list, click **Delete**, and then click **OK** to confirm the deletion.

The toolbar is deleted.

25 Click **Close** to close the **Customize** dialog box.

26 In the presentation window, click the **Close Window** button.

Close Window

BE SURE TO display the Standard and Formatting toolbars on two rows if you want your screen to look like those in this book.

Changing the Default Settings for Objects

When you create an object such as a text box, PowerPoint applies a set of default attributes to it. These attributes include settings such as the fill color, shadow style, and line style. For text boxes, the attributes also include font settings such as the font, size, and style—regular, bold, and italic—as well as other effects—underline, small capitals, embossing, and so on. If your presentation will include objects with attributes that are different than PowerPoint's defaults, you can change the defaults for that presentation to save yourself some formatting steps.

Tip To learn the current font default settings for your presentation, you can draw an object or create a text box and then check the state of the buttons on the Formatting or Drawing toolbar.

In this exercise, you will change the default font and other default object attributes.

BE SURE TO display the Drawing toolbar before beginning this exercise.
OPEN a new, blank presentation, and if necessary, close the task pane.

Text Box

1 On the Drawing toolbar, click the **Text Box** button.

2 In the **Slide** pane, click the upper-left corner of the title slide to create a text box.

3 Type Current default font.

4 Click the text box's frame to select the box, and then on the **Format** menu, click **Font**.

The Font dialog box appears, showing the current default font settings.

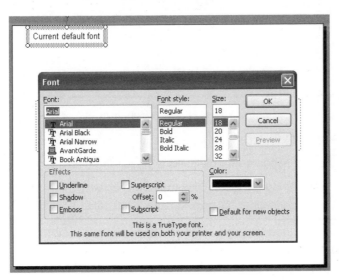

5   In the **Font** list, click **Book Antiqua**.

6   In the **Font style** list, click **Bold**.

7   In the **Size** list, click **20**.

8   Click the down arrow to the right of the **Color** box, and click the **Dark Blue** box in the color palette.

9   Select the **Default for new objects** check box, and click **OK**.

The new settings are applied to the selected text box.

10   On the Drawing toolbar, click the **Text Box** button, and on the slide, click to the right of the existing text box to create a new one.

11   Type Book Antiqua is now the default font.

The text appears with the new default settings.

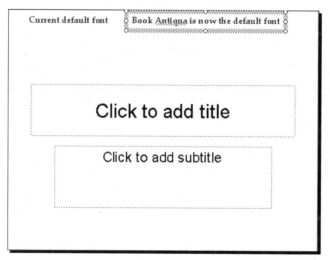

12   On the Drawing toolbar, click the **Oval** button.

Oval

13   In the lower-left corner of the slide, drag to draw an oval.

The oval appears with the current default fill color, shadow style, and line style.

Fill Color

14   On the Drawing toolbar, click the down arrow to the right of the **Fill Color** button, and click the **Lime Green** box on the color palette.

Shadow Style

15   On the Drawing toolbar, click the **Shadow Style** button, and in the second column of the top row, click **Shadow Style 2** on the style palette.

Line Style

16 On the Drawing toolbar, click the **Line Style** button, and click **3pt** on the line palette.

Tip You can make additional changes to the object, such as font attributes and line color, to suit your needs.

17 On the Drawing toolbar, click **Draw**, and then click **Set AutoShape Defaults**.

18 On the Drawing toolbar, click the **Oval** button, and drag a new oval object in the slide's lower-right corner.

Both oval objects have the new default attributes.

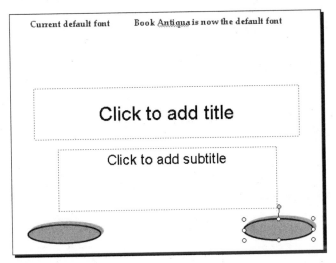

Close Window

19 In the presentation window, click the **Close Window** button, and then click **No** when you are prompted to save changes to the presentation.

BE SURE TO turn off the Drawing toolbar to save screen space.

Simplifying Tasks with Macros

If you perform a task often, you can record a *macro* that automates the task. A macro is a series of commands and functions, stored in a *Visual Basic* module, that you can run with one step whenever you need to perform a task. You can record a macro in PowerPoint to combine multiple commands into one, to speed up routine editing and formatting tasks, or to make a dialog box option more accessible.

Before you record or write a macro, you need to plan the steps and commands that you want the macro to perform. After you record a macro, it is listed in the Macro dialog box, and you can run it from there.

In this exercise, you will record a macro and then run it. You will then delete it.

OPEN a new, blank presentation, and if necessary, close the task pane.

1   On the **Tools** menu, click **Options**, and on the **View** tab, select the **Slide Layout task pane when inserting new slides** check box (if it is not already selected), and click **OK**.

2   On the **Tools** menu, point to **Macro**, and then click **Record New Macro**.

The Record Macro dialog box appears.

3   In the **Macro name** box, type InsertTitleOnlySlide.

Tip   Macro names cannot contain spaces.

4   Click **OK**.

The Stop Recording toolbar appears, containing nothing but a Stop Recording button.

5   On the Formatting toolbar, click the **New Slide** button.

PowerPoint inserts Slide 2 with the "Title and Text" layout and opens the Slide Layout task pane so that you can change the layout of the new slide if the default is not what you want.

6   In the **Text Layouts** area of the **Slide Layout** task pane, click the **Title Only** layout.

The layout of Slide 2 changes to reflect your selection.

Stop Recording

7   On the Stop Recording toolbar, click the **Stop Recording** button.

The Stop Recording toolbar closes.

8   On the **Tools** menu, point to **Macro**, and then click **Macros**.

The Macro dialog box appears, with *InsertTitleOnlySlide* highlighted in the "Macro name" area.

9   Click **Run**.

The Macro dialog box closes, and PowerPoint executes the macro, inserting a new Slide 2 with the Title Only layout, and renumbering the old Slide 2 to Slide 3.

Slide created by running macro   Slide created while recording macro

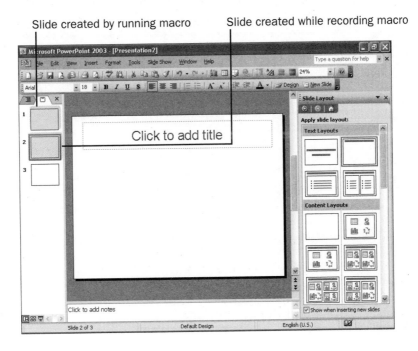

> **Tip** If you know how to program in Visual Basic, you can use the *Visual Basic Editor* to edit a macro you have recorded. To edit a macro, click Macro on the Tools menu, click Macros to open the Macro dialog box, click the macro you want to edit, and then click Edit to open the macro in Visual Basic Editor. You can also open the Visual Basic Editor without opening an existing macro by pointing to Macro on the Tools menu and then clicking Visual Basic Editor on the submenu. (You can also use the Visual Basic Editor to write a new macro from scratch.)

10 On the **Tools** menu, point to **Macro**, and then click **Macros**.

The Macro dialog box appears, with InsertTitleOnlySlide highlighted in the "Macro name" area.

11 Click **Delete**.

PowerPoint asks you to confirm that you want to delete the macro.

12 Click **Delete** again.

13 In the presentation window, click the **Close Window** button, and then click **No** when you are prompted to save changes to the presentation.

Close Window

Adding Functionality to PowerPoint with Add-Ins

You can use supplemental programs, called *add-ins*, to extend the capabilities of PowerPoint by adding custom commands and specialized features. PowerPoint add-ins might be available on The Microsoft Office System 2003 CD-ROM or on the Microsoft Office Online Web site. Otherwise, you can obtain add-ins from independent software vendors, or if you are proficient in Visual Basic, you can write your own add-ins by using Visual Basic Editor.

To use an add-in, you must first install it on your computer and then load it into your computer's memory. PowerPoint add-ins have the file-name extension *.ppa*.

Tip To conserve memory and maintain PowerPoint's running speed, it's a good idea to unload add-in programs that you don't use often. When you unload an add-in, its features and commands are removed from PowerPoint, but the program itself remains on your computer for easy reloading.

To install and load an add-in program:

1 On the **Tools** menu, click **Add-Ins**.

The Add-Ins dialog box appears.

2 Click **Add New**.

The Add New PowerPoint Add-In dialog box appears.

3   Click the down arrow to the right of the **Look in** box, and then click the folder where you have stored PowerPoint add-in programs.

4   In the list of file and folder names, click the add-in you want.

5   Click **OK**.

The Add New PowerPoint Add-In dialog box closes, and in the Add-Ins dialog box, the new add-in now appears in the list of those that are available for loading into memory.

6   In the **Available Add-Ins** list, click the add-in you want to load, and then click **Load**.

The add-in program is loaded.

7   Click **Close**.

The Add-Ins dialog box closes, and the add-in is available for use in PowerPoint.

To unload an add-in:

1   On the **Tools** menu, click **Add-Ins**.

The Add-Ins dialog box appears.

2   Click the add-in you want to unload.

3   Click **Unload** to remove the add-in from memory but keep its name in the list, or click **Remove** to remove the add-in from the list entirely.

4   Click **Close** to close the **Add-Ins** dialog box.

Key Points

- In addition to displaying and hiding toolbars, you can move them to locate them conveniently.

- You can create new toolbars that contain the buttons you use most frequently. You can customize the arrangement of buttons on a new or existing toolbar, and you can move buttons from one toolbar to another.

- You can change the default settings for new objects, such as text boxes, to the attributes you prefer.

- You can record a macro in PowerPoint to automate a repetitive task.

Glossary

action button Navigation buttons that can be added to slides.

active cell A selected cell.

Active Directory A network service that stores information about resources, such as computers and printers.

add-ins Supplemental programs that extend a program's capabilities.

adjustable objects Objects with an adjustment handle (a small yellow diamond) that allows you to alter the appearance of the object without changing its size.

adjustment handle A small yellow diamond that indicates a shape is adjustable. You can use this handle to alter the appearance of the shape without changing its size.

agenda slide A slide used at the beginning of a presentation that outlines in bulleted points the presentation's material.

animated pictures GIF (Graphics Interchange Format) or digital video files that you can insert into a slide presentation as a movie.

animation scheme A set of professionally designed animations divided into three categories: Subtle, Moderate, and Exciting.

arc A curved line whose angle you can change by dragging an adjustment handle.

attribute A changeable characteristic of a shape—such as fill, line, and shadow—or of text—such as style, font, color, embossment, and shadow.

AutoContent Wizard A wizard that takes you through a step-by-step process to create a presentation, prompting you for presentation information as you go.

AutoCorrect A feature that corrects common capitalization and spelling errors (such as changing as *teh* to *the*) as you type them.

automatic layout behavior A feature that recognizes when you insert an object onto a slide and changes the layout to fit the objects on the slide.

background The underlying colors, shading, texture, and style of the color scheme.

bullet points A list of items in which each item is preceded by a symbol.

button A graphical image or text box that executes a command. Buttons appear on toolbars, in dialog boxes, and in other display elements.

case The capitalization (uppercase or lowercase) of a word or phrase. Title case has the first letter of all important words capitalized. Sentence case has only the first letter of the first word capitalized. *ZIP* is all uppercase and *zip* is all lowercase. Toggle case changes uppercase to lowercase and vice versa.

cell   The intersection of a row and a column.

change markers   Icons that indicate where reviewers have made a revision to a slide.

chart   A diagram made up of different elements that help display a datasheet's information.

clip art   Professionally designed images that can be incorporated into PowerPoint presentations.

color menu   The color palette associated with Drawing toolbar buttons, such as Fill Color, Line Color, or Font Color.

collate   To assemble or print in order.

color scheme   A set of eight complementary colors available for designing your PowerPoint slides. A color scheme consists of a background color, a color for lines and text, and six additional colors balanced to provide a professional look to a presentation.

connection pointer   A small box pointer with which you drag a connection line between two connection points.

connection points   Small blue handles on each side of a shape that you use to add a connection line between two shapes.

comments   Notes that can be written and viewed by multiple reviewers, and hidden or displayed as needed.

compress   To reduce the file size of an image. Sometimes picture quality is compromised for smaller file size.

control boxes   The gray boxes at the beginning of a row or column in a datasheet that correspond to the different data series.

crop   To trim the edges of an image by hiding parts of it.

data marker   A graphical representation in a chart of each data point in a data series. The data is plotted against an x-axis, a y-axis, and—in three-dimensional charts—a z-axis.

datasheet   A numerical representation of chart data in a grid of rows and columns.

data point   The value in a datasheet's cell that, together with other data points, comprise a data series.

data series   A group of related data points.

data series marker   A graphical representation of the information in a data series.

demote   To indent a title or bulleted item on a slide, moving it down in the outline to a lower-level item (a bullet item or sub-point).

design template   A presentation with a designed format and color scheme.

digital signature   An electronic, secure stamp of authentication on a document.

docked toolbar   A toolbar that is attached to the edge of the PowerPoint window.

dotted selection box   The border of a selected object that indicates that you can manipulate the entire object.

embedded object   An object created with another program but stored in PowerPoint. You can update an embedded object in PowerPoint.

encrypted   Encoded for privacy protection.

export   The process of converting and saving a file format to be used in another program.

File Transfer Protocol (FTP)   A communications method that you use to quickly transfer and save files over the Internet.

First Line Indent marker   The small upper triangle on the horizontal ruler that controls the first line of the paragraph.

floating toolbars   A toolbar that is not attached to the edge of the PowerPoint window.

FTP   See *File Transfer Protocol.*

graphics   Non-text pictorial or geometric images.

grayscale   A black and white image that displays shades of gray.

grouping   An action that allows a set of shapes to be handled or changed as a single unit. See also *ungrouping.*

Handout Master   The part of a template that controls the characteristics (background color, text color, font, and font size) of the handouts in a presentation. To make uniform changes to the handouts, you change the Handout Master.

hanging indent   Paragraph formatting adjusted by small triangles on the horizontal ruler where the first line of text is indented less than the subsequent lines.

Hanging Indent marker   The small lower triangle on the horizontal ruler that controls all lines in a paragraph except the first.

home page   The first page of a Web site or PowerPoint presentation.

hovering   Pausing the pointer over an object for a second or two to display more information, such as a submenu or ScreenTip.

HTML   See *HyperText Markup Language.*

HTTP   See *HyperText Transfer Protocol.*

hyperlink   A "hot spot" or "jump" to a location in the same file, another file, or an HTML page, represented by colored and underlined text or by a graphic.

HyperText Markup Language (HTML) The language used to create pages on the World Wide Web.

HyperText Transfer Protocol (HTTP) The World Wide Web's formatting protocol that determines how commands are executed and how browsers interact.

import The process of converting a file format created in another program.

indent marker A marker on the horizontal ruler that controls the indent levels of a text object.

insertion point The blinking vertical line that appears in the presentation window, indicating where text or objects will appear when you type or insert an object.

landscape Horizontal orientation (10 x 7.5 inches) of an image on the output media.

Left Indent marker The small square on the horizontal ruler that controls how far the entire paragraph sits from the edge of the text object. The Left Indent marker moves the First Line Indent marker and the Hanging Indent marker, maintaining their relationship.

legend A list that identifies each data series in the datasheet.

linked object An object created in another program that maintains a connection to its source. A linked object is stored in its source document, where it was created. You update a linked object within its source program.

lobby page An information page that appears on the server before the broadcast starts.

macro A command or series of commands (keystrokes and instructions) that are treated as a single command and used to automate repetitive or complicated tasks.

margin markers Small squares on the ruler that move both the upper and lower indent markers.

master A design pattern that is uniformly applied to slides, handouts, and speaker notes.

menu A list of commands or options available in a program.

Microsoft Clip Organizer A tool that enables you to collect and organize clip art images, pictures, sounds, and motion clips.

Microsoft Visual Basic for Applications (VBA) A high-level programming language developed for creating Windows applications.

more colors Additional colors that you can add to each color menu.

move handle The four vertical dots at the left end of a toolbar by which you can move the toolbar around.

navigation frame   A graphical panel used for navigating from slide to slide in a PowerPoint presentation on the Web.

Normal view   A view that contains all three panes: Outline/Slides, Slide, and Notes.

Notes Page view   A view where you can add speaker notes and related graphics.

Notes Pages Master   The part of a template that controls the characteristics (background color, text color, font, and font size) of the speaker notes in a presentation. To make uniform changes to the speaker notes, you change the Notes Pages Master.

Notes pane   Area in Normal view where you can add speaker notes.

object   In PowerPoint, any element that you can manipulate.

Office Assistant   A help system that answers questions, offers tips, and provides help for Microsoft Office XP program features.

Office Clipboard   A storage area shared by all Office programs where multiple pieces of information from several different sources are stored.

Office Online   A clip art gallery that Microsoft maintains on its Web site. To access Office Online, you click the "Clip Art on Office Online" link at the bottom of the Clip Art task pane.

offset   The direction and distance in which a shadow falls from an object.

Outline/Slides pane   Area in Normal view where you can organize and develop presentation content in text or slide miniature form.

Package for CD   A feature that helps you ensure that you have all the presentation components you need when you have to transport a PowerPoint presentation for use on a different computer.

paragraph   Text that begins and end when you press Enter.

password   A unique set of letters and characters used to allow access to documents or processes.

Places bar   A bar on the left side of the Save As and Open dialog boxes that provides quick access to commonly used locations in which to store and open files.

photo album   A personal collection of digital images to use in presentations.

portrait   Vertical orientation (7.5 x 10 inches) of an image on the output media.

PowerPoint Viewer   A program that allows you to show a slide show on a computer that does not have PowerPoint installed.

presentation window   The electronic canvas on which you type text, draw shapes, create graphs, add color, and insert objects.

program window   An area of the screen used to display the PowerPoint program and the presentation window.

promote   To remove an indent on a bulleted item or sub-point of a slide, moving it up in the outline to it a higher-level item (a bulleted item or title).

properties   Information about a PowerPoint presentation such as the subject, author, presentation title, and so on.

pure black and white   A black and white image that displays only black and white without any shades of gray.

range   A block of cells in a worksheet or datasheet.

read-only   The designation of a file that can be viewed but not altered.

RGB (Red, Green, and Blue) values   The visible spectrum represented by mixing red, green, and blue colors.

rich media   The combined use of motion and sound in media.

Rich Text Format (RTF)   A common text format that many programs can open.

rotating handle   A small green handle around a shape used to adjust the angle of rotation of the shape.

scalable font   A font that can be represented in different sizes without distortion.

scaling   To size an entire object by a set percentage.

ScreenTip   Information displayed about a button, icon, or other item on the screen when you point to the item.

security level   A setting that determines whether presentations that contain macros can be opened on your computer.

selecting   To make an object, graphic, or text active, usually by clicking it with the mouse, so that it can be moved or modified.

selection box   A gray slanted line or dotted outline around an object.

shape   An object that can be drawn free-form or created using tools provided by PowerPoint. Shapes can be sized, moved, copied, and formatted in a variety of ways to suit your needs.

sizing handle   A white circle on each corner and side of a shape that you can drag to change the shape's size. To preserve the shape's proportions, you can hold down the Shift key while resizing a shape.

slanted-line selection box   The border of a selected object that indicates that you can edit the object's content.

Slide Master   The part of a template that controls the characteristics (background color, text color, font, and font size) of the slides in a presentation. To make uniform changes to the slides, you change the Slide Master.

Slide Master view   The view from which you make changes to slides, using the Slide Master View toolbar. You switch to Slide Master view by pointing first to Master and then to Slide Master on the View menu.

Slide pane   Area in Normal view where you can view a slide and add text, graphics, and other items to the slide.

Slide Show view   A view where you can preview slides as an electronic presentation.

Slide Sorter view   A view where you can see all slides in a presentation in miniature.

slide timing   The length of time that a slide appears on the screen.

slide transition   The visual effect when moving from slide to slide in presentation.

Smart Tag   A button that helps you control the result of certain actions, such as automatic text correction, automatic layout behavior, or copy and paste.

source document   The original document, created in the source program, to which an object is linked.

source program   The program that created the document that has been linked to a slide object.

status bar   The bar at the bottom of the presentation window that displays messages about the current state of PowerPoint.

subfolder   A folder within a folder.

subpoints   Indented items below a bulleted item.

summary slide   A slide that lists titles of slides in a presentation and which can be used as a home page or an agenda slide.

tags   Codified characters that determines how text and graphics are displayed in a Web browser.

task pane   A pane that enables you to quickly access commands related to a specific task without having to use menus and toolbars.

template   An applied pattern used in creating the slides, handouts, and speaker notes in a PowerPoint presentation. A template uses masters—sets of colors, text formats, and graphics to achieve different designs. You can use a template provided by PowerPoint or create your own.

text animation   An effect applied to text that makes it appear on a slide in increments: one letter, word, or section at a time.

text label   A text object used primarily for short phrases or notes.

text object   A box that contains text in a slide and is handled as a unit.

text placeholder   A dotted-lined box that you can click to add text.

Thesaurus   A feature that looks up alternative words or synonyms for a word.

thumbnails   Miniature representations of graphics or slides.

tick-mark labels   The labels that identify the data plotted in a chart.

Title Master   The part of a template that controls the characteristics (background color, text color, font, and font size) of the title slides in a presentation. To make uniform changes to the title slides, you change the Title Master.

title slide   The first slide in a presentation.

title text   Text that identifies the name or purpose of a slide.

toggle   An on/off button or command that is activated when you click it and deactivated when you click it again.

toolbar   A graphical bar in the presentation window with buttons that perform some of the common commands in PowerPoint.

Toolbar Options button   The button at the right end of a toolbar that provides access to hidden buttons and other toolbar options.

transparency film   Clear sheets for use in overhead projectors that can be written or printed on like paper.

ungrouping   An action that allows grouped shapes to be restored to individual shapes that can be handled independently. See also *grouping*.

Uniform Resource Locator (URL)   An address on the World Wide Web.

URL   See *Uniform Resource Locator*.

VBA   See *Microsoft Visual Basic for Applications*.

Visual Basic Editor   The environment in which VBA programs are written and edited.

Web browser   An application, such as Microsoft Internet Explorer, used to find and display Web pages.

WordArt   Stylized text for enhancing titles and headings in PowerPoint presentations.

word processing box   A text object used primarily for longer text.

word wrap   A feature that automatically moves the insertion point to the next line within an object as you type.

World Wide Web (WWW)   A network of servers on the Internet that support HTML-formatted documents.

WWW   See *World Wide Web*.

x-axis   The horizontal plane in a chart on which data is graphically represented. Also called the category axis.

y-axis   The vertical plane in a chart on which data is graphically represented. Also called the value axis.

Index

Numerics

C

H

I

K

L

PowerPoint Viewer, 238, 240, 297
presentation windows, 297
presentations. *See also slide shows*
  adding slides to, 23
  blank, creating, xxx, 20–21
  broadcasting over networks (see
    online broadcasts)
  closing, xxix
  collating, 229
  color schemes (see color schemes)
  comments (see comments)
  comparing, 214
  copying to folders, 239
  creating blank, xxx
  creating, from Microsoft Word
    outlines, 54
  creating, with AutoContent
    Wizard, xxix, 15–17
  creating, content, 14, 17
  digital signatures (see digital
    signatures)
  due date, setting, 212
  e-mailing, xlv (see also e-mailing
    presentations)
  embedding fonts in, 238–39
  encrypting, 206 (see also
    passwords)
  ending, 240
  fonts, embedding, 238–39
  graphics, saving in PNG format, l
  headers/footers (see
    headers/footers)
  jumping to first slide, 270
  merging, xlv, 214
  opening, xxix, 14, 240 (see also
    PowerPoint Viewer)
  outlines (see outlines)
  packaging for CDs, xlvii, 238–40
  password protecting (see
    passwords)
  permissions (see permissions)
  previewing, xlvi, 224
  printing, xlvii, 221–34
  properties, viewing, 271
  read-only, 206, 208
  recovering after a crash, 21
  saving, xxix, 6
  saving as outlines, in Word, xxxii
  saving as templates, 98–99
  saving as Web pages (see Web
    presentations)
  self-running, 254
  sending for review, 210
  sending to printer, 228

  sharing (see sharing presentations)
  slides (see slides)
  starting, with design
    templates, xxx
  taking on the road, 238–40
  templates for (see templates)
  tracking changes (see tracking
    changes)
  transporting, 238–40
  unpacking, 238
  viewing, 9, 238 (see also
    PowerPoint Viewer)
Presenter view, and multiple
  monitors, 245
presenting slide shows. See
  delivering slide shows
Preserve Master button (Slide
  Master View toolbar),
  xxxiv, 88
preserving masters, xxxiv, 88
previewing
  animation effects, 183
  animation schemes, 182
  color slides, for printing, 224
  design templates, 19
  headers/footers, 222
  presentations, xlvi, 224
  Web presentations l, 270, 272
Previous Page button (Print
  Preview toolbar), 226
print preview, xlvi, 224–26
Print Preview button (Standard
  toolbar), 225
printers, xlvii, 229, 231
printing
  animated slides, 185
  black and white, 230
  collating, 229
  color slides, previewing
    before, 224
  comments, 230
  grayscale, 225, 233
  handouts, 225, 229
  headers/footers, on every
    page, 223
  hidden slides, 230
  notes pages, 229, 234
  outlines, 229
  presentations, xlvii, 221–34
  range, setting, 229
  settings, changing, xlvi
  slides, 229–30, 234
program windows, 297
programs, add-in. See add-ins

Promote button (Outlining
  toolbar), 42
promoting, 40, 298
  text, 42
  proportional shapes, 120
protecting Slide Master, xxxiv
protecting presentations. See
  passwords
publishing Web presentations, 274
punctuation, checking, 77
pyramid diagrams. See diagrams

R

radial diagrams. See diagrams
ranges, 170, 298
read-only presentations,
  xlv, 206–208
reapplying
  slide layout, 84
  original slide formatting, xxx
rearranging
  org chart boxes, 175
  paragraphs, xxxii
  slides, xxxi, 32
Recolor Picture button (Picture
  toolbar), 145–46
recoloring pictures, 145–46
Record Narration command, 194
recording
  macros, liii, 288
  narration, xliii, 194
recovering presentations, 21
Redo button (Standard toolbar), 46
redoing edits, xxxi, 46
Rehearse Timings button (Slide
  Sorter toolbar), 251, 253
rehearsing slide shows, 251, 253
rejecting changes, 213, 217 See
  also tracking changes
removing. See deleting
re-ordering
  animation effects, 186
  movies, 196
replacing. See finding and replacing
Reset Picture button (Picture
  toolbar), 152
resetting
  menus, to original appearance, lii
  pictures, 146, 152
  tips, 78
  toolbars, to original
    appearance, lii, 282

Get a **Free**
e-mail newsletter, updates,
special offers, links to related books,
and more when you
register online!

Register your Microsoft Press® title on our Web site and you'll get a FREE subscription to our e-mail newsletter, *Microsoft Press Book Connections.* You'll find out about newly released and upcoming books and learning tools, online events, software downloads, special offers and coupons for Microsoft Press customers, and information about major Microsoft® product releases. You can also read useful additional information about all the titles we publish, such as detailed book descriptions, tables of contents and indexes, sample chapters, links to related books and book series, author biographies, and reviews by other customers.

Registration is easy. Just visit this Web page and fill in your information:

http://www.microsoft.com/mspress/register

Microsoft

Proof of Purchase

Use this page as proof of purchase if participating in a promotion or rebate offer on this title. Proof of purchase must be used in conjunction with other proof(s) of payment such as your dated sales receipt—see offer details.

Microsoft® Office PowerPoint® 2003 Step by Step
0-7356-1522-5

CUSTOMER NAME

Microsoft Press, PO Box 97017, Redmond, WA 98073-9830